TEXAS
MARKET HUNTING

TEXAS MARKET HUNTING
STORIES OF WATERFOWL, GAME LAWS, AND OUTLAWS

R.K. SAWYER
Foreword by Rick Pratt

EAKIN PRESS Fort Worth, Texas
www.EakinPress.com

Originally published by Texas A&M University Press as part of their Gulf Coast Books series and sponsored by Texas A&M University-Corpus Christi. This was the twenty-fourth book in the series and edited by John W. Tunnell Jr.

Copyright © 2013
By R.K. Sawyer
Published By Eakin Press
An Imprint of Wild Horse Media Group
P.O. Box 331779
Fort Worth, Texas 76163
1-817-344-7036
www.EakinPress.com
ALL RIGHTS RESERVED

Paperback ISBN 978-1-68179-371-9
Hardback ISBN 978-1-68179-442-6
eBook ISBN 978-1-68179-373-3

ALL RIGHTS RESERVED. No part of this book may be reproduced in any form without written permission from the publisher, except for brief passages included in a review appearing in a newspaper or magazine.

CONTENTS

Foreword vii
Preface ix

1 Introduction 3
2 Sowing the Seeds of Texas Market Hunting 9
3 A National Appetite 39
4 Fowl as Fad and Fashion 87
5 The Window Closes 101
6 The Law and the Outlaw 121
7 Epilogue: The Last Big Sting 143

Notes 147
Index 173

FOREWORD

With his book *Texas Market Hunting*, R. K. "Rob" Sawyer has freed an unwritten part of our history from exile.

The practice of market or commercial hunting of wildfowl—through the eyes of many of today's sportsmen and conservationists—is considered offensive, a part of our past they don't wish to acknowledge. Some revisionists would even have us expunge any memory of it. But it was a very large and important part of our history, a history in which America's wealth of wild game animals, birds, and migratory waterfowl was seen as just one more bounty of a bountiful land, to be gathered and used. The taking of wildlife for the table was simply a part of everyday life in the United States.

I have long waited for this book to be written. For years before Rob walked into my Port Aransas Museum office, I wondered why no one had tackled the subject. I even considered writing it myself. Tomes on America's market hunting history have been written for many regions of the United States and include chapters on the Atlantic Coast from New York to Florida and the famed waterways of Chesapeake Bay, the central United States from the Great Lakes to Louisiana, and the West to California. But no one wrote of Texas.

Those who settled the Lone Star State had the frontier drive to survive and prosper, and their chosen homeland had abundant natural resources of wild game, with as many, perhaps more, waterfowl than any other place in the nation. The stories had to be there, I reasoned.

I was right. Rob begins the story with the importance of waterfowl as sustenance to settlement Texas and follows the state's market hunting to its peak, when it helped supply the nation's demand for ducks, geese, and shorebirds in restaurants and on dining room tables. From the very beginning the income generated through market gunning kept many watermen and their families from winter hunger. By the turn of the nineteenth century it grew to be a major part of the Texas coastal economy.

Rob reminds us there was so much more to market hunting than just the killing of waterbirds. It employed local boat builders, decoy makers, suppliers of guns and ammunition, and a well-established shipping and transportation network. Local women gathered and sold down and feathers to the clothing, bedding, and fashion industries. It was a practice woven into the very fabric of the coast. But the record remained mute, the story untold.

My interest in the subject comes from many directions. I love history, waterfowling, classic shotguns, wooden decoys, and small, hand-built boats. I am an outdoor writer, former editor of two hunting magazines, and a contributor to many more. Among my responsibilities as the Port Aransas Museum director is to search for traces of our past through interviews with the living.

Many of the Port Aransas old-timers remembered their parents' part in the commercial harvest of wildfowl. Decades later, some of their memories remain vivid: of rising before dawn in the wet and cold to load boats with gear and guns, or, as children, of being pressed into service to help pluck and clean the birds and get them ready for their trip on the market train. One remembered a gunning skiff, rotting away in his yard, equipped with a rusting old four-gauge punt gun. But no one wrote about it—until at last Rob took up the challenge and produced what will without doubt come to be seen as one of the finest books on the subject ever written. It was worth the long wait.

The morning I finished this piece, I took a small, locally built skiff to the Quarantine Island shore just north of Port Aransas, where Lydia Ann Channel becomes Aransas Bay. I beached the little boat and sat watching flights of birds and listening to their sounds. This is the place where a remarkable mile-long elevated-rail train track ended. It was here at this remote spot that local market gunners delivered their take to the train each morning before the cleaned and dressed birds began their trip north, destined to feed city folks who otherwise would never have tasted canvasbacks or redheads, rails or curlews. Once the center of a thriving local industry, it is now mostly silent. Only a trace of the once busy overwater rail line remains. Ducks are now scarce by the measure of that long-ago time, shorebirds and cranes are no longer legal game, and waterfowl cannot be sold.

The era of the market hunter, so different from our own, has long ended. And it would likely have been forgotten but for *Texas Market Hunting*. Thank you, Rob.

Rick Pratt

PREFACE

Texas Market Hunting: Stories of Waterfowl, Game Laws, and Outlaws, like its preceding tome, *A Hundred Years of Texas Waterfowl Hunting*, was written primarily for duck hunters. Its audience is also meant to include wildfowlers everywhere who are passionate about North America's waterfowling history. Too, it is intended for the Texas history reader who savors stories of land and water, settlements as they became towns and cities, the progression of maritime transportation from sail and steam to the gasoline engine, and railroads that took the place of oxen and ponies.

This book is primarily about waterfowl and the people who made a living from the migratory bounty during the nineteenth and early twentieth centuries. Located at the southern terminus of North America's Central Flyway, Texas was a wintering ground for millions of geese, ducks, and shorebirds and thousands of cranes and swans. The huge flocks of migratory birds that once rose from Texas bays, wetlands, and prairies are no more, the land that sustained them but a fragment of its former character. Gone, too, are the people who killed, sold, and shipped waterfowl—the Texas market hunters.

The market hunter is an entity well known to the public in nearly every state located along America's waterfowl flyways. I grew up in the shadow of the Chesapeake Bay market hunter and followed it for half a century from Maryland to Florida, Louisiana, and finally Texas. There was, however, no shadow cast in Texas. I wrote this story because no one else had.

Texas market hunting proved to be an esoteric topic. The Lone Star State, it seemed, did not often chronicle the people who made a living from land and sea. Most of Texas' watermen were just fishermen or hunters, and usually nameless. These pages attempt to weave the available historical information into the story of Texas market hunting. The effort results from a number of people, and the author is extremely grateful to those willing to recall, provide, or search for written material, oral histories, and historical photographs. Great thanks go to them for their labors.

The author particularly recognizes Robin Doughty, professor emeritus, The University of Texas at Austin; Rudy Rosen of the Meadows Center for Water and the Environment, Texas State University at San Marcos; Fred Bryant of the Caesar Kleberg Wildlife Research Institute, Kingsville; and Jeff Churan, former Missouri conservation commissioner. All four suffered through early manuscript drafts and took the time to make them better. The book exists mostly through the vision of Shannon Davies of Texas A&M University Press, who thought the market hunter's story should be told.

Contributions to information on the Texas upper coast in Jefferson and Chambers Counties result from efforts by Bill Quick, Judy Linsley of the McFaddin-Ward House, Herb Stafford, Randy and Brook Chatagnier, Lillian Richards, Greg Keddy, E. G. Gerry Cordts Jr., J. P. "Pink" Logan, J. Steve Kole Jr., Peter Stines, John Kemp, Evelyn Standley, Kevin Ladd at the Wallisville Heritage Center, Doug McLeod of the Moody Foundation, author Melanie Wiggins, *Houston Chronicle* outdoor writer Shannon Tompkins, Jim Bob Jackson, Freddie Abshier, Joe Whitehead, Jack Holland, Gene Campbell, Ralph Leggett, Forrest West, Clyde "Boots" Faggard, Joe Faggard, Claud Kahla, Kendon L. Clark, and Sylvia Lamb. Material on Harris and Galveston Counties was shared by Cliff Fisher, Alex Wolff, James Smock, Joel Draught of the Houston Public Library, and Casey Greene and Carol Wood from the Rosenberg Library, Galveston.

I extend my appreciation for materials on the middle coast and Coastal Bend to Michael Bailey and Jamie Murray of Brazoria County Historical Museum, Bill Womack, George Ann Cormier of the Calhoun County Museum, Dean Johnstone, J. C. Melcher, Steve Fisher, Ronnie O. Luster, Eagle Lake's Louis Schorlemmer, Janie White of the Aransas Historical Commission, Gordon Stanley, Gary Chambers, Rockport's Johnny Atwood and James Fox, Rick Pratt of the Port Aransas Museum, Byrd Lee Minter Jr., and Jamie and Gordon Spears from Aransas Pass. I am deeply indebted to Corpus Christi's Jim Moloney, who kindly made available the entirety of his extensive Coastal Bend photographic collection.

Material covering the Texas lower coast, from Corpus Christi to Brownsville, was provided by Corpus Christi's Billy Sheka Jr. and Murphy Givens, Cameron County historian Norm Rozeff, and Kate Moore from the Brownsville Historical Association.

I am indebted for the sections on inland coastal prairies to Lyle and Pat Jordan, Jim Warren, Carol Beauchamp of Fort Bend County Libraries in Richmond, and Bill Stein of the Columbus Nesbitt Library. Market hunting stones were upturned on Caddo Lake by Andrea Weddle from the James Gilliam Gee Library of Texas A&M University–Commerce, Jonathan Gerland of the History Center in Diboll, and James Conrad.

A number of natural history experts provided assistance in the group effort to keep the author out of biological and botanical trouble. Thanks are extended to retired Texas Parks and Wildlife Department (TPWD) biologists Charles Stutzenbaker and David Lobpries, Ducks Unlimited's Todd Merendino and Matt Kaminski, and Warren Pulich Jr. of The Meadows Center for Water and the Environment, Texas State University at San Marcos.

Additional photographic and document archives were scoured by Dreanna Belden at the University of North Texas; the US Fish and Wildlife Service in Elkins, West Virginia; the Texas History Center in Austin; Darwin Morris of Tyrrell Historical Library in Beaumont; and Tom Shelton from the Institute of Texan Cultures in San Antonio. Jeff Pelayo of the Canvasback Gallery in Cambridge, Maryland, and Joe Walsh, from Easton, Maryland, kindly allowed use of their collections from Chesapeake Bay. Ron Gard, senior consulting specialist of Sotheby's American Folk Art Department, and Todd Steele of Todd Steele PhotoArt provided the punting skiff lamp image.

Last, I am indebted to my parents, who lit the fire in a very young boy by encouraging me to prowl the waters and shorelines of Chesapeake Bay, and to my wife, Wendy, and daughter, Christen, who tolerated my doing the same in Texas.

TEXAS
MARKET HUNTING

CHAPTER 1

INTRODUCTION

On each side of the flat-bottomed skiff lay the guns, a Winchester Model 1893 pump and an old side-by-side ten-gauge, their barrels rusted from salt water that leaked through planked floorboards. The night was cold, the north wind blowing hard after a front. But the moon shone through herringbone clouds that made it easier to row from the anchored sloop to the flats where, the day before, the market gunner watched a big flock of redheads mixed with pintails and wigeons. The hunter positioned his skiff upwind to drift into their masses, darkness masking his approach. If he timed it right, daybreak's splintered sunlight would help him retrieve the results of his seven shots.

He waited, prone in the little skiff, listening to the catlike sounds of contented redheads that always gave their location away. Water seeped through his canvas jacket, and he turned his collar up against the wind, remembering a time when the morning chill didn't feel as cold. Gnarled fingers clenched the wooden paddle as he guided the skiff into position, and his back ached as he turned to reach for the first weapon. "Thirty-nine," he said to himself, "is just too old for this."

Aboriginal Indians followed by the Spanish, French, and Mexicans trapped or hunted waterfowl on the Gulf Coast for sustenance or barter long before arrival of Anglo-Americans. The Anglos were, however, the first to look upon nature as a commodity, finding a place for it initially in local then later national economies. Those who made their living by killing and selling waterfowl for profit were at first called huntsmen. The name *market hunter* did not often appear until the late 1800s, when efforts to control declining natural resources brought a largely ignored segment of society to the forefront of a great conservation and legislative tug-of-war.

The best known of the market hunting operations gained their foothold in the 1700s along the East Coast of the United States. The Texas market hunting period started much later, its foundation laid by privateer Jean Lafitte in the late 1810s, followed by Stephen F. Austin's colonists in the early 1820s. Oysters, fish, native game, and migratory flocks of wading birds and shorebirds, puddle ducks, diving ducks, geese, swans, and cranes were integral to survival of Texas' early settlers. A single discharge of black powder and chilled shot fired through the middle of a flock of wildfowl assured food for a family, and extras could be bartered or sold in the nearest village. Galveston visitor Matilda Houstoun in the 1840s wrote: "No one must be surprised at our attempts to eat nearly everything we shot." Galveston meals, she noted, were either wild game or wild cattle, with no domestic meat other than pigs that "fed so uncleanly, upon snakes and dead dogs that recourse to them was not to be thought of."[1]

Along the Brazos and Colorado Rivers, waterfowl fed the planter culture of a cotton and sugarcane economy built by the sweat of slave labor. James F. Perry's Peach Point Plantation, between the Brazos and San Bernard Rivers, was like many, where "the Perry boys and some of the slave men . . . hunted on a regular basis, and venison or wildfowl often found their way to the Peach Point kitchen." Others of Brazoria County's blacks, usually unable to possess guns and certainly unable to afford them, trapped large numbers of teal using primitive deadfall traps "in the common contrivance called a 'figure of four.'"[2]

Ducks and geese also fed armies, from the Texas Revolution to the Civil War. When Gen. Sam Houston sent a detachment of men to the village of Copano to meet Col. James Fannin, they lived off fish and game before setting out to Goliad and into immortality. One of Fannin's soldiers described fowl on the prairie so thick "we might have loaded our horses down with wild geese." Zachary Taylor, landing his troops in 1845 during the Mexican War on the peninsula between Nueces and Corpus Christi Bays, found the "tall grass was buzzing with rattlesnakes" and supplied his army with rations made up in large part of wild ducks and geese.[3]

As port settlements and crossroads became towns, huntsmen peddled game door-to-door or from wagons on the side of the road, or sold their wares in town marketplaces, market stalls, and meat markets. Every form of wild game was found in Texas during the 1800s. Large game included deer, pronghorns, and bears; smaller animals were rabbits, squirrels, raccoons, opossums, and muskrats. There was every bird imaginable: whooping cranes, sandhill cranes, swans, geese, ducks, nearly every type of shorebird—of which snipes, plovers, and curlews were most common—upland birds such as woodcocks, passenger pigeons, prairie chickens, wild turkeys, quail, doves, and a variety of songbirds.

Before the Civil War, transportation and preservation limitations restricted sale of most game in Texas to local markets. It often took days to reach the nearest town on foot or by pony, ox- or horse-drawn wagon, rowboat, or sail. The risk of spoilage between field and market was always high. The most efficient method to preserve the kill was by brining it, but salt was often hard to obtain and always expensive. Instead, birds were often gutted and sacked or packed in ventilated, slatted barrels with preservation left to a prayer for cool weather.

Despite abundant natural resources, Texas in the first half of the nineteenth century lagged far behind much of the United States in the economy of waterfowl. The Lone Star State was still part of Spain when wildfowl and other game were sold in established marketplaces along the northeastern Atlantic seaboard. In the early 1800s settlers were taming the frontier of Mexican Texas as wintertime shoppers packed sophisticated big-city markets in Boston, New York, Philadelphia, Baltimore, Washington, Chicago, Saint Louis, and New Orleans.

Texas entered the national, and even global, trade in wild game during the late 1870s to early 1880s, as post–Civil War economic expansion afforded a growing segment of Texas and the United States with disposable cash to spend on luxury items. One of those items was wildfowl, popularized as a vital seasonal ingredient in the nation's pursuit of trendy and refined dining.

Demand was the catalyst for Texas' burgeoning late-1800s trade in wild game, but it was postwar advancement in technologies that delivered it. Inefficient black powder and muzzle-loading shotguns were swapped for repeating firearms and factory-loaded shotgun shells. Hooves on the prairie, and sail and steam on the waterways, gave way to a network of railroads that shipped products quickly to market. Salt was replaced by ice-making machinery used to refrigerate rail cars and cold storage houses. The combination of ice and rail did away with the uncertainty of getting birds to market without spoiling, or even getting them there at all.

As quickly as rail tracks were laid, nearly every sizable Texas coastal and inland town joined in the harvest, packing, and transportation of wildfowl to cities across America. The birds in highest demand were canvasbacks, redheads, plovers, and curlews. Of these, it was America's seemingly insatiable appetite for the canvasback that allowed Texas a prominent place in the wild game industry. By the late 1800s express railroad cars moved barrels of Texas canvasbacks to all points on the national compass. The big red, black, and white diving duck also found its way to Europe; when Texas shipped its first cargo of refrigerated meat across the Atlantic by steamship in 1887, on the ship's manifest were seventy canvasbacks that sold "like wildfire" in London's Leadenhall Market.[4]

The Texas trade in wildfowl also included plume-bearing and ornately feathered birds for the fashion industry and secondary markets in bird skins, eggs, and wing feathers for quill pens. By the late 1880s demand for plume feathers by the millinery trade—mostly for ladies' hats—developed into a fad not unlike what the canvasback was to America's dining table. At the top of the feather list were long, delicate plumes of the snowy egret. Plumes sold for hundreds of dollars per pound and were in such high demand that the egret was sometimes dubbed the "bonnet martyr." Snowy egrets were hunted so intensely that, by the early 1900s, the white bird was uncommon in Texas.[5]

Whether they were hunting for the meat market or the plumage market, or for the local or export trade, market gunners harvested wildfowl by whatever means they could, and it was not sophisticated and not sport. The big birds—whooping cranes, sandhill cranes, swans, and geese—were rifled or shot with scatterguns from horseback. Ducks were usually killed by shotguns fired from the shoulder and most often shot while they were on the water. Large bags were made by gunners who raked shot across feeding and resting flocks from behind slow-moving oxen. Birds were hunted at night, sometimes by sneaking into flocks of rafted birds in sculling skiffs, with weapons that included shotguns, eight- to four-gauge swivel guns, and punt guns. Ducks were netted, trapped, and baited to the gun. Texas market hunters, like those across the United States, did whatever it took to earn a living from the harvest of nature's bounty.

With the late nineteenth century came recognition that numbers of many of America's game animals and birds were declining, and some were already eradicated. The market hunter's occupation came to be viewed as one of the major causes, and increasingly maligned. More insidious than his guns, however, was the destruction of habitat by a progressive nation. But the market man, certainly not wealthy, and poorly represented in the halls of business and politics, was an easier target.

Sportsmen, whose tenure afield paralleled that of market hunters throughout the late 1800s, were among the most vocal opponents to the market hunter's trade. Theirs was not an issue of conservation, but more a matter that market men were a competitor for the same declining game and bird resources. When the sport hunter's crusade was joined by naturalists, farmers, and a growing segment of the population with the means to enjoy wildlife not as food, not for profit, but on its own merits, they formed a forceful but unlikely coalition that brought game protection to the forefront of American consciousness.

Texas' efforts to curtail sale of wild game began as early as 1874, but protection of migratory waterfowl managed to pass through slippery lawmaking fingers for another thirty years. The legal reign of the market hunter in the Lone Star State ended when Texans passed a Model Game Law in 1903 and a Permanent Game Law in 1907. The noose around the neck of the national migratory bird trade was tightened with the federal government's passage of the Lacey Act in 1900, the Weeks-McLean Law or Federal Migratory Bird Act in 1913, and the Migratory Bird Treaty Act in 1918.[6]

The Texas market hunter had a choice to comply with each new state and federal law, and many quit; those who continued were outlaws. Outlaw hunters enjoyed several years of near impunity; sale of wild game in the first decades of the twentieth century was still legal in much of the United States, and if Texas gunners could export their wildfowl across state lines, they found ready buyers.

Too, there was little law enforcement. In 1903 the Texas State Fish and Oyster Commission, predecessor to today's Texas Parks and Wildlife Department, had only five game wardens to cover the entirety of the Texas coast. As their numbers increased after 1907, the stage was set for a decades-long showdown between game wardens and those who still made a living from nature's migratory bounty.[7]

The fire lit under the Texas market hunting business burned brightest between 1880 and 1903, but the flame was largely extinguished after 1918 with the advent of federal regulation. In many ways the era of the market hunter was similar to that of the great cattle drives in Texas. Both occupied only a brief period of Lone Star State history but were steeped in legend and lore. The travails of the cowboy spawned spellbinding legends of men on mustangs who pushed the edge of a frontier. Equally engaging stories emerged from market gunners who supplied the frontier, and later a nation. This book attempts to tell their story, spanning the time from when waterfowl were sustenance, then income, to a new era in which they were, at last, protected.

CHAPTER 2

SOWING the SEEDS of TEXAS MARKET HUNTING

On his ill-fated expedition along the Texas coast in 1685, French explorer René Robert Cavelier, Sieur de La Salle, witnessed limitless herds of buffalo and deer and swarms of turkeys, quail, waterfowl, and prairie chickens, which the French called grouse. Little had changed nearly 150 years later, when Stephen F. Austin's colonists settled between the Brazos and Colorado Rivers. In addition to native wild game, each fall they saw a sky filled with huge numbers of migratory wading birds and shorebirds, puddle ducks, diving ducks, geese, swans, and cranes.[1]

Early Texans knew only that migratory birds, in flocks that at times blackened the sky, arrived from the north. It would not be until later that the birds' route south from northern breeding grounds would be mapped by biologists who in the late 1920s gave it a name: the Central Flyway. Waterfowl nearing the end of their Central Flyway journey passed over northwestern Texas' rolling plains, where wet years brought playa potholes to life. At times they paused along wide spots of the red, silty Panhandle river waters or flooded hardwoods along the upper Red, Trinity, Brazos, and Colorado Rivers until the first hard frost drove them farther south.[2]

South of the Central Texas Balcones Escarpment, wildfowl gorged on acorns beneath oak trees that lined floodplains wide with meanders, oxbows, and overbank ponds along the Guadalupe, Colorado, San Bernard, and Brazos Rivers. To the east, they flocked to growths of duck potato in flooded hardwood and cypress trees along the Trinity and Sabine Rivers. A swirling skyline of ducks often animated horizons over natural lakes such as Mitchell Lake near San Antonio and Caddo Lake in East Texas.

Finally the journey brought them to the coast. There an unbroken marsh extended from the Sabine to Lavaca River of the upper and middle coasts, where shallow, fringing shorelines of spartina grasses, bulrushes, spikerushes, millet,

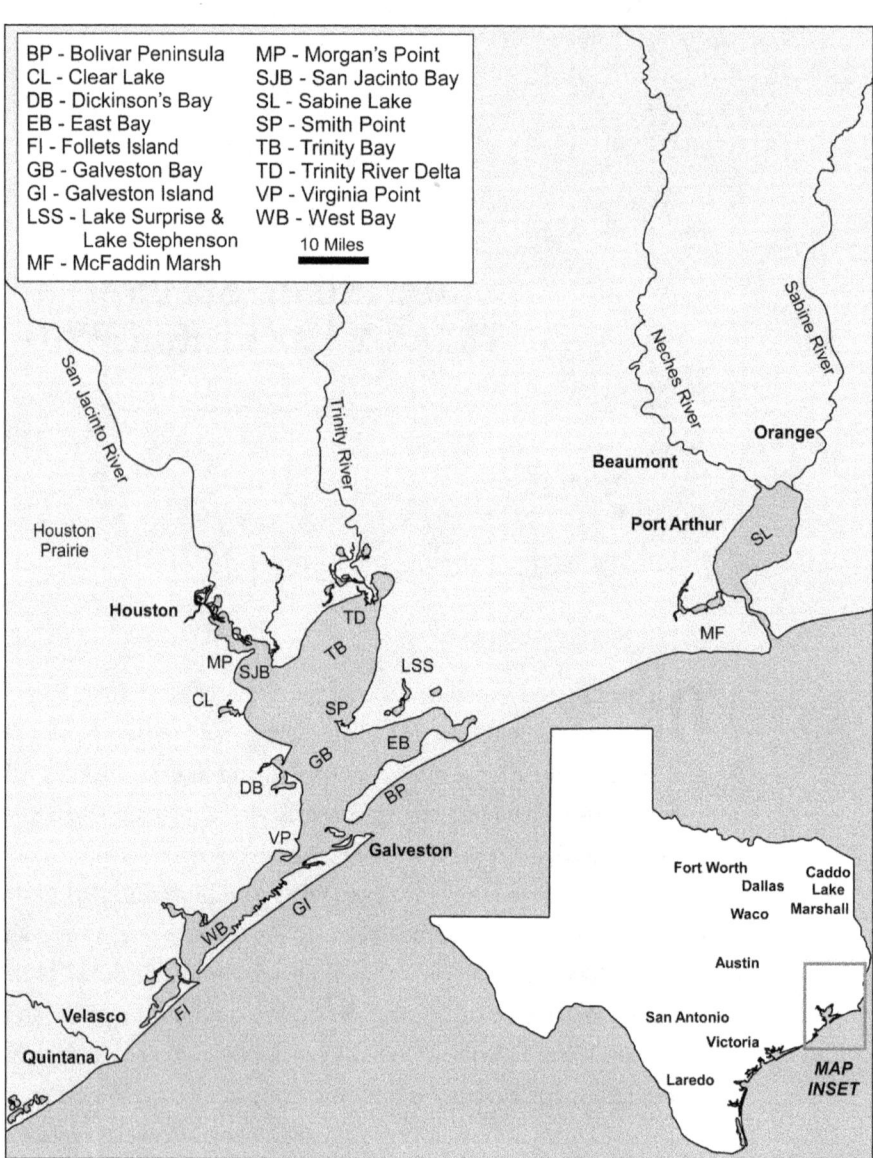

Texas Upper Coast. *Major market gunning and/or shipping towns and cities of about 1900 are shown on both inset and index maps.*

phragmites, and three-square grasses concealed bayous and coastal ponds adjacent to the estuaries of Sabine Lake and Galveston, Matagorda, and Lavaca Bays. Stretching from the edge of Galveston Bay to near Lavaca Bay, the inland prairie freshwater habitat of Houston Prairie and Big Prairie was a sea of bluestem, switch, yellow Indian, and eastern grama grasses covering a topography of low-relief knolls and shallow ponds. Abundant aquatic vegetation in the prairie's large natural lakes, notably Orchard Lake and Eagle Lake west of Galveston Bay and Green Lake on the Lavaca River, held uncountable numbers of birds.[3]

The coastline morphology of the Coastal Bend and the northern part of the lower coast was made up of San Antonio, Copano, Aransas, and Corpus Christi Bays, protected from the ravages of the sea by Matagorda, St. Joseph, and Mustang Islands. With fewer rivers than along the upper coast, bay waters here were

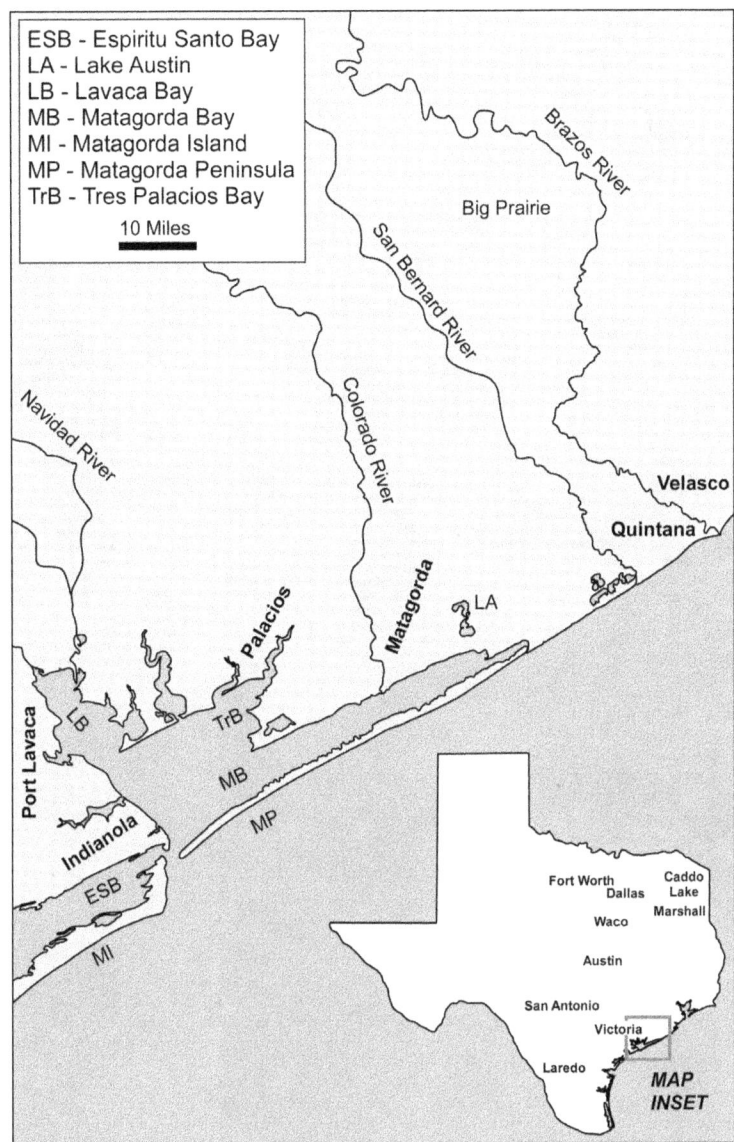

TEXAS MIDDLE COAST. *Major market gunning and/or shipping towns and cities of about 1900 are shown on both inset and index maps.*

more brackish than those to the north and east. More saline still were Baffin Bay and Laguna Madre of the lower coast. Shallow waters of Laguna Madre, paralleling Padre Island for more than a hundred miles, supported rich growths of widgeon, shoal, turtle, and manatee grasses. Past shoreline clay and silt dunes, and tidal and algal mud flats, were extensive quartz sand deposits of the coastal plain, its terrain of cactus and mesquite dotted with freshwater ponds filled intermittently by rainfall and natural springs. The mainland sand sheet was interrupted in two places, cut by rich delta deposits of the Arroyo Colorado and Rio Grande, their floodplains covered in dense vegetation along banks of meandering streams, ponds, and oxbow lakes.

From the upper coast to the lower coast, the geomorphology of prairie, floodplain, river, delta, coastal plain, and estuary complexes created unrivaled habitat

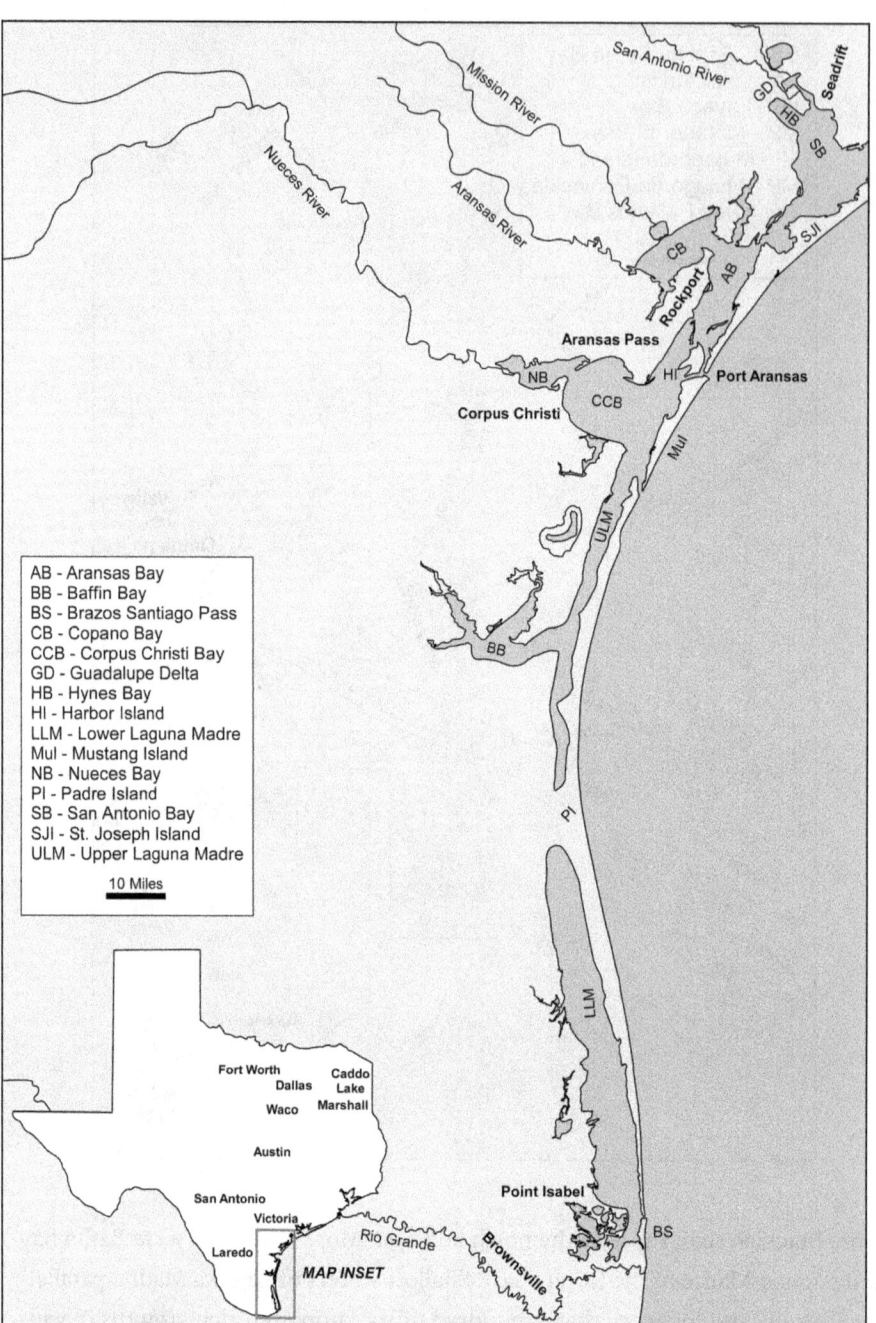

TEXAS COASTAL BEND AND LOWER COAST. *Major market gunning and/or shipping towns and cities of about 1900 are shown on both inset and index maps.*

for great skeins of wintering Central Flyway waterfowl. Fresh water delivered by rainfall and rivers was the ecosystem's lifeblood. Rainwater saturated the organic-rich soils of the upper prairie, its runoff so slow that early ranching families joked that the land could bog down a snipe. Rivers overstepped their banks at times, with sheets of floodwater that covered miles of prairie. Small rises that poked through the ephemeral inland sea were the only high ground for quail and prairie chickens, which became easy prey to circling eagles, hawks, and falcons. As fresh water continued to make its way to the coast, it was prevented from quickly reaching the Gulf by the same shallow, silled inlets that caused deep-draft sailing ships to bounce hard on the bottom during their crossings.

EARLY FOWLING ACCOUNTS

Descriptions from pioneering travelers paint a rich picture of the numbers of birds that migrated to a pristine Texas coast. On the upper coast, mariners rounding Bolivar Point in the early 1800s located the pass to Galveston Bay by the skeletons of grounded schooners, their standing rigging rising as silent sentinels above the sea. Surviving a harrowing passage through the pass during a storm in 1828, J. C. Clopper wrote: "Four or five of us went ashore with our guns and lay till morning on the soft grass shooting at geese, ducks, and other waterfowl which collect here in innumerable multitudes every morning to feed on marine substances that are left on the beach by the tide." That night the sailors, who had been living off salted and dried sea rations, indulged in a feast of ducks, geese, oysters, and redfish.[4]

An unnamed writer visited West Galveston Bay between Dollar Bay and Clear Lake on a hunting excursion during the 1840s. His party hired a "five-oar cutter" in Galveston provisioned with a keg of powder, shot pouches, powder horns, three muskets "to serve as fowling-pieces," a double-barreled gun, and ample supplies of lead "in the shape of shot, bullets, and bars." Sailing up the shoreline, they described a coastline with only a few low, stunted trees on a "monotonous prairie, which spread . . . as far as the eye can reach."

The travelers anchored off Edwards Point and rowed into Edwards, or Dickinson, Bay, where "a dense cloud" of geese and ducks passed only a few yards over their heads. They shot for twenty minutes, "killing the stupefied birds by dozens, until we ceased from sheer inability to carry any more." On another hunt they pursued a flock of several hundred swans, with the discharge from two barrels at seventy yards producing three of the great white birds.

At the head of Dickinson Bay they negotiated the tree-lined bayou of Dick's Creek, now called Dickinson's Bayou, from a small rowboat. Canvasbacks filled wide spots in the creek, where the author "gave them one barrel after another, and seven killed and wounded were left upon the field [and] captured with difficulty." The only residents of Dick's Creek at the time of this excursion were an old Irishman and his son, Jim Rock, who hunted game for Houston and Galveston markets, and Capt. John G. Tod, a retired officer of Sam Houston's navy.[5]

Sailing the western shoreline of Galveston Bay, travelers passed Morgan's Point and the estate of Col. James Morgan at the mouth of San Jacinto River. Morgan was an avid duck hunter, his schooner a familiar sight on the shallow oyster reefs and shoals of Trinity and Galveston Bays in the 1840s and '50s. He wrote letters describing his fowling observations for local newspapers, such as the report published by the *Houston Telegraph and Texas Register* in 1845: "Important to

Sportsman—We learn that many of the inlets of Galveston Bay are literally filled with wild ducks, brant, geese, etc. Several thousand are often seen in a single flock. Col. Morgan informs us that one of his slaves lately killed sixty-five ducks in about two hours." Colonel Morgan is well known for his mulatto servant Emily West Morgan, seized by Mexican general Santa Anna on his march to San Jacinto in 1836 and who lives on in Texas lore as the Yellow Rose of Texas.[6]

Up the San Jacinto River, the town of Houston was carved between clear running streams that led from the inland prairie to Galveston Bay. About the time of Texas independence, a Mr. A. Malsch hunted at Old Bayou, east of town where Buffalo Bayou drained into Burnett Bay. He wrote that at night ducks and geese "would sound like thunder as the ducks came to roost and we could hardly sleep for the noise they made." After a two-hour morning shoot, Malsch picked up 180 mallards and left behind all the "small ducks."[7]

Texas Independence and Civil War hero Gen. Albert Sidney Johnston made his home at China Grove Plantation on Oyster Creek, east of the Brazos River. Before it was converted to cropland, the Brazos floodplain was a "primeval forest ... almost pathless, filled with all manner of wild beasts and game, thick-set with jungle, and concealing miasmatic swamps caused by the annual overflow of the river." In winters, uncountable numbers of wildfowl "circled and settled in the shallow pools left by the winter rains." General Johnston once rifled a goose on the prairie at 140 yards and found in "a healed wound ... several long slugs, which he recognized as Canadian in manufacture."[8]

Upriver from China Grove, Dr. Benjamin Harris Neal poked his fowling piece from the window of an old wood-planked building on the prairie in West Columbia and killed seven sandhill cranes with one shot. The dilapidated structure where he made the shot had been the first capitol building of the Republic of Texas' elected government.[9]

On Matagorda Bay a resident of the settlement at Decrow's Point described waters "covered with ducks, geese, brant, swans, and other waterfowl" and, embellishing on the numbers of canvasbacks, said he killed them with a stick. Across the bay on the mainland, seven frame and log houses made up the port town of Lavaca in the 1840s. There, visitors found resident Captain Smith "seated in front of his door with a Kentucky rifle resting in a ... fork from the branch of a tree," waiting for geese. He once fired at a line of the big birds, and "three geese fell, shot through the neck with the same rifle ball."[10]

Percy St. John, traveling to Corpus Christi on the schooner *Santa Anna*, provided an absorbing account of St. Joseph's Island in 1842. Carrying a heavy fowling gun loaded with "swan shot," borrowed from a bar pilot named Mackenzie, St. John set out in a flat-bottomed dugout canoe fitted with a jib and mainsail to Aransas Pass. He hunted on the south side of St. Joseph's Island, which he described as a "multitude of islands, shoals, flats, false channels, etc., which I undertake to say, would have puzzled a smuggler's pilot." St. John wrote of his hunt:

I crept with my double-barreled gun to the crest of the bank, and cautiously peeped over, beneath the shelter of a knot of prickly pears. Before me was a swamp half dry, half wet, so covered with ducks, geese, pelicans, snipes, and sandhill cranes, as literally to confuse me. None but those who have sported in regions where the fowling-piece is not heard perhaps twice in a year can conceive the amount of wild-fowl to be found in these sequestered spots during cold weather.

I leveled my gun, and watched patiently [for] the proper moment to fire; my object was to seize an opportunity when the greatest possible number were in line within range of my gun.... I pulled both triggers. Never before or since did I witness the confusion which ensued—thousands and tens of thousands of ducks, geese, swans, etc., were on the wing from every brook, pond, swamp, and morass in the neighborhood, screeching, cackling, uttering a series of cries most inharmonious and unmusical, fulfilling the expression, for an instant, of darkening the sky.

St. John's single discharge produced twenty-three ducks and snipes, eight geese, and a swan, all a welcomed addition to the galley of the *Santa Anna* on his return.[11]

When Zachary Taylor made his encampment on the Nueces River and Corpus Christi Bay during the Mexican War, hunting parties sent up the Nueces were astonished at the abundance of wild game. A soldier wrote that officers shot geese, snipes, curlews, and plovers on Corpus Christi Bay "every day, with no apparent diminution of their numbers." Kentuckian William McClintock, on a shooting excursion in 1846 led by Texas Ranger captain Grey, wrote: "Earth and water were covered with infinite numbers, of ducks, geese, cranes, and swans. At the fire of our pieces, they rose in such dense clouds, as for a time to darken the air."[12]

SETTING THE STAGE

As they settled along navigable rivers and near the coast, early Texas explorers and pioneers considered native and migratory wildlife a practical matter: what they gathered from land and sea was necessary to their survival. Autumn flights of migratory birds brought a change in diet, replenishment of the homestead's feathers for pillows, and rendered lard used for cooking and making soap.

As pioneer Texas evolved into settlement Texas, its small, isolated communities created a demand for all manner of goods, and essential to that list was native wild game and migratory wildfowl. Early Texas trading centers were established in river communities in East Texas, Austin's Colony between the Brazos and Colorado Rivers, DeWitt's Colony between the Lavaca and Guadalupe Rivers, and James Power and James Hewetson's grant between the Guadalupe and Nueces Rivers.

Ports, crossroads, and trading posts of settlement Texas became towns between the 1840s and the Civil War. As Texas' population grew, so did the number of men who made at least a part of their income from the harvest and sale of wild game. Some of those behind the guns were farmers; others were watermen who, between winter flights of ducks, netted fish, tonged oysters, and harvested green turtles and terrapins.

The wild game trade was, at first, an informal affair. Hunters hauled their harvest to town in small sailing sloops or by horse-drawn wagons and sold it by the side of the road. They were called game hawkers, and as town boundaries expanded, they followed rutted, dirt-track trails to peddle their wares door-to-door to boardinghouses, taverns, and merchants.[13]

FIRST MARKET GUNS

The first professional hunter in Texas was probably Burrell Franks. An accomplished Louisiana marksman, Franks was hired by privateer and pirate Jean Lafitte to provision nearly a thousand convicts, outlaws, and fortune seekers who made up Lafitte's community of Campeche at the site that later became the city of Galveston. Franks's was a harsh existence, one he shared with Karankawa Indians, hordes of mosquitoes, rattlesnakes, cottonmouths, and alligators. There was little respite from summer's heat and winter's freeze and no warning of coming northers or summer storms, such as the 1818 hurricane that flattened Lafitte's outpost.[14]

Anson Taylor was another professional hunter who, like Burrell Franks, shot game for the Campeche outpost. Both men were often accompanied on their hunting expeditions by others of Lafitte's motley band; one later recalled their favorite gunning spots were Pelican Island, Eagle Grove, Bolivar Point, Virginia Point, Red Fish Bar at the mouth of San Jacinto River, and the Trinity Bay headlands they called "the great wild geese and wild duck nations." For years Lafitte's hunters used the hulks of burned and scuttled ships, dilapidated trophies of Campeche's plunder, as markers to navigate Galveston Bay.[15]

Lafitte's settlement in many ways laid the foundation for the Texas market hunting industry. Several associated with the community—some pirates, others merely procurers—remained in Texas after Lafitte's hasty departure at the insistence of the US government in 1821. One of Lafitte's crewmen, whose name was never printed, was some seventy or eighty years old but still able to support himself by harvesting and selling game to Galveston markets in the early 1840s.[16]

Other of Lafitte's men who stayed behind harvested game for Austin's Colony. According to author Gary Cartwright, it was a vague confederacy of men, living mostly off the land, who provided Austin's settlers with venison, redfish, trout, perch, oysters, crabs, shrimp, and turtles. Fall through spring, a plethora of migratory waterfowl, mostly geese, canvasbacks, and teal, was sent to small community market outposts.[17]

Mary Austin Holley, on a visit to Bolivar Plantation on the Brazos River in 1831, described the professional hunters of Austin's Colony. She wrote that plantations often hired a hunter to provision the family, hired hands, and slaves, and considered these hunters "very profitable to their employers, and much cherished by the family, and often become spoiled by familiarity and indulgence. . . . They are a sort of privileged character." Most, she said, were Indians or Mexicans. "But it sometimes happens that a white man from the states who has become somewhat de-civilized . . . is substituted."[18]

Before they were called market hunters, they were huntsmen, an occupation listed in census records along with farmer, sawyer, seaman, and merchant. The hunter in the first half of the 1800s experienced a Texas very different from today's. There were the smells: damp oilskins and canvas, horses, leather, and black powder. There were the sounds of a coast devoid of manmade noises other than the luffing of a canvas sail during a tack or the knock of an oar against the gunwale of a wooden skiff. Nature, however, was a prolific noisemaker, from the cacophony of crickets to the scream of the panther and the raucous sounds of huge flocks of fowl lifting from their resting places.[19]

No lights illuminated the Texas night. Boatmen used the moon and stars for navigation unless the weather closed in. By darkness or daylight, the coastline could be a dizzying maze of bayous, lakes, and bays. The way light reflected off the water told them its depth, and the rubbing sound of the keel let them know if the bottom was sand, oysters, or the edge of a mud flat. A change in wind direction might mean they were close to a body of land, and often they could smell it. If they were wrong, they could strand—always inconvenient, and sometimes deadly.

There were few comforts. On land, hunters lived in "a crude shanty of logs and branches" or in a wooden wagon covered with a canvas tarp. For days at sea "the hard, rounding floor of the cabin, with a blanket over it, serves as a bed." Provisions were typically no fancier than salted meat, bread, hardtack, onions, garlic, potatoes, and coffee. There was little protection from the heat, cold, and water that crept into their world from rain, sleet, or snow and from poor clothing and leaks in their boats.[20]

In summer and early fall, coastal Texas' hot, humid air was a gumbo of deer flies, greenhead horseflies, and mosquitoes. A Galveston Bay hunter called the hordes of mosquitoes "winged tormentors" that "almost drove me crazy ere morning, when I could scarcely see out of my eyes, so swollen was my face." A nine-day mosquito plague on the shores of Sabine Lake made the sun appear to be in eclipse. One Chambers County hunter recalled that mosquitoes swarmed muzzles of newborn calves and suffocated them and that "cows would walk themselves to death. Mothers would walk off and leave their calves." Some market men seemed immune to the mosquito swarms, as "their blood has become so thin that no swelling or irritation follows the bite."[21]

Texas land and water could be alive with alligators, rattlesnakes, cottonmouths or water moccasins, copperheads, and occasional coral snakes. A store owner on Sabine Lake kept his daughters indoors during summer as a precaution against alligators and snakes that at times filled oystershell streets. There is a Jefferson County legend of an alligator that dragged off one of W. P. H. McFaddin's cowboys during the night, after which others in camp were kept awake by the sound of bones breaking in the distance.[22]

Winter northers that roared into Texas were the bane of watermen. A fresh south wind, warm temperatures, and restless fowl gave a sense of false security before the fast-moving line of the storm front. Northers turned bays into mud flats that stranded gunners in their boats, and with the cold that followed, they sometimes froze to death. Inland hunters drowned when spring rains turned rivers and streams into raging torrents of water. On the coast, as the first shots aimed at the early fall migration rang out, hunters occasionally perished when their vessels were dashed to pieces during West Indian cyclones, before they were known as hurricanes.

THE QUARRY

The market hunter closely followed the feeding habitats of wintering puddle and diving ducks, geese, swans, cranes, and wading birds and shorebirds. Before the planting of agriculture grains, the main diet for several species of puddle ducks was acorns. English market man Capt. Frank W. Flack, in his *A Hunter's Experiences in the Southern States of America* (1866), observed that ducks in early fall always congregated on woodland lakes and river bottoms, where they gorged on mast and, once the supply was exhausted, "resort[ed] to the prairie ponds and sloughs." Near Gonzales, as thousands of wild ducks swarmed Peach Creek and Sandy Fork, farmers were concerned they were robbing acorns from their hogs. After killing all the ducks they could eat, the farmers left them in piles for their pigs "in place of the acorns they have stolen." On the lower Texas coast, acorns from blackjack and post oaks were as important to ducks as grain became during the twentieth century.[23]

Whether fattened on acorns, aquatic vegetation, prairie grasses, or later rice and other agricultural grains, the most common puddle ducks hunted for the market in Texas were mallards, pintails, and teal. Two ducks were called mallards: the greenhead and the black or summer mallard, better known to today's sportsmen as the mottled duck. Both ducks were found throughout Texas, with the biggest concentrations in the marshes of the upper coast. Greenhead mallards were migratory, while mottled ducks were resident to the Louisiana and Texas coast.

Northern pintails in Texas were always called sprigs or sprig tails. The chestnut and white drakes and drab-colored hen birds were widely distributed across

HUNTERS' NAMES FOR CENTRAL FLYWAY WATERFOWL	
Common Name	Texas Hunters' Name
Mallard	Greenhead
Northern Pintail	Sprig, Sprig tail
Mottled Duck	Black or summer mallard
Northern Shoveler	Spoonbill
American Wigeon	Baldpate
Gadwall	Gray duck
Lesser Scaup	Bluebill, Blackhead
Ruddy Duck	Butterball
Snow Goose	White brant or brant
Blue Goose	Gray brant
Lesser White-fronted Goose	Specklebelly, Spec, Gray or black brant
Greater Canada Goose*	Ringneck, Honker
Lesser Canada Goose**	Cackler, Hutchins's Canada goose
Tundra Swan	Whistling swan
Upland Sandpiper (Plover)	Grass plover
Upland and Wilson's Sandpiper	Papabot (Rio Grande Valley)
Killdeer	Ringneck plover or plover
Wilson's Snipe	Jack snipe

Branta canadensis   ***Branta hutchinsii*

the state, frequenting timber bottoms, prairie potholes, and marshes, and along with redheads they were found in enormous flocks on seagrass flats from Matagorda Bay to Laguna Madre. With the advent of rice agriculture in the 1850s, and other grains planted later, huge flocks of pintails joined mallards and other puddle ducks over inland crops.

Because of their twisting flights, the diminutive blue-winged, green-winged, and less common cinnamon teal were shot only when they grouped in large flocks on the water. The blue-winged teal was the first migratory duck to arrive on the Gulf Coast, usually as early as August. Green-winged teal appeared later but remained throughout much of winter. Cinnamon teal were never common in Texas, with most harvested south of San Antonio Bay.[24]

Wigeons, gadwalls, and northern shovelers—always called spoonbills—were sold in early local markets, but with a flavor inferior to that of other puddle ducks, they were the ducks the market hunter most often took home to supply the family larder. Colorful wood ducks were uncommon on the coast; with a preferred habitat of acorn-rich flooded river bottoms, they were mainly sold in inland markets.

Diving ducks, which traditionally frequent deeper water than most species of puddle ducks, were hunted on coastal bays and deep inland lakes. In Texas, wintering diving ducks, sea ducks, and stiff-tailed ducks included, in relative abundance, lesser scaup, redheads, canvasbacks, ruddy ducks, buffleheads, goldeneyes, and ring-necked ducks. The canvasback was the most favored of the diving ducks in local and later national markets. The red, black, and white diver once ranged from Sabine to Laguna Madre, with its preferred feeding areas in waters rich in growths of wild celery, sago pondweed, and banana water lily.

Redheads were the second most sought diving duck. They fed in huge rafts on shallow seagrass flats along the entirety of the coast, with the biggest numbers from Lavaca Bay to the Rio Grande delta. Redheads had a habit of "knotting up" before they landed, and the market man who timed his shot could kill several with a single pull of the trigger. Lesser scaups, or bluebills, were probably the most abundant duck on the coast, but with a diet that included mollusks and other invertebrates, they were not rated highly on the table. Ruddy ducks, buffleheads, goldeneyes, and ring-necked ducks, rarely mentioned by name in market accounts, were priced in the category "all other ducks." Market hunters did their best to avoid shooting them.

Whistling ducks, both black-bellied and fulvous, were abundant summer residents of the Rio Grande delta, with the range of the fulvous extending up the coast as far north as Louisiana. In much of Texas they were called tree ducks, and on the lower coast, where they were a popular staple in Brownsville markets, they went by the name "cornfield ducks."[25]

Geese of the Central Flyway included snow geese, Canadas, white-fronted or specklebelly geese, and small numbers of the dark-phase snow goose, or blue goose. Early accounts did not differentiate between the big Canada geese, later referred to by sportsmen as greater Canadas, and the smaller, or lesser, Canada geese. Texas hunters called big Canada geese ringnecks, sometimes honkers, but these names were not used in the marketplace—they were just geese. Specklebelly and blue geese were always gray geese, gray brant, and even black brant. Snow geese were white brant, and certainly the most abundant goose in Texas, but they were not favored on the table; their dark-colored meat was considered "most fishy, and worthless."[26]

Although less abundant than snow geese, Canada geese were much more common in the marketplace. They were considered excellent table fare because their diet was dominated by native grains, seeds, and shoots of new-growth grasses. Green grass sprouts were a preferred food choice, and by the early 1800s hundreds of acres of new-growth grass, created by overgrazing and the burning of wetlands and salt marsh, formed a patchwork across the upper prairie. Market hunter Frank Flack found flocks of "hundreds of thousands" of greater Canada geese on the prairies of Matagorda and Brazoria Counties and observed: "At night they generally seek the bays or lakes, but by day they graze upon the short grass of the prairies, preferring those spots where the grass has been burnt off, and where the new grass is greenest."[27]

Trumpeter and whistling swans, the latter more commonly known now as tundra swans, wintered from Sabine Lake to the Rio Grande delta and all inland points between. On the upper coast, "vast numbers" of wild swans frequented Jefferson County. It was the same on Galveston Bay, where hunters found them near Anahuac, on gravel bars between Virginia Point and Clear Lake, and on appropriately named Swan Lake. At the mouth of the Trinity and San Jacinto Rivers, a traveler in 1866 wrote: "I remember being once on a steamboat which plied between Galveston and Houston, and which ran aground in the night at the head of Galveston Bay. In the morning, upon going on deck, we were all astonished to see vast numbers of swans around us, and, as far as we could roughly guess their numbers, we estimated that at least two thousand were in sight from the deck."[28]

During his travels to Texas in 1835, Gideon Lincecum was so taken by the number of swans on the beach near the San Bernard River in Brazoria County that he wrote in his diary: "I have witnessed the stampede of a thousand buffaloes; at another time six or eight hundred mustangs. I had a million wild pigeons pass over in a few minutes; but they all dwindle to insignificance when compared to the flight of the southern division of American swans, on the Texas Gulf Coast."[29]

Swans continued to winter in Brazoria County until the early 1900s and were often found just outside the Velasco town limits. Swans were mentioned as early as 1840 on Matagorda Bay and were still common to the south in Lavaca Bay until 1920. Along the lower coast, the big white birds were hunted from Corpus Christi Bay to the Rio Grande delta near Brownsville. Inland, swans frequented Colorado County's Eagle Lake and were often shot by market men and sport hunters on lakes near Dallas and San Antonio.[30]

Wintering cranes included whooping and sandhill cranes. Accounts of whooping cranes, sometimes called trumpeter cranes, suggest that they once ranged from Galveston Bay to the Rio Grande. Whooping cranes were called "noble and majestic targets" and covered a lot of the sky in flight, their calls unmistakable, "somewhat resembling the sounds made by a block when hoisting a sail." Russell Clapper, the first manager of Anahuac and McFaddin Wildlife Refuges, recalled, "They were big and they were white and they used to kill them for the market." The smaller sandhill crane was described as "a light-blue coloured bird, with short red hair or feathers upon its head, which feels to the touch like velvet." More abundant and easier to kill than whooping cranes, they were "very good eating" and a favorite in local markets throughout the 1800s.[31]

On fall nights, flocks of shorebirds at times migrated down the Central Flyway in such numbers that for hours their silhouettes blotted out the light of the moon. Year-round there was always some species of shorebird in the marketplace, and of the varieties the most commonly referenced were upland sandpipers or plovers, Wilson's snipes, curlews, and yellowlegs. Upland sandpipers, or plovers, were "very fat, good, eatable birds" and the best-tasting shorebird, with snipes evidently a close second. Eskimo curlews were prized by epicures as "palatable and sizable," while long-billed curlews were "by no means a favorite for culinary purposes," their meat "tough but still desirable." Also good on the table were yellowlegs, and a market man who knew his birds could differentiate between the greater or "winter" yellowlegs and the lesser or "summer" yellowlegs. The little piping plover was "most excellent eating," while the killdeer, or ringneck plover, was an inferior bird, its flesh dry and tough.[32]

Most of those who hunted shorebirds 150 years ago didn't know their proper names and instead developed their own vernacular. In much of Texas the upland sandpiper was called a grass plover, but in the Rio Grande Valley, it and the Wilson's sandpiper, were both papabots. Any ploverlike bird went by names such as gray plover, prairie plover, sand-snipe, yellow-shanked tattler, prairie runner, spring plover, tilt-up, beach bird, prairie pigeon, doughbird, or prairie snipe. Killdeer were ringneck plovers or just plovers. Both long-billed and short-billed dowitchers were called Dolwich snipes, and Wilson's snipes were often either English snipes or jack snipes, the latter mistaken for its European cousin. The name tattler or tell-tale was given by waterfowlers to lesser yellowlegs, willets, and upland sandpipers, the name arising from their shrill alarm call, with the approach of a hunter, that was a warning to other waterfowl. Gallinules and rails were rarely mentioned by name in markets, but the latter likely would have included king, clapper, Virginia, and sora rails.[33]

MAKING A LIVING FROM DUCKS

Arrival in late August of the first early waterfowl flights was the sign that it was time to prepare for the main fall migration—the time for gunners to purchase a keg or more of powder and gather shot pouches, powder horns, and ample supplies of lead shot, which they either bought or made themselves. Homemade shot was prepared by pouring molten lead into a bucket of wet sand crisscrossed with holes made by poking wire through the mixture. It produced shot that was square-ended and looked very different from factory-made shot pellets. Manufactured shot was produced in commercial shot towers built in industrialized northern and Great Lake states by the early to mid-1800s. Shot pellets were called drop shot, the name derived from the process of pouring molten lead from the top of the shot towers, generally over a hundred feet high. By the time the lead reached the bottom, it had formed a hard, round pellet.[34]

Hunters' guns were considered an agricultural implement, available from mail-order catalogs or sold locally in general merchandise and hardware stores. The weapons of choice for early market hunters were long-barreled eight- and ten-gauge muzzle-loading shotguns, both flintlocks and later percussion locks with external hammers. Loading of these guns was a time-consuming process that required an exact amount of black powder (a mixture of saltpeter, sulfur, and charcoal), chilled or soft shot, and wadding that were sequentially tamped down the barrel into the chamber by ramrod. In all muzzle-loading guns the powder had to be kept dry, no small achievement during hunts in rain or over water.[35]

POWDER AND SHOT—29 kegs superior powder, 26 bags assorted Buck and Bird Shot. Just received and for sale by VANWINKLE, BROTHERS.

(Modified from *Civilian and Galveston Gazette*, Oct. 19, 1838)

RECEIVED per late arrivals and for sale low for cash
20 kegs Duponts FFFG Powder,
26 bags buck and drop Shot.
A & G BALL.

POWDER AND SHOT *were shipped from industrial centers in the north by oceangoing schooner and steamers.*

(Modified excerpt from A & G Ball advertisement, *Civilian and Galveston City Gazette*, Jan. 28, 1843)

The inefficiency of early 1800s firearms was, in part, offset by the sheer numbers of wintering Gulf Coast puddle and diving ducks, geese, swans, cranes, wading birds, and shorebirds. The variety of birds covered an equally varied landscape, and both influenced what was hunted for the market and how they were hunted. At times the hunters' quarry swarmed prairie potholes or fresh burns; at other times the birds were in deep coastal marshes, rafted on shallow bays, or in flooded timber.

From river bottom to bay, early market men shot waterfowl by day and at night by the light of the moon. The simplest and most common operation was one man and a pony, the mainstay of the small market hunting operations from the Sabine to the Rio Grande. Logistically confined to prairie, potholes, and the edge of coastal marshes, most hunters stalked or "snuck" their quarry, hid in natural cover, or shot from the saddle with rifles or long-barreled shotguns.

Hunters found that waterfowl, perhaps accustomed to herds of wild horses and longhorn cattle, were often easily approached and "killed by a man on horseback." Mounted gunners usually took their first shot at ducks on the water, with the more birds grouped together, the better. Before pulling the trigger they whistled or yelled; alerted, the birds raised their heads, increasing the effectiveness of the first volley. The number of ducks mounted hunters harvested in a day was limited to the amount the pony could carry, usually forty to sixty birds.[36]

Plovers and snipes were also hunted from horseback. Plovers were said to be hard to approach on foot, giving "a good deal of trouble to the unmounted shooter," but were effortlessly killed from "your shooting pony's back." When plovers were hunted from wagons, the wheels practically had to overrun them before they would flush. Spring was the preferred time to shoot plovers, snipes, and curlews, as the birds were then at their fattest. In the days of muzzle-loading weapons, shorebirds were only shot when they grouped in large flocks.[37]

The big birds—whooping cranes, sandhill cranes, swans, and geese—were either shot with scatterguns or rifled from horseback. Sandhill cranes were more susceptible to the hunter's rifle than were whooping cranes, reputedly a more

EARLY TOOLS OF THE TRADE: *a side-by-side shotgun, a pony loaded with about forty mallards, and a transport wagon (background). Shown here is Bolivar Peninsula market hunter Fred Kahla, probably in the early 1900s. (Courtesy Melanie Wiggins, originally donated by Odessa Mouton)*

> Caution to Sportsmen. . . . The swarms of plover upon the prairie keep hunters continually employed, and many families live in fear of accidents.

(Modified from *Civilian and Galveston City Gazette,* Apr. 15, 1843)

challenging quarry because of "their superior height and great . . . timidity." Market man Frank Flack did not kill more than fifteen during as many years of hunting in Texas.[38]

Besides being less desirable on the table than Canada geese, snow geese were usually more difficult to shoot because they frequented deep marshes, places always hard for hunters to access. Canada geese were usually found "on the first ridge out of the marsh," coastal prairies, and beaches and shoreline bluff banks where they found grit, places that could be easily reached by horse and wagon. Captain Flack described his method for shooting Canada geese on the prairie near West Columbia. After locating a flock, he rode his horse in a tight circle around them, then "at the proper moment the horse is halted, and a little hailstorm of five-and-twenty small buckshot are rained upon the compact mass of twenty or thirty geese, and the other barrel, with a like charge, is worked at them when their wings are extended to rise. This often proves more destructive than the first fire."[39]

Wooden boats were to the coastal hunter what the pony and wagon were to inland and prairie hunters. Gunners who plied shallow waters used rowing and sailing skiffs, while broad-water operations employed sloops and two- or three-

Shallow-draft, single-mast sloops in the Port Lavaca shipyards, early 1900s. (Courtesy Dean Johnstone, File No. 0045 PL)

masted schooners that towed rowboats or single-masted, centerboard sailing skiffs, both called tenders. Galveston market men built fast, twenty- to twenty-five-foot cat-rigged sailing skiffs, while in the Coastal Bend and the lower coast the prevailing sailing craft was a square-bowed, hard-chined scow. It was common for sail-based excursions to last days or even weeks—as long as the weather, in the days before ice, remained cold enough to prevent spoilage of the harvest.[40]

Night shooting was widely practiced along the Gulf Coast, both on land and over water. Hunters shot by the light of the moon, behind skiff-mounted fire boxes, and with handheld torches. Captain Flack crossed Matagorda County's Great Bay Prairie on horses laden with double-barreled shotguns, bags of shot, and cattle horns filled with gunpowder for night shoots on Lake Austin in the late 1850s. Lake Austin was then two bodies of water, and hunters, he wrote, spread out on the narrow strip of land between them. To prevent birds from settling out of gun range, half a dozen local African American gunners were dispersed around the shoreline in an effort "to keep the fowl on the wing."

As the sun rose after one hunt, Flack's party launched an old cypress dugout pirogue to retrieve the night's kill, and "those collected we count, and then tie upon our saddles to carry home." Their total for the night was 347 birds. Flack considered night shooting "a very wasteful method, as scarcely one in three of the killed or badly wounded birds are ever bagged," and he added that "hundreds of the wounded have concealed themselves in the sedges, in the rushes, or have wandered out into the prairie grass to die."[41]

In addition to ducks, geese, and swans, another popular nighttime quarry was woodcocks, the successful harvest of which required only a torch and a stick.

SOWING THE SEEDS

Example of a hunting lantern *used on the bow of sculling boats for night shooting. The hen pintail decoy shows the scale. (Collection of Ron Gard, Dallas, Texas; photo by Todd Steele)*

Torch hunters found the small shorebird vulnerable to light, which "so bewilders them that they are easily shot or beaten down with clubs." One visitor wrote that woodcocks were "often killed in large quantities by the negroes [sic], who, carrying a torch held high up above their heads, are enabled to see them running down between the cotton rows, and, having a long bamboo cane in their hand, tap them on the head, and so kill them."[42]

On shallow waterways, night hunting was done from sculling skiffs. In sculling, the hunter lay prone or on his back in a rowboat, drifting slowly with the current or wind into flocks of rafted and resting birds until close enough for the shot. The skiff was steered with either short, wooden paddles or a transom-mounted sculling oar, and often a fire pot or fire box with a bright piece of reflective metal was mounted on the skiff's bow. As waterfowl were highly susceptible to lights at night, the method allowed for an easy approach. The fire pot evolved into the gunning lamp, and before kerosene, it was illuminated with charcoal and wood or candles made of pine tar, beeswax, or tallow.[43]

Hunting over live or wooden decoys appears to have been uncommon before the Civil War. Gunners on foot or horseback preferred not to be encumbered by decoys' weight and bulk. Instead, they watched the skyline and went to the birds, and if decoys were used at all, they staked out a few dead birds. There is a puzzling lack of references to the use of decoys on bay waters from the first half of the nineteenth century. The fact that, by the late 1800s, large decoy spreads were used to attract the sometimes immense coastal flocks of redheads and pintails might point to an earlier history, but it would only be an inference. It is possible there were so many ducks that decoys were not needed.

FROM FLYWAY TO MARKET

Whether on land or sea, by day or by night, at the end of a hunt cranes, swans, geese, ducks, and shorebirds were gathered, gutted, and sometimes plucked. They had to reach the marketplace before spoiling, and before factory ice, most fowl was preserved by brining with salt in wooden barrels. Used as a preservative for meat, tallow, and hides, salt was critical to early Texans, and an entire industry developed around its production and transportation. Salt could be hard to find, always difficult to transport, and often expensive. For market hunters, the only alternative was to pack ducks in ventilated slat barrels with preservation left to a prayer.[44]

Commercial hunters procured salt from vendors who delivered their cargoes by wagons or sailing sloops. An early salt trader named Captain White made trips in 1824 from Lavaca Bay to Austin's colonists on the Colorado River, facing challenges along his route from fickle weather to Karankawa Indians. Corpus Christi's Captain Anderson of the schooner *Flour Bluff* collected salt from the upper Laguna Madre, then sailed up the coast, where he sold it for ten cents a bushel. Salt was such a precious commodity that Capt. Peter Johnson, who hauled salt from Lamar on Aransas Bay to San Antonio by wagon and a team of horses, sold it for as much as a dollar a pound in the 1860s.[45]

Much salt, before it was mined and transported in bulk, was produced locally. The earliest and least efficient method was to scrape sea salt from salt flats. During the early 1800s wagons and sloops converged on Oyster Lake in Matagorda, and within just a few years over ten thousand barrels of salt were collected before rainwater diluted the deposit. Another salt deposit, formed by evaporation of seawater during high tides, was mined on the shore of Captain Mifflin Kenedy's Laureles Ranch, later part of King Ranch, on the upper Laguna Madre. A storm in 1874 washed the salt away.[46]

Salt was also produced by evaporation from seawater, a labor-intensive process in which bay water was run into evaporating pits and the salt was collected and ground in crude mills powered by men, horses, or windmills. These factories, called saltworks, produced small volumes of salt in several port towns along the Gulf Coast. Brazoria County had three saltworks during the 1830s and '40s. Two were in operation in Matagorda by the 1830s, with several in the Coastal Bend, including Mission Lake on north Copano Bay and Lamar on Aransas Bay.[47]

By the early 1840s the largest coastal port towns had an alternative to salt preservation: ice. Cut from frozen ponds in New England by horse-pulled plows,

> ## SALT, SALT, SALT.
> THE subscribers have just received pr. Sloop Phoenix from Corpus Christi, sixty sacks Texas Salt, a very superior article which they offer for sale at low rates.
> June 4; SYDNOR & STREET.

(Modified from *Galveston Civilian and Gazette,* July 24, 1842)

> **ARRIVED YESTERDAY.**—The bark Trinity, Capt. Leah, from Boston, with 300 tons ice for the Galveston Ice Company.—Agents, Messrs. E. B. Nichols.

(Modified excerpt from *Civilian and Galveston City Gazette,* April 20, 1858)

> ## ICE!—KEEP COOL—ICE!
> **500** TONS ICE, in the Houston Ice House—
> SAN JACINTO STREET.
> All orders filled promptly for any point on the railroad, either in hogsheads, barrels or boxes—when accompanied with the cash.

(Modified excerpt from *Civilian and Galveston City Gazette,* August 21, 1866)

huge square or rectangular slabs of ice made their way south in the insulated holds of schooners, frigates, and steamships. New England ice was stored in icehouses, their thick walls insulated with sawdust. Some of the leading refrigerator firms of the day were the Houston Ice House, Port Lavaca's Poindexter Ice Company, the Indianola Ice House, and the Galveston Ice House, which in the 1840s promoted its product as essential to "comfort and health."[48]

Ice companies posted advertisements whenever cargoes of ice were destined in port, the largest in shiploads of up to three thousand tons. Because supply was intermittent and uncertain, it was common for companies to ration ice by selling "coupon retail ice tickets." Only the leading coastal game and fish houses used New England ice in the commercial trade, with price as much as availability the main deterrent to widespread use.[49]

Whether brined, salted, iced, or left to the whims of weather, waterfowl next had to be transported to market. At first, game procured on the coast made its way inland by small, shallow-draft stern-wheel steamers and by freighters, big bois d'arc wagons pulled by half a dozen oxen. Steamer journeys were often burdened by shifting river channels and point bars, logjams, and low-hanging tree limbs. At night, vessels navigated by the light of bonfires built in iron baskets loaded with pine knots; placed on the bow of the boat, they created "a dangerous combination on wooden steamers." The biggest challenge for wagon travel was mud; oxen stuck along inland trails created huge roadblocks. Teams doubled up to extract the struggling beasts, and if they failed, the oxen were killed and left in the muck.[50]

Trade between coastal port towns on the Gulf of Mexico was by sail and steam. Eighteen thirty-seven saw the first steamship that ran between New Orleans and Galveston, and soon side- and stern-paddlewheel steamers shared the Gulf with brigs, barks, frigates, and two- and three-masted schooners.[51]

TEXAS MARKETS

Wild game was a mainstay on the family table and in saloons, eateries, hotels, and boardinghouses, their menus in the early years limited to whatever wildfowl was available. Wildfowl was bartered or bought from game hawkers as well as from open-air markets established in the public square of almost every Texas village and town. Early marketplaces consisted of rows of wooden-frame market stalls with makeshift canvas roofs, and later evolved into more formal structures with indoor and outdoor stalls. The public marketplace was the social center of the community, where shoppers gathered along oystershell and dirt-packed streets to trade stories, gossip, political views, or the latest advances and retreats in Texas' War for Independence and the Mexican and Civil Wars.

Early markets carried general merchandise, agricultural products, home furnishings, and food staples requisite to life in 1800s Texas. Perishable goods were grouped together, with wild game sold near assortments of fruit, vegetables, butchered meat, and seafood. Whether in markets large or small, shoppers usually found a large variety of wild game animals and birds. Migratory waterfowl included whooping cranes, sandhill cranes, swans, geese, ducks, snipes, plovers, and other shorebirds. Featured migratory game birds were mainly passenger pigeons, doves, and woodcocks, while resident game birds included wild turkeys, prairie chickens, and quail. Other offered birds commonly included robins, flickers, meadowlarks, and blackbirds.

Colonial Texas

Many of Texas' early colonies prospered as trading and market centers before the Civil War. The town of Brazoria in Austin's Colony, shaped from the canebrakes and pecan and oak forests and nearly "impassable in time of floods on account of the mud," was for a time a vibrant river trading town with wharves, a market, and stores. Jane Long, the Mother of Texas, ran a Brazoria hotel about 1830 that was known for fine dinners that featured local fish and game.[52]

Matagorda, on the Colorado River, was one of the main seaports for settlers immigrating to Austin's settlement. With its planter, mercantile, and shipping economy, the port town had fourteen hundred residents by 1832. Waterfowl was sold in the town square and served in boardinghouses, and by 1852 it was on the menu of one of the finest hotels in Texas, the Texas House.[53]

At the mouth of the Brazos River, Quintana and Velasco handled much of the seagoing trade that supplied Austin's colonists. The Velasco waterfront in the late 1830s was lined with beachfront residences, wharves, warehouses, a customhouse, Asa Moses's saltworks, boardinghouses, and the American Hotel. Shoppers who gathered at the large local marketplace in Monument Square found it stocked with oysters, turkeys, curlews, snipes, quail, passenger pigeons, bears, venison, a half dozen types of fish, and ducks of every type, from teal to canvasbacks.[54]

Called Bad Luck Island by Cabeza de Vaca when he landed there in November 1528, the peninsula west of Galveston was named for the Follet family of boat builders. The Follets Island town of San Luis in the late 1830s was the largest trading center between Matagorda and Galveston, and by the early 1840s it had two thousand residents. Visitors arrived by stagecoach, the Follet family ferry from Galveston, or schooners that docked at the town's thousand-foot wharf. The port town boasted several hotels where fish, oysters, and wild game were nearly always available.[55]

The village of Linnville was one of the first trading towns in DeWitt's Colony, on the edge of Lavaca Bay. In the early 1830s locally procured fin and fowl were transported from John J. Linn's wharf to inland destinations "in rude carts on solid wheels sawed from large trees and drawn by several yoke of oxen." A Comanche raid in 1840 ended Linnville's brief reign as an early center of trade. The town of Lavaca, on the west shore of Lavaca Bay, fared better. In the 1830s Lavaca was only a small landing, but within a decade it had a new name—Port Lavaca—along with a wharf and two hotels. One was the Brower House, its table in the 1850s "supplied at all times with the best the market affords." A small number of trading and forwarding companies were opened that moved goods by sea and to the interior by long wagon trains. By 1857 Port Lavaca's coastal trade in fish and fowl got a boost with New England ice available from the Poindexter Ice Company.[56]

The fishing village of Decrow's Point shared Matagorda Peninsula's sand dunes and back barrier marsh with rattlesnakes, horseflies, and mosquitoes. By the 1840s Decrow's Point was a thriving seaport visited by vessels from throughout the Gulf Coast and Atlantic seaboard. Visitors dined on fish and fowl at Huff's Hotel at Decrow's Point in the 1850s. Saluria, across from Decrow's Point on the north side of Matagorda Island, was part of James Power and James Hewetson's holdings. By the early 1800s Saluria's trade infrastructure included Judge Hawes's warehouse and a wharf at the end of Resaca Street that bustled with oceangoing schooners, steamships, and a ferry that connected the island to the mainland at Alligator Head. During the 1850s, fine duck and snipe dinners were on the menu at S. S. Givens's Sea Breeze Hotel.[57]

A number of small coastal villages prospered for a time on the Power and Hewetson grant around Aransas and Copano Bays. They included El Copano, Blacks Point, and Saint Mary's on Copano Bay, Lamar and Aransas City on Aransas Bay, and the town of Aransas on St. Joseph Island. Aransas was a settlement of ship captains, bar pilots, lightermen, watermen, and hunters. Residents Peter and Theodore "Charlie" Johnson ran the main shipping and transport business. The Johnsons' operation included schooner service from Indianola to Saluria and a mule-drawn stagecoach line connecting Saluria to Aransas town. There, Capt. Peter Johnson provided lodging in a two-story boardinghouse, and the next morning he unfurled his sails for the remainder of the journey to Corpus Christi. Aransas town was short-lived, its demise during the Civil War a result of a Yankee blockade, bombardment, and burning. Captains Peter and Charlie moved to Lamar, from where Charlie continued a life at sea, sailing the length and width of Aransas and Copano Bays to deliver mail, and worked as a market hunter and sport hunting guide.[58]

Early Texas Cities

The city of Galveston, platted by the Galveston City Company in the late 1830s, owed its rapid rise to maritime trade made possible by a natural deep harbor. Galveston's Tremont House was the first and for a short time the only boardinghouse in town. A two-story frame building with four sleeping rooms, it was located next to the town's sole wharf, long and narrow with loose, plank boards, where small sloops docked to deliver fish and fowl. A visitor in 1837 wrote that the Tremont's menu was not fancy but "could not be excelled, however, as to the fish, oysters, geese, ducks, turkeys, and venison." Eggs from domestic fowl were so scarce that the Tremont served tern, pelican, and gull eggs gathered by the bushel on nearby Pelican Island.[59]

The first public marketplaces in Galveston were shanties near the wharves on Market Street, followed in 1837 by a market building at Market and 20th Street. By the 1860s the two-story brick Market House, with its belfry on the top floor, opened at Mechanic and 11th Streets. On the ground floor near the crawfish and vegetable stands, butcher stalls during winter months offered a "liberal supply and great variety [of game], embracing almost everything that the climate and season affords, from the juiciest of venison to the rabbit, and from the swan to the jacksnipe." Shoppers on Christmas mornings during the 1860s found the market filled with venison, bears, ducks, geese, brant, quail, "partridges," and fish of almost every variety.[60]

Galveston's local markets were served by a rapidly expanding transportation infrastructure. New wharves built on the bayfront extended into water deep enough to berth oceangoing steamers. Small sailing vessels with their loads of fish and game docked next to newly constructed warehouses, plucking sheds, and salt packers, and a fleet of waiting wagons lined up to cart their bounty to

Galveston harbor's *Central Wharf as it looked in 1861. The side-wheel steamer is thought to be part of the Morgan fleet. (Courtesy Rosenberg Library, File No. G-2274.2 FF1, Item No. 3)*

the city center. Gaslights lit avenues along the Strand, with its dozens of boardinghouses and hotels that listed seafood and waterfowl on their menus. One of the city's hotel proprietors was J. S. Sydnor, who opened the Sydnor House in 1866. In his first advertisement he exclaimed, "The War Is Over!" and invited city residents to celebrate their success in "repair[ing] our lost fortunes [and being freed from] military rule" with his seventy-five-cent meals of fish, oysters, and game.[61]

North of Galveston, sloops and schooners rounded Morgan's Point, traversing shallow bays and bars up the San Jacinto River to Buffalo Bayou and the trading port of Harrisburg, its few houses built mostly of logs. Houston quickly usurped Harrisburg, by 1837 growing from twelve residents and one log cabin to fifteen hundred people and a hundred houses, a place that "thronged with statesmen, politicians, and merchants, and [was] noted for its wickedness." Hunters brought their wares to town from the cypress tree–covered landing near the foot of Main Street or joined long lines of prairie schooners and ox-driven carts, traveling streets that after a rain were "bog holes, and well nigh impassable."[62]

Houston established an open-air, public market in Market Square between Congress and Preston Streets in 1854. With it came the city's first efforts to regulate its markets. The city's riotous collection of street vendors, for example, were

> **MERCHANTS' RESTAURANT**
> AND
> **"THE LUNCH,"**
> ANTONIO MORGAN,
> Market street—one door west of the Austin House,
> OYSTERS,   GAME,   FISH,
> FOWLS,   MEATS,   FRUITS,
> All kinds of WINES and REFRESHMENTS of
> all kinds.
> Parties and Families supplied with OYSTERS
> as desired.

(Modified excerpt from *Flake's Bulletin* [Galveston], Aug. 27, 1867)

forbidden to sell their wares anywhere except Market Square, and only within the hours between four and nine in the morning. With the best interest of the public in mind, another ordinance prevented sale of "unsound meat, decaying fish, or other unwholesome food." Local newspapers kept track of the market supply and prices. Shoppers in the 1860s, anxiously awaiting fall's first deliveries, heralded the news that "five or six dray loads of game," mostly squirrels, geese, ducks, and prairie chickens, had arrived in the city and would keep residents "well supplied with these delicacies for two or three weeks."[63]

The number of the city's wild game dining establishments certainly rivaled Galveston's. As early as the 1840s, patrons of W. T. Cates's Bar Room on Main Street enjoyed "all varieties of wild game in season." Fish, oysters, venison, ducks, and geese were on the menu in 1860 at Antonio Morgan's by the Austin House and at James Robertson's Our House Restaurant, where "nothing that a reasonable man could ask for is wanting."[64]

Indianola, on Matagorda and Lavaca Bays, grew from a plague-infested immigrant camp into a prosperous city of fifteen hundred by the 1850s. As it was located behind Matagorda Peninsula and adjacent to Powderhorn Lake, commercial hunters did not have far to travel to supply its markets or hotels. Henry Runge of H. Runge and Company opened Indianola's first commission house and wharves in 1845. Mexican carts moved goods from the harbor to inland points; it took them a week to reach markets in San Antonio, although the Wells Fargo Company made the trip in less time using special wagons drawn by sixteen mules.[65]

Indianola residents followed prices and availability in the *Indianola Courier*, such as the report from September 1858 that markets were flush with plovers, curlews, and prairie chickens, which the game merchants called grouse. Shoppers bought their fish and game from the City Meat Market and the Bayou Market, both owned by August Schwartz, or from W. Volk's Indianola Market House. In addition to his retail market, Volk provisioned hotels and oceangoing vessels that called on town wharves. Well-stocked bills of fare greeted visitors at Indianola's

McCulloch House and Casimir Villeneuve's Casimir House, the latter considered the finest city eatery during the 1850s. Casimir also ran Indianola's Alhambra House, where a dollar and seventy-five cents paid for a night's lodging and "one single meal" from a menu of fish, oysters, and game.[66]

To the south, on the edge of Corpus Christi Bay, Henry L. Kinney in 1839 established his shellcrete trading post in a no-man's land claimed by both Mexico and the Republic of Texas and still wild with smugglers and thieves. The private army Kinney hired for protection was the only market for wild game until Zachary Taylor's army arrived in 1845 at the start of the Mexican War. The population of the trading post that would eventually become Corpus Christi grew overnight from a hundred residents to four thousand before the troops departed as swiftly as they had arrived.[67]

California gold brought the next wave of settlement to Corpus Christi in 1849, as gold-seeking forty-niners turned Kinney's trading post into a major supply center for the western frontier. The Corpus Christi Hotel was the only hotel in town, and to ensure that proprietor George Noessel had enough fresh fish, oysters, turtles, ducks, geese, and shorebirds to handle his surging business, he signed contracts with nearly all of the area's fishermen and hunters. The population of Corpus Christi grew to a thousand residents by 1867, before three hundred died in a yellow fever epidemic.[68]

Brownsville and Point Isabel were the major markets for waterfowl sold in coastal South Texas. Brownsville watermen got their foothold when the US Army built Fort Brown in 1846. Fort Brown soldiers were supplied with redheads and pintails from the Rio Grande delta and Laguna Madre by military hunting expeditions and by Mexicans who hauled the birds in mule-drawn two-wheeled carts. Only two roads, the old Spanish road from Alice and Military Telegraph Road along the Rio Grande, allowed market men to move their products through cactus and mesquite scrub to Fort Brown. It is likely that waterfowl were also part of the cargo carried by Capt. Mifflin Kenedy, Richard King, and Charles Stillman, who were contracted to supply the army at Fort Brown by steamboats sailing between Point Isabel and Rio Grande City. Brownsville got its first public marketplace in the early 1850s.[69]

The importance of wildfowl to early Texas was not limited to coastal towns. Jefferson, on Big Cypress Bayou in East Texas, was one of the state's most prosperous early inland trading and market centers. Linked to the rest of the Gulf Coast by a fleet of river steamers, the cosmopolitan city had a robust plantation and mercantile economy by the 1830s. Adjacent Caddo Lake's abundant wildfowl, particularly mallards and canvasbacks, fed boat captains, merchants, travelers, fishermen, and slaves. For Caddo Lake gunners, with their long-barreled, muzzle-loading shotguns, the only practical way to shoot ducks was on the water. In the winter of 1855–56, John Haywood and Port Caddo blacksmith James Penny killed 133 ducks with only two shots. Not to be outdone, another group boasted that, between the four of them, they killed between 250 and 400 ducks every day, each never firing more than two shots.[70]

Waterfowl were also a part of the market trade in thriving San Antonio, one of the largest Texas cities before the Civil War. Alamo City residents bought waterfowl in a number of hotels and restaurants and in the city's public market, the Market House. Tom Grayson ran his meat business in the late 1850s from the north stall of the Market House, promising patrons he could be "found at early hours, ready to serve his friends and the public." During winters, his stall was packed with geese, ducks, quail, and snipes. The most renowned city restaurant was the Colonial Dining Room in the Menger Hotel on Alamo Square. Opened in 1859, its menu included wild game and snapper soup made from turtles caught in the San Antonio River. Dinners were taken in a setting with a solid cherry bar, cherry-paneled ceiling, French mirrors, and gold-plated spittoons.[71]

The scene was similar throughout Texas towns large and small. Victoria, on the Guadalupe River, had its public Victoria Market House by 1851, and the Globe House and Railroad House, which in the 1850s advertised tables always supplied "with all the luxuries and delicacies that can be procured in this or any other markets." In 1850s Austin, John Lewis's saloon on Congress Avenue provided a bill of fare that included ducks, snipes, and plovers; among his regular patrons were capital city legislators. Dallas and Fort Worth, which were both to become important shipping centers in the late 1800s, were only just stretching their urban wings before the Civil War.[72]

WATERFOWL PRICES

In early Texas, cash was rarely used to buy wild game. Mary Austin Holley observed, "No one will receive money for anything taken by his gun, but will cheerfully give as much as you will take, and feel insulted, if you offer him money in return." Part of the reason was lack of currency in Mexican Texas and the nearly worthless redback currency of the Republic of Texas. As an alternative, trade was often consummated with foreign currencies or by barter. As late as the mid-1800s, Mexican silver was acceptable medium of exchange in South Texas. Cattle and hogs were common currency between the Brazos and Colorado Rivers, with a cow and a calf in pioneer Texas "passing as ten dollars." Barter continued to prevail for a long time in rural communities; in Chambers County legend has it that a pound of duck feathers could be traded for a sixteen-year-old bride.[73]

However it was paid, a pair of ducks by the 1850s cost approximately fifty cents in Indianola and Houston, thirty cents in Galveston, and twenty-four cents in Matagorda. One hunter wrote that, in the town markets along the lower Brazos River, "wild ducks, or widgeons, averaged a quarter of a dollar" and "geese and cranes half a dollar; and we thought ourselves lucky to be able to dispose of quails, plovers, or snipes at a dime . . . each." Little distinction was made between species of wildfowl before the 1860s; they were just ducks, geese, brant, swans, cranes, or shorebirds. The only advice shoppers were given was to look at the legs of ducks, as those with a fishy taste had "black legs."[74]

FOOD, FEATHERS, AND FAT

Nearly as important as meat to pre–Civil War Texas were wildfowl feathers, used to fill mattresses, pillows, and bolsters; it was tradition for brides to receive feather pillows when they married. Waterfowl down and feathers were more highly esteemed for the home than farm-raised poultry, and the 1862 *Chambers Encyclopedia* explained the difference: "At the present day, goose-feathers are preferred, the white rather than the gray. What are called poultry feathers, such as those of the turkey, duck, and fowl, are less esteemed, on account of their deficient elasticity. Wild-duck feathers are soft and elastic, but contain oil difficult to remove."[75]

Wildfowl feathers sold for fifty cents a pound in the 1840s, and Henry Jordan, whose family settled in the village of Decrow's Point on Matagorda Peninsula, estimated it took three hundred pounds of feathers to meet their needs. With only a few dollars in cash when they landed in Texas, the Jordans could not afford the $150 it would have cost to furnish their homestead. Instead, they procured their own waterfowl, and it would have taken more than three thousand ducks to meet their requirements for feathers.[76]

By the 1850s demand for feathers in growing urban centers was met by wholesale merchants who purchased feathers packed in bales and shipped by the half ton. Local stores charged shoppers about twenty-five to thirty-five cents a pound. In the 1860s the *Galveston Daily News* advised young men about to marry to travel to Marlin, south of Waco, where so many wild geese feasted on corn crops that they could quickly gather a good dowry of feathers.[77]

Early Texans also relied on waterfowl for cooking fat. Henry Jordan said settlers stored gallons of cooking oil "tried out," or rendered, from the fat of ducks, geese, and swans. A Trinity River delta market hunter wrote: "I killed a very heavy swan, and to escape the fatigue of carrying it, I gave the bird to an old German woman, who had as much idea of the art of cooking as a pig." But she knew about fat. She parboiled the bird and skimmed off three pints of grease.[78]

A FOUNDATION LAID

Despite its abundant natural resources, Texas in the first half of the nineteenth century lagged far behind much of the United States in the economy of waterfowl. What later became the Lone Star State was still part of New Spain when, in the late 1700s, a vigorous trade in wildfowl and other game was already established in

> FEATHERS—10 Bales of Live Geese Feathers, just received and for sale at the House Furnishing Warehouse.
>
> (Modified from *Civilian and Galveston Gazette*, Nov. 23, 1852)

marketplaces along the northeastern Atlantic seaboard. By the early 1800s, when settlement Texas was part of Mexico, shoppers were jamming sophisticated big-city marketplaces in Boston, New York, Philadelphia, Baltimore, and Washington.

Fleets of sailing ships and steamers made it possible to supply markets up and down the Atlantic seaboard with birds shot in the renowned fowling regions of the day: Cape Cod in Massachusetts, New York's Long Island Sound and Great South Bay, Barnegat Bay in New Jersey, Delaware Bay, Chesapeake Bay, and Back Bay to Currituck Sound from Virginia to North Carolina. Those gunning regions provided markets with a remarkable diversity of wildfowl. Thomas F. De Voe, in his survey of New England butcher stalls in the 1860s, counted two species of swans, four of geese, twenty-six of ducks, forty-three different marsh and shorebirds, and dozens of game and nongame birds.[79]

The assortment and quantity of wild game in Saint Louis and Chicago rivaled East Coast markets. John James Audubon commented on the abundance of locally procured geese, ducks, and canvasbacks in Saint Louis markets in his visit to the city in the late 1850s. The impressive numbers he saw were mainly supplied by gunners who hunted just a short distance from the city along the Missouri and Mississippi River floodplains. Chicago city markets were supplied mostly from Wisconsin's Horicon Marsh, Sandusky Bay on Lake Erie, Michigan's Saginaw Bay and Lake Saint Clair, and glacial pothole ponds throughout Minnesota.[80]

New Orleans had the largest markets on the Gulf Coast in the late 1700s. Cobblestone streets fronted the city's two main open-air marketplaces, the French Market and Jackson Square, on the banks of the Mississippi River. Market men delivered ducks by the hundreds by wagon or via the Mississippi River in trade boats of all shapes and sizes. The maritime flotilla included skiffs with gaff-rigged sails, square-bowed and flat-bottomed chaland skiffs, and square-sailed New Orleans luggers that threaded their way through oceangoing schooners, brigs, and barks to wharves adjacent to the French Quarter.[81]

By the early 1800s the New Orleans French Market was one of the leading game markets in the world. Past the vegetable and fish stands were row upon row of meat and game stalls, the most renowned of which were manned by professional butchers who hailed from Gascony, France. Sunday was the main shopping day, and fall through spring, shoppers in their Sunday best were feted with an assortment of cranes, geese, ducks, coots, and shore and wading birds. Game birds included wild turkeys, pigeons, quail, and doves as well as a host of colorful songbirds. The array of wildfowl offered in New Orleans markets induced artists

Alexander Wilson and John James Audubon to buy several bird specimens used in their famous illustrations.[82]

Having evolved from predominantly a means of sustenance to a growing local industry, the Texas wildfowl trade had established a firm foothold by the early 1860s. With its abundant natural resources and developing transportation infrastructure, the Lone Star State was poised to join the wild game shipping business to northern and eastern states. But first came a Civil War, and it took Texas, like most of the South, a long time to recover.

CHAPTER 3

A NATIONAL APPETITE

Market hunting, like almost everything about America, changed greatly and hurriedly in the decades after the Civil War. The wild game trade became a growing industry, brought about, in part, by postwar economic expansion that afforded a growing segment of Texas and the United States disposable cash to spend on luxury items. For urban Americans, wildfowl was one of those extravagances. In part, too, the wild game trade benefited from postwar advancement in technologies. Inefficient black-powder muzzle- and breech-loading shotguns were replaced by repeating firearms using factory-loaded shotgun shells. A national network of railroads provided for the shipment of products quickly to market and, along with invention of ice-making machinery, did away with the uncertainty of getting birds to market without spoiling, or even getting them there at all.

Popularized as a vital seasonal ingredient in the culinary culture of nineteenth-century America, game birds and animals were a regular feature on the household dining table. Extensive attention was paid to the best ways for the homemaker to prepare and cook them. In an 1866 *Good Housekeeping* article, readers were reminded that "game is healthful and easily digested," and the "housekeeper should supply her table with it frequently." An 1891 account by Mrs. M. E. W. Sherwood covered pages of newsprint with practical advice, such as cooking woodcocks, snipes, and most "common" ducks the day they were shot, but noted that canvasbacks would "bear keeping." The *Dallas Morning News* in 1903 dedicated a full page to cooking wild ducks and instructed that plovers should be cooked with the head on, as the "brain is considered a great luxury." Such advice was repeated in media all across America.[1]

Waterfowl graced menus of hundreds of restaurants, from humble boardinghouses to some of America's finest. The gastronomic standard for fine dining was set by restaurants in the eastern seaboard cities of Washington, Baltimore, Philadelphia, and New York and those in Saint Louis, Chicago, and New Orleans. Texas hunters supplied many of them, although probably none of the market men ever attended a dinner like the exclusive Annual Game Dinner hosted at Chicago's Tremont Hotel, with its dazzling array of game shipped from throughout the United States. Wildfowl entries on the menu in 1868 included nine species of ducks, "dark goose," snow goose, roasted cranes, snipes, yellowlegs, plovers, and more esoteric servings of rice, reed, and marsh birds. Likely, too, they never sat at a table at Randolph Guggenheimer's supper at New York's Waldorf Astoria in 1899. Guggenheimer's ten-thousand-dollar dinner bill covered a huge staff of prep cooks, chefs, and waiters who prepared game that was shipped from all over America, including ruddy ducks sent by express to New York in small portable refrigerators.[2]

The supply of wild game was carried by America's railroads. Expansion of the nation's rail network after the Civil War made it possible to deliver wildfowl to East Coast cities from across the country. Large numbers of birds came from the southern Atlantic seaboard, the Great Lakes region, the Mississippi River valley, and Texas. While Washington, Baltimore, Philadelphia, and New York maintained their preeminence as the largest marketplaces, the sale of wild game grew to include nearly every city and town with rail connections on the East Coast.

By the second half of the 1800s railroads converged, like spokes of a wheel, on both Chicago and Saint Louis city centers. Particularly significant were railroad connections to the Southern states, as they enabled access to rich gunning grounds in the lower Mississippi River valley, notably southern Reelfoot Lake in Tennessee and Arkansas' Big Lake and the "Sunken Lands" along the Saint Francis River. In the 1880s Chicago received what were probably the first regular shipments of ducks from Texas: canvasbacks shot on Lake Stephenson in Chambers County and shipped by rail out of Galveston.[3]

In the southern United States, railroads advanced the geographic reach of the New Orleans market trade and by the late 1880s included fowl shipped from the upper coast of Texas. Much of New Orleans' supply was dominated by French Acadian hunters, the Cajuns. Wildfowl in city markets had always carried local names that reflected Indian, French, Spanish, slave, and Creole heritage, and with the Cajuns came a distinct dialect, part French-Canadian and part developed in the Louisiana swamp. A Parisian would wince at their pronunciation of *canard cheval* for canvasbacks, *canard gris* for gadwalls, *dos gris* for scaup, and *poule d'eau* for the popular American coot. New Orleans markets were so flush with game that, according to one visitor, the prices "would astonish an eastern man, who finds ducks as low as two bits [twenty-five cents] per pair, and even ten cents in hot weather."[4]

On the Pacific Coast, railroad depots in California's largest cities, notably Sacramento, Oakland, Los Angeles, and San Francisco, handled large volumes of birds shipped from the Sacramento–San Joaquin River delta, San Francisco Bay, the length of the Central Valley, and as far away as Tule Lake and Oregon's Klamath Lake. Early 1900s California markets carried canvasbacks, mallards, "sprigs," teal, redheads, wigeons, gadwalls they called gray ducks, northern shovelers or spoonbills, ring-necked ducks or blackjacks, bluebills, and "small ducks." Small ducks included goldeneyes, which went by the local name of whistlers or brownheads; ruddy ducks, which they called either dollar ducks or martelles; or butterballs, although the latter name was also used for buffleheads. Markets sometimes carried wood ducks, called summer ducks, and "Mexican tree ducks." Merchants nearly always advertised snow geese as white geese, white-fronted geese as gray geese, and Canada geese as honker geese. Both sandhill cranes and shorebirds were market staples, the latter including sand plovers, which were called bullheads, and others locally known as brown curlews, jack snipes, robin snipes, and half snipes.[5]

Gifted with copious natural resources and a railroad transportation network after the Civil War, Texas joined the national and even trans-Atlantic trade in wildfowl. The cross-country trade in Texas wildfowl was made up mostly of canvasbacks, redheads, plovers, and curlews. Swans, cranes, and geese were not commonly shipped across state lines. Too, until the late 1890s transportation costs limited the distances that low-demand birds such as gadwalls, wigeons, and bluebills, and low-price birds such as teal, pintails, and mallards, could be shipped for profit. That changed near the turn of the century, when prices for many waterfowl increased to the point that nearly every species was sold.[6]

TEXAS TRADE

The Lone Star State's export business ran parallel to an equally vibrant in-state shipping business. Before railroads, nearly all of Texas' waterfowl shipments were confined to within the state. The foundation for the intrastate trade was laid by river steamers that, on routes between Texas port towns, regularly listed wild ducks in their bills of lading. Among the manifests of the steamer *T. M. Bagby*, which arrived from Houston to the Port of Galveston in 1872, were two sacks, one barrel, and one box of ducks. Throughout the 1870s the cargo of winter steamships usually listed ducks by the sack, although the number of ducks packed per sack is unknown.[7]

Growing towns and cities were the destination for most wild game. The largest quantities were sold to hotels, restaurants, and retail meat and produce markets. In some ways, late-nineteenth-century Texas marketplaces resembled those of settlement Texas. Game hawkers still prowled the edges of the main marketplaces. Others hawked their wares on street corners, such as Sabine market hunters who "brought wagon upon wagon loads of ducks, mostly mallards," and sold them in Port Arthur for fifty cents a pair. Two boys in the 1890s who killed a

NEEDVILLE MEAT MARKET, *year unknown. Nearly every Texas town by the mid- to late 1800s had a meat market that sold wild game. Buildings varied from stalls to indoor-outdoor markets and even grand two- and three-story buildings. (Courtesy Fort Bend County Libraries, Genealogy and Local History Department)*

DIRT-PACKED STREETS *turned to mud after rains. Beaumont, possibly Pearl Street, about the 1890s. (Courtesy Tyrrell Historical Library, Beaumont, Texas, File No. GPA.1-016-BJ-335a)*

wagonload of swans brought them to Galveston, stopping at each of the city's boardinghouses until their cart was emptied. In Brownsville, any buyer willing to pay six cents each could purchase ducks by the wagonload from hawkers parked at the edge of town.[8]

There was, however, noticeable progress in many larger towns as hastily constructed outdoor stalls and open-air markets in the public square gave way to indoor stalls under the roof of a central market building. Oystershell and packed-dirt streets were, like the muddy tracks of the first half of the nineteenth century, still filled with shoppers, wagons, and carts, but increasingly cities on the cutting edge of transportation infrastructure had mule- and horse-drawn streetcars.

Weekly commodity reports in big-city Texas newspapers kept shoppers abreast of wildfowl prices and availability. The duck nearly always listed first in market reports was the canvasback. Galveston customers in the 1870s paid the remark-

> "A few teals have found their way into the market and, what is still more wonderful, can be bought for a little less than their weight in fractional currency."
>
> (Modified from *Galveston Daily News*, Sept. 11, 1869)

> "Texas is still the promised land. . . . Our market is supplied with great numbers of wild geese at 50 cents, wild ducks at 50 cents a brace, . . . All these things are the substantials on which we live."
>
> (Modified excerpt from *Galveston Daily News*, Dec. 4, 1867)

ably high price of seventy-five cents to a dollar for a pair of the white, black, and red-headed duck. Listed next were greenhead mallards, mottled ducks, pintails—always called sprigs—redheads, and teal, which cost from thirty to ninety cents a pair according to quality. The only bird called a goose was the Canada; all others were brant, and usually they sold by the dozen. Swans in Galveston markets sold for seventy-five cents to a dollar. Snipes usually sold for a dollar a dozen, and the price was similar for plovers, curlews, woodcocks, and passenger pigeons.[9]

Prices in Galveston and Houston were much higher than in coastal towns to the south. A pair of "fat ducks" in 1870s Rockport, for example, cost twenty-five cents, and mallards during the 1890s sold in the game houses of Corpus Christi, Rockport, and Port Lavaca for only about two dollars a dozen. Historian Murphy Givens said that Corpus Christi hunters sold their piles of redhead ducks to a San Antonio game firm for just twenty cents a pair.[10]

Prices were so low in Brownsville that the *Galveston Daily News* boasted "northern people" would never believe that "snipe are selling here for two cents apiece [and] canvasback for half a dime each." A *Brownsville Daily Herald* market report of 1892 listed canvasback for ten cents each, teal for three cents, and gadwall—"gray ducks"—for two and one-half cents. Snow geese were twelve cents a dozen, and wild "gray geese"—either specklebellies or Canada geese—were twelve cents each. Snipes sold for two cents apiece, and a dozen upland sandpipers—or

> Game—Retail prices: Canvas-back ducks, $1.00 per pair for choice; mallards, 50 to 65c.; sprigs, 50 to 60c.; red-heads, 75c.; gray ducks and widgeons, 40 to 50c.; teal, 25c. Snipe, 75c to $1.00 per dozen. Quail, $1.00 to 1.25 per dozen. Wholesale prices are lower.
>
> GALVESTON WILD BIRD *prices in 1879.*
>
> (Modified from *Galveston Daily News*, Dec. 18, 1879)

> Game—The market was bare to-day, but supplies are due to-morrow. Ducks—canvas-back, per pair, $1; teal, 25 to 30c.; spring bald-pates (or widgeons) and gray ducks, 40 to 50c.; mallards, 60 to 75c. Wild geese, 50c to $1 each. Snipe, $1.00 per dozen; English snipe, $1.50; Dolwich snipe, $1. per dozen. Quail, $1. Venison scarce at 10c. per lb. retail.
>
> A SCARCE MARKET *greeted Galveston shoppers in November 1880. English snipe are today called Wilson's snipe, and Dolwich snipe are probably both long-billed and short-billed dowitchers.*
>
> (Modified from *Galveston Daily News*, Nov. 20, 1880).

A NATIONAL APPETITE

PRICES FOR WATERFOWL *in the Brownsville City Market were much lower than those on the upper and middle coast and in inland cities during the same time period.*

(Modified from *Brownsville Daily Herald*, Dec. 16, 1893)

MARKET REPORT.

Following is a list of some of the articles sold in the city market with prices at which they sold:

Ducks, canvas back, a piece	10c
" teel	3c
" grey	2½c
Snipe, per dozen	10c
Brant " "	12c
Gray geese a piece	12c
Ham venison "	37c
Shoulder of venison a piece	18c

papabots—cost seventy-five cents. Prices were actually lower than they seemed; Brownsville posted its market prices in Mexican currency, with one Mexican dollar worth sixty-five cents.[11]

At times prices fluctuated wildly in local markets. Highest prices corresponded to Thanksgiving and Christmas holidays or when birds were scarce. Scarcity was the cause of lofty prices in January 1895, when no mallards, plovers, or geese were in the market and canvasbacks were "scarce and high." In Port Lavaca, the *Lavaca Sea Breeze* pronounced the scarcity of geese in 1887 with a sense of humor, writing "geese are too high at present to sell at any price, unless sold on the wing." High prices were sometimes a result of market monopolies, such as the one built by two brothers who dominated Galveston markets in 1879. As the only suppliers of canvasbacks to the city that year, they sold their birds through only one city dealer, and their hold on the market forced customers to pay exorbitant prices.[12]

The peak waterfowl migration, with its increased supply, brought lower prices not only for wild birds, but even for farm-raised animals. In December 1871 a surplus of wildfowl caused a 20 percent decline in domestic chicken prices in parts of the state. Port Aransas merchants fretted that the local cattle and poultry industry was "seriously damaged" on account of the overabundance of wildfowl in local markets during the 1890s. In 1893 so many ducks flooded markets along the coast that the price in Velasco fell to a nickel apiece. Gluts sometimes extended to the entirety of the US market. During one market surplus, a Rockport hunter netted only a five-dollar profit from 430 canvasbacks he shipped to New York. He quit.[13]

Sometimes when the market was slow, it had nothing to do with holidays, monopolies, or availability. In November 1867, wildfowl hanging from the posts of market stalls in Galveston attracted few buyers. Merchants blamed it on the fact that "the country people did not come in." And the country folk had good reason not to come to town; that autumn Galveston was still reeling from a yellow fever epidemic that had decimated its population, one of half a dozen deadly outbreaks that plagued the city since 1855.[14]

> **Texas Express Company,**
>
> **FORWARDERS**
>
> of Merchandise. Specie and Valuables of all kinds, to all points in Texas, and (in connection with other Express Companies,) to all points in the United States, Canada and Europe.
>
> *Makes Collections of paper, either with or without goods,*
>
> AND
>
> Transacts a GENERAL EXPRESS BUSINESS,
>
> PRINCIPAL OFFICE:
>
> **Houston, - - Texas,**

THE TEXAS EXPRESS COMPANY *was one of three in Texas that shipped fish, oysters, and wild game. (Morrison and Fourmy's General Directory of the City of Houston, 1899 [Galveston: Morrison and Fourmy, 1899], Appendix C)*

SUPPLYING THE NATIONAL TABLE

Texas after the Civil War had only a few rail lines that connected the coast to inland markets, notably Sabine Pass to Beaumont, Galveston to Houston, and Houston to the inland prairie towns of Hockley and Eagle Lake. Between the 1870s and late 1890s, however, rails began to link major Texas cities to the rest of America. As quickly as tracks were laid, nearly every sizable coastal town and inland city joined the burgeoning wild game enterprise. Railroads made it possible to transport wild ducks from Texas to a nation.[15]

The backbone of the supply network was railroad express agencies. Called express shippers, these operations moved perishable goods rapidly, with few if any connections between depot and destination city. Three express forwarding agencies dominated the shipping business in Texas: Adams Express Company, the Texas Wells Fargo Express Company, and the Texas Express Company.[16]

Railroads delivered the volume, and it was ice that kept game from spoiling. Salt and expensive New England ice began their descent into obscurity with the first ice-making technology in the 1860s. Widely credited for its invention were brothers James S. and David Boyle, who built early plants in New Orleans and Jefferson, Texas. Cost and availability, however, limited use of early manufactured ice in the game trade.[17]

In the late 1870s the Louisiana Ice Manufacturing Company of New Orleans developed an ice plant capable, at last, of producing commercially viable volumes of manufactured ice. The chill of commercial refrigeration was met with a warm reception. When mass-produced ice reached Galveston in 1878, it was greeted with accolades such as "one of the greatest blessings ever enjoyed by people." Ice plants were quickly built in nearly every major Texas port and inland city. Fish, oyster, and game purveyors embraced the new technology, paying between three and eight dollars a ton by the late 1800s to railroad companies with refrigerated cars.[18]

A NATIONAL APPETITE

WOODEN BARRELS *were always in demand to transport fish, game, and a host of other things and were manufactured in several Texas port towns. (Directory of the City of Galveston, 1899–1900 [Galveston: Morrison and Fourmy, 1899], 39, courtesy Rosenberg Library, Galveston)*

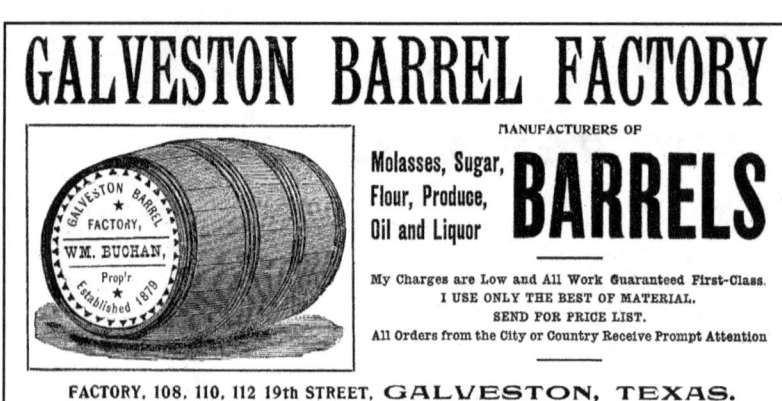

The wooden barrel filled with crushed ice became the standard for long-distance shipment of game. The process for packing ducks, according to Smith Point market hunter Forest McNeir, was first to line empty barrels with cotton bagging. Then a sawed block of ice was wrapped in burlap and placed in the middle of the barrel before it was filled with ducks. Burlap filled the remaining space, the top was secured by a wooden ring pushed down over the slats, and the top of the barrel was nailed shut. McNeir packed forty-five to fifty canvasbacks to a barrel, while other market men averaged up to sixty.[19]

Many small seaside communities never had ice-making capabilities during the legal market hunting years and had to rely on ice delivered by wagons, sloops, and steam launches. Market hunters and transport vessels from High Island and Smith Point on the upper coast bought ice transported from Galveston by the half ton at a cost of ninety cents per hundred pounds. In Point Isabel the ringing of the ice wagon bell announced deliveries from the Frontier Ice Works at one and one-half cents "Mexican coin" per pound.[20]

Ice stored in the holds of sloops and schooners allowed market men to preserve their kill during extended shooting trips. Port Lavaca market man A. L. Canfield was like many who filled his new "common ice chest" year-round with oysters, fish, and ducks. Rockport's Capt. Ed Armstrong fitted his ice box amidships, filling it with 150-pound blocks of ice. Because of its bulk, and the fact that it melted, ice remained impractical for hunters who hunted from horseback and small sloops or lived for days and weeks in isolated camps. Bolivar's Herman Johnson, who hunted McFaddin Marsh in Jefferson County, brined ducks as late as the turn of the century. Every few days he packed his salted ducks in barrels and sent them by sail to Galveston.[21]

Manufactured ice by the 1880s gave rise to another industry important to the trade in waterfowl: the cold storage plant. At first called "refrigerator meat markets," they allowed game merchants and hotels throughout Texas to advertise availability of fish, oysters, and game almost year-round. With cold storage, wild game could be kept for several months, and game dealers who timed its entrance in the marketplace at periods of peak demand fetched the highest prices.[22]

Ducks were brought *to harbor, then loaded onto piers or horse-drawn wagons for transport to the packing house. This Port Lavaca photo from about 1900, possibly taken by Charles Boyd, shows many of the boats of the time: wooden skiffs (foreground), sloops (at the wharf), and two-masted schooners (anchored in the harbor). (Jan Regan Collection, courtesy Dean Johnstone, File No. 0189)*

Cold storage had a major impact on the Texas export business. In 1889, Texas game was kept until summer in a New York cold storage plant, its inventory consisting of twelve hundred canvasbacks, thirty thousand plovers, over fifteen thousand snipes, and forty-two hundred prairie chickens. In the fall of 1897, Texas market men supplied ten thousand ducks and an astonishing eighty thousand geese to a New York merchant who stored them until Christmas that year. One Houston cold storage house handled twelve thousand plovers in a single week for a Northern shipper.[23]

Cold storage was swiftly adopted by the maritime shipping industry. In the 1890s, Maj. Henry E. Alvord of the US Department of Agriculture arrived in Galveston with a plan to ship Texas farm products around the world. He dispatched two oceangoing, refrigerated steamers from Canada, proclaiming, "I understand that any number of wild ducks may be had for export at this place. There is a demand for them and it should be supplied." It was.[24]

Demand in distant marketplaces quickly expanded the ranks of Texas game merchants. Originally known as commission merchants or forwarding agents, they handled a variety of perishable products and general merchandise in addition to wild game. By the late 1870s, most dealt exclusively in fin and fowl, their moniker changed to "fish, oyster, and game dealers." Wharves and buildings sprouted along the waterfront of most major coastal towns, where watermen brought kills of waterfowl and catches of oysters, turtles, fish, and crabs for cleaning and packing before shipment by waiting refrigerated railroad cars.

Fish, oyster, and game dealers relied on a maritime industry of "buy boats" that linked their picking and packing houses to suppliers. Sailboats and steamers of the buy boat fleet fanned out from major port towns to prime hunting locations along the coast, where hunters, fishermen, and oystermen delivered their wares. After taking on a full load, the captain and his vessel set sail for port.[25]

Unloading barrels in Galveston harbor at Pier 19's floating market. (*A Souvenir of Galveston, 1893* [Galveston: Galveston Evening Tribune, 1893], 21, courtesy Rosenberg Library, Galveston)

Picked and cleaned ducks were packed by fish, game, and oysters dealers in ice in wooden barrels, covered in burlap, and shipped by express rail cars (background) to northern points. This shipment is from Port Lavaca's Gentry Fish and Oyster House, with the goods being handled by the local Wells Fargo Express agent. (Courtesy Dean Johnstone, File No. 0311)

Typical Galveston Bay *oyster lugger. The Erett, shown in 1920, belonged to a Captain Arvidson during the market hunting era.* (Galveston Daily News, *Feb. 20, 1909, John Winter Collection, courtesy Cliff Fisher*)

Buy boats were a great advantage to hunters, who, because they no longer had to return to town to sell their harvest, could remain afield longer. For game merchants, buy boats cut down on spoilage. But not always; buy boats frequently faced bad weather or unfavorable winds that caused the total loss of the shipment. Market man Forest McNeir remembered seeing a spoiled shipment of five hundred pairs of cleaned ducks thrown overboard in Galveston harbor, the result of transport on a sloop that "bucked two days of headwinds and tides coming down from High Islands, only fifty miles away." By the turn of the century, steam- and sail-powered buy boats began to give way to ones with gasoline engines; typical early-1900s buy boats were thirty-six-foot oyster luggers with a ten-horsepower inboard engine.[26]

At its peak, the many moving parts of the Texas wildfowl business are well illustrated by a group of Orange market gunners who hunted Sabine Lake in 1901. They killed nearly a thousand ducks and, with their sloop filled to the gunwales, sailed to meet the buy boat *J. I. Griffith*. The steamer set a course for Orange, where the ducks, packed in ice, filled sixteen barrels. By the time those ducks were hauled by wagon to the express depot and on to New Orleans, they had afforded income to shooters, buy boat captain and crew, pickers, ice company employees, barrel makers, packers, teamsters, railroad men, and game merchants.[27]

EVOLUTION OF THE HUNT

Demand and technology had an impact not only on the way game was hunted, but also on who was hunting the game. Late-nineteenth and early-twentieth-century technology made it possible to put relatively inexpensive, mass-produced, and efficient firearms into the hands of a growing number of men involved in the market trade. To accommodate their numbers, guns now blazed in places that,

> "Farmers are troubled now with large flocks of wild geese. They have taken a liking to corn, the complaint is that the hands will have to be taken from the cotton, and put to gathering corn."
>
> (Modified from *Galveston Daily News*, Dec. 12, 1869)

only a few years before, were considered too harsh or simply too hard to reach. Many of the new guns now belonged to professional or commercial hunters, who shot birds twelve months a year.

Progress, too, was altering the hunting landscape. The breaking of native prairie for agriculture was one of the biggest changes, and it was to have a profound effect on waterfowl feeding patterns. Entirely new shooting grounds were opened to hunters as ducks and geese began to shift inland to feed on crops of corn, sorghum, wheat, barley, peanuts, and soybeans. The foremost grain on the upper and middle coasts, from Orange to Port Lavaca, was rice. First cultivated in Beaumont in 1850, it was called "providence" rice because farmers relied on rainwater for irrigation.[28]

Every step in the rice-growing process provided feeding opportunities for wildfowl. When fields were first flooded in spring, they attracted resident mottled ducks, whistling ducks, and purple gallinules, the latter called tangle birds because their nests got caught up in farm machinery. As seed matured in late summer, fields were infested with more mottled ducks, blue-winged teal, and early arriving pintails and mallards. Blackbirds and cowbirds blackened the sky over standing rice. Ronnie Luster, who moved to Port Lavaca as a boy, remembers that when his mother saw her first big, twisting flock of red-wing blackbirds over rice, she thought it was a tornado and took shelter with her son in a ditch.[29]

Most irresistible to waterfowl was the rice harvest, when, each fall, long lines of mule-pulled binders wound their way into the fields, bundling cut rice stalks into shocks that were left upright to dry for up to six weeks. The waiting food source was an opportunity seized upon by ducks, geese, and other birds. Flocks of ducks were known to "destroy in one night almost a whole crop of rice. Rice farmers often awaken to find their fields, which were ready for the threshing machine in the previous afternoon, appear as though a mowing machine had just run over a huge field of hay. The neatly stacked shocks of the evening before have been found scattered all over the fields, all grains from which having been picked clean by ducks."[30]

Ducks caused rice farmers no end of lost revenue. Under the heading "Trouble in Texas," the *Louisiana Planter and Sugar Manufacturer* called attention to "the great injury" caused by immense flocks of ducks to upper coast rice fields at the turn of the century. Market hunter and game dealer Nat Wetzel recalled how ducks razed a hundred-acre upper coast rice field during a single night, and east of

MULE-PULLED BINDERS *were a big improvement over hand harvesting of rice with sickles. Every step in the rice-growing process provided feeding opportunities for wildfowl. (Photo from Garwood, Colorado County, early 1900s, courtesy Nesbit Memorial Library, File No. 04058)*

Houston another hunter witnessed the destruction of forty acres of shocked rice in just one night. On the middle coast, a prominent rice farmer from Wharton County called ducks "winged pests." At Clark's rice farm outside of Port Lavaca, neighbors assisted in the slaughter of hundreds of wild ducks, geese, and prairie chickens in 1903 in an effort to save Clark's uncut rice from total destruction.[31]

Market hunters began to follow the birds to rice. In 1902, Jefferson County hunters who traditionally worked on the coast were "anxious as to the result of the rice fields on their business." They had good reason; the year before, ducks were said to be "unusually scarce, and it is believed that they will desert the salt water [for rice] more and more each season."[32]

Whether they hunted agricultural fields, native prairie, or over water, the main difference in the way market men killed waterfowl during the late nineteenth century was in the tools they used. It was a big leap forward when black-powder flintlocks, muzzle-loaders, and early breechloader shotguns were replaced by hammerless firearms and factory-loaded shells. The first hammerless shotguns were manufactured in the 1870s. Although they still used black powder, their shells could be loaded in advance or, for those with the money, purchased from catalogs and hardware stores.[33]

Long-barrel and two-barrel muzzle- and breech-loading guns, stock–in-trade for market hunters using shoulder-fired weapons, were superseded in the 1880s by mass-produced repeating shotguns. Spencer introduced the first pump gun in 1882, and it was followed in quick succession by Winchester's Model 1887 lever-action repeater, John M. Browning's Winchester 1893 pump gun, and its successor, the Winchester 1897 built for smokeless powder. By the turn of the century Browning developed the first semiautomatic shotgun, manufactured in the United States as the Remington Model 11. After decades of inefficient black powder fired from single- or double-barreled guns, the five-shot pump gun and semiautomatics with white smokeless powder became the weapons of choice for nearly all of Texas' commercial hunters.[34]

Market men with their new weapons made some phenomenal harvests. Sabine Pass gunner John J. "Jack" Johnson was said to have killed 135 ducks with only five shots. Using a ten-gauge repeater, Jefferson County's J. D. Lane killed 105 ducks with just thirty-three shells. However hunters got to the birds, and wherever they hunted, harvests like Johnson's and Lane's were repeated across Texas.[35]

Efficient shotguns also turned shorebird shooting into a widely practiced and highly profitable venture. In contrast to the days when a single shot was fired across grouped birds, hunters with modern weapons increasingly turned to wing shooting over decoys. Seasoned snipe hunters shot one or two from a flock, then waited for them to return to "settle down again in a body close to their dead companions, giving the hunter shot after shot." Preferred plover and curlew decoys were crippled, wing-tipped live birds that shooters would "always preserve and tie out among his flock." It was characteristic for entire flocks to hover around a screeching, wounded bird until most of their numbers were killed.[36]

Pump and semiautomatic shotguns increased the effectiveness of gunners who shot from horseback and were the gun of choice for hunters using trained steers in the late 1800s. In steer hunting, gunners loaded into wagons behind a team of mules with an ox tied alongside and slowly scoured inland and coastal prairie to find potholes with concentrations of birds. Once they located a flock, they "made a sneak," in which one of the hunters controlled the steer with a halter and stick while another walked behind the big animal until they were close enough to fire. One hunter made his shot by resting his fowling piece on the steer's back, and even after the volley the ox never stopped feeding.[37]

The versatility of guns that could be held to the shoulder, whether side-by-side or repeating, made them the preferred weapons. Some Texas hunters also used big guns, both swivel and punt guns. The punt gun was the most infamous, considered "the deadliest weapon known for waterfowl bagging." Its description makes it easy to understand why; punt guns were six to nine feet long, with a half-inch- to two-inch-diameter bore and chambers that held up to a pound of powder and two pounds of shot to the charge. Because they weighed from fifty to two hundred pounds, the only practical way to use them was in a small sculling skiff. The big gun was rested on chocks with the large barrel pointed over the bow and the stock wedged against sand-filled burlap tow sacks and a bulkhead, or kickboard. A single discharge by the gunner, who drifted or paddled quietly into resting flocks, sometimes left several hundred birds belly up on the water.[38]

The punt gun was probably never as common on the Texas Gulf Coast as it was on the Atlantic seaboard. It was cumbersome, not just because of the weight

MARKET HUNTER'S *punt gun and sculling or punting skiff, from Chesapeake Bay. No pictures of punt guns from Texas are known to exist. (The Harry Walsh Collection, courtesy Joe Walsh and Jeff Pelayo, Canvasback Gallery, Cambridge, Maryland)*

and bulk, but also because it had to be beached for loading. The gun was entirely too much trouble to use on the muddy shallows of upper coast marshes, but the hard-bottomed estuaries of the Coastal Bend and lower coast were well suited for the punting rig.

The big gun most preferred in 1800s Texas was the swivel gun. Swivel guns were smaller than punt guns—usually eight- to four-gauge single- or double-bore guns set on a swivel system designed to handle their weight and to increase mobility. The guns were used in sculling skiffs but could even be held to the shoulder by gunners who hunkered down in the prairie, pulled skiffs up on shorelines, or shot from wooden duck blinds.

By the late nineteenth century, the use of decoys to attract ducks and geese was much more common than it had been in the years before the Civil War. Factory-made decoys evolved in the 1870s and were a great advantage over hand-carved decoys painstakingly whittled from locally available cypress, tupelo, and driftwood. Lathe-turned mallard, black duck, canvasback, scaup, and redhead decoys, for example, could be ordered from New York in 1878 at a price of from four to six dollars a dozen. About the turn of the century, cedar and white pine decoy stools were churned out of factories from several key waterfowling states. The best known were the Mason and Dodge decoy factories in Michigan. Hunters sometimes added live decoys, usually "English callers," to their puddle duck spreads.[39]

Sometimes big decoy spreads surrounded sink boxes, which had been popularized on Chesapeake Bay's Susquehanna Flats in the early nineteenth century. A sink box was a narrow, floating box in which the hunter lay on his back below water level. Hunting with sink box rigs was labor intensive, requiring a schooner, sloop, and large crew to run the operation, but the phenomenal kills that could

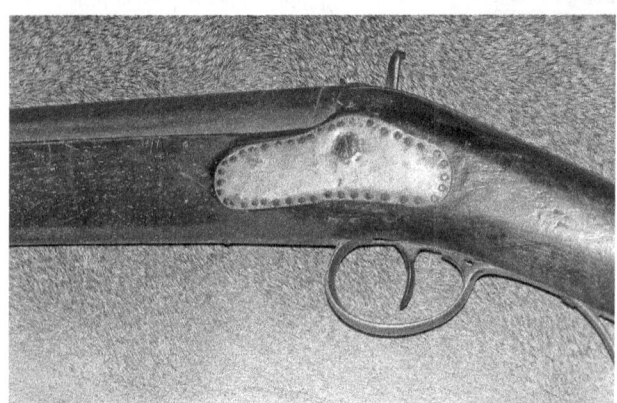

SWIVEL GUN *from Kamey Island, Guadalupe Bay. The bore diameter is 1 inch, and length of the gun is 68.5 inches. (Collection of Gordon Stanley, Rockport, Texas)*

EXAMPLE OF A SINK BOX RIG *from Chesapeake Bay. The shooting box was below the surface and weighted down with iron wing decoys. (Photo by A. Aubrey Bodine, Jennifer B. Bodine Collection, courtesy Jeff Pelayo, Canvasback Gallery, Cambridge, Maryland)*

be made usually justified the effort. There were several known sink box operations in Texas, notably on Lake Surprise in Chambers County and at Harbor Island in Aransas County, but in Texas this shooting rig never reached the level of popularity that it did on the East Coast.[40]

The late 1800s brought changes not only in how birds were hunted, but also in who was hunting them. Early market gunners on the coast were traditionally watermen, and inland they were farmers. Both usually gunned only part-time between the demands of their regular occupations. Only when fall skies turned black with ducks was the time right to put away nets or plows. Increasingly, the local market hunter was joined by commission hunters, and for these men there was nothing part-time about their business. Most were employed by game merchants or shipping companies and were paid a percentage of the kill. Some were local, such as the Galveston "delicatessen dealer" who paid four hunters at the turn of the century to deliver as many as three hundred ducks a day. The majority were from other states, and upper coast guide Jack Holland says many of them hunted year-round as they followed the flyway from Canada to the Gulf of Mexico, traveling with their guns, ammunition, decoys, and live decoy English callers.[41]

Not all of the hunters who sold their harvest in Texas markets were professional market men. Although loathe to admit it, many sport hunters sold part of their kill as well. They often shot far more waterfowl than they could ever consume at home, and the revenue from their kill helped defray the cost of their sport. Galveston game dealer J. Miller was evidently targeting sportsmen's spoils with his 1867 advertisement: "Sportsmen will rejoice to know that a fine life-boat will ply between Galveston and Bolivar during the season," and his forwarding company offered to "furnish trip tickets so that anyone may be supplied with ducks, snipe, curlew, etc."[42]

PLACES AND FACES OF TEXAS MARKET HUNTING

It was not long after the first rail shipments of ducks left Galveston, about 1880, that other Texas towns and cities joined in the wild game supply to America's cities. Galveston, Rockport, and Port Lavaca were the state's largest gunning, packing, and export centers at the turn of the century. Significant market hunting and shipping businesses were also established in Orange, Beaumont, Port Arthur, Velasco, Indianola, Aransas Pass, Corpus Christi, and Brownsville. Houston and San Antonio were not as much gunning centers as they were shipping and distribution hubs, a role shared by Dallas, Fort Worth, and Victoria. The largest Texas cities leave for posterity a fairly rich historical record of the importance of wild game in their society and economy. Only fragments remain from smaller towns, colorful historical morsels that provide hints of the days when waterfowl filled the sky and marketplace.

Orange and Jefferson Counties

The towns of Orange, Beaumont, and later Port Arthur were at the heart of the Jefferson County wildfowl trade. Profiting from wild ducks and geese said to have migrated by the millions to the upper coast in November 1886, Orange game merchants that year shipped birds to all parts of the country. Beaumont established its main markets in New Orleans and Houston, supplying "immense quantities of game" during the 1890s via the Texas and New Orleans Railway. Kansas City became a major buyer of upper coast canvasbacks, redheads, and mallards after Arthur Stilwell's Kansas City, Pittsburg, and Gulf Railroad—later the Kansas City Southern—connected Port Arthur to the US interior in 1897.[43]

Dozens of Orange and Jefferson County men made a living from the harvest of wildfowl. An unnamed Sabine Pass market hunter killed and shipped more than 1,500 in twenty-two days in 1900. J. D. Lane, who organized a hunter's union that provided Kansas City markets with ducks "big and fat," killed 800 ducks over a few weeks in 1901. Lewis Lowell Johnson, a veteran of the Spanish American War who rode with Teddy Roosevelt, ran the stagecoach from Sabine Pass to Galveston and shot ducks along his route. On one hunt he reined in his team to sneak a flock of ducks on Long Lake, and in the teeth of a howling north wind he killed 246 ducks in two hours.[44]

J. P. "Pink" Logan grew up listening to stories from his father, James Pinckney Logan, who moved as a young boy from Grand Chenier, Louisiana, to Port Arthur around the turn of the twentieth century. J. P. says that when they first moved to Texas, his father and uncles made their living from the land, mostly by trapping and hunting. They frequented Sabine Lake, riding horses through tall marsh grass until they located flights of birds that they then followed on foot. Like most who hunted from horseback, they limited their morning harvest to fifty ducks each. The Logan brothers shipped their birds to New Orleans, J. P. says, and were paid a quarter for mallards and pintails, fifteen cents for gadwalls and wigeons, and a dime for teal and spoonbills.[45]

Outdoor writer Ed Holder interviewed a Mr. Charlie who shot ducks for the Sabine Hotel and the local Beaumont and Port Arthur markets. Mr. Charlie said he limited his kill to what he could carry out of the marsh, which was fifty teal or twenty-five big ducks. In nearby Groves, Herb Stafford grew up listening to stories from two Cajun market hunters, Messrs. Thibodeaux and Billeaud. Herb says they hunted around Sabine Lake on a commission basis for a buyer who provided them with twenty shells each day. "The object was to kill as many ducks as possible with those shells," they told Herb, and they did so by crawling flocks in the marsh. Herb says they preserved their ducks in wooden barrels with lard before they were repacked in ice by local distributors.[46]

Legends were made from the shooting prowess of the marksmen who supplied Jefferson County marketplaces. A single shot across a flock of ducks on the water provided John J. "Jack" Johnson with eighty-one ducks. It was the same for Joe Marty, whose single discharge secured fifty-five mallards. A Beaumont market hunter in 1899 killed twenty-seven ducks with only two shots "while they were feeding" and sold the entire lot for three dollars.[47]

Galveston Bay

Public wild game markets, hotels, and restaurants provided Galveston residents with an almost year-round supply of wildfowl. Eateries lined the streets of the city's business district, the Strand, enticing customers with wild game window displays. The culinary bounty was described by one writer as "delicacies that tempt the appetites of hungry citizens," and "to see them so temptingly displayed in the windows and on the counters is more than the frail human nature can bear." Businesses also competed for the attention of diners in newspapers and city directories, in which elaborate engravings of fin and fowl accompanied culinary praises and promises. Advertisements included such places as Henry and Joe's Restaurant, John M. Laens and Frank Giozza's Epicurean Restaurant at Market and 24th Streets, and William O'Farrell's Elite Restaurant, in which a five-dollar "commutation ticket" was good for twenty-one meals from a selection of oysters, fish, and game.[48]

Galvestonians shopped at the two-story brick Market House in the Central Market near the Strand, its presentation of wild game carefully arranged to "satisfy the most fastidious taste." The Market House in 1873 boasted of "wild geese by the score and ducks by the thousands," the amount "more than were ever seen before at once." Galveston opened another public market area in the Second Ward during the late 1880s, and a few years later the Galveston Committee on Markets established an all-day Saturday market in the Third Ward. There, hunters from the mainland brought wagonloads of wild game across the wooden trestle bridge to a centralized location where retail dealers bought in bulk.[49]

Galveston shoppers also frequented the floating market, locally called the "vegetable" or "mosquito" slip, between 19th and 20th Streets. On any given morning a hundred or more sloops that tacked through the breakwater at Pier 19 could be found moored six deep in the harbor waiting for buyers. A visitor in the 1880s wrote: "One may find here a load of oysters, there potatoes, in another boat cauliflower and pigs, chickens here and terrapins there, ducks, and crabs, fish and milk." According to historian Melanie Wiggins, the ladies of Galveston who shopped there in mornings carefully inspected offerings that covered sailboat decks, along with "cleaned birds and animal carcasses" that hung in bunches from the standing rigging.[50]

A number of Galveston shops dealt exclusively in wild game. There was N. B. Jaas of the Third Ward, League and Company at 21st and Market Streets, William Nelson's Old Reliable Game Stand, and the Model Market on Center Street, in which wild game "can be had any time of day." One of the largest city dealers

Galveston's floating market *at Piers 19 and 20, early 1900s. All the moving parts of the market infrastructure are visible: sloops, wagons, and rail cars, with a steamer and the masts of large sailing ships in the background. (Courtesy Rosenberg Library, File No. 56FF 1, Item 3)*

handled as many as twenty-five varieties of wildfowl. Game from Peter Gengler's Fine Groceries was fully prepared "for picnics and sailing outings," with specialty items such as pâtés of woodcock and quail, wild duck pâté with truffles, and truffled larks.[51]

Galveston was the largest waterfowl distribution center in Texas, its harbor on the bayfront the beating heart of the shipping business. Acres of waterfront were covered by wharves, warehouses, and a network of rail tracks all seemingly brought to life by the bustle of steamers, schooners, and frigates, horse-drawn wagons and carts, trolleys, longshoremen, and shoppers. Watermen in their sloops and buy boats called on Galveston harbor from places as far away as a day or two's sail.

> THE OLD RELIABLE GAME STAND—W. G. Natson, 123 Center street, near Market, is constantly receiving fresh supplies of game, poultry, etc. Venison, canvas-back ducks and dressed poultry are specialties. All orders, wholesale or retail, filled promptly. Telephone connection.

Advertisement *for canvasback ducks from W. G. Nelson's meat market in Galveston in 1882. In the original advertisement the newspaper misspelled Nelson's name as "Natson."*

(Modified from *Galveston Daily News*, Dec. 26, 1882)

GAFF-RIGGED *sailing skiff of the mosquito fleet, Point Bolivar, early 1900s. (Courtesy Rosenberg Library, File No. 52303 FF2, Item 14)*

CAPT. WILL STINES SR.'s *transport boat* Ida Mae. *This photo, taken years after the close of market hunting, shows rabbits hanging from the back. (W. J. Stines Jr. Collection, courtesy Peter Stines)*

The fluid confederacy of Galveston Bay market boats was called the mosquito fleet, and by the 1880s it numbered two hundred sloops from mostly Galveston and Bolivar. The mosquito fleet transported fish, oysters, and waterfowl from nearly all points of the upper coast, sailing north to Houston and Wallisville, west as far as Matagorda, and east to Double Bayou and East Bay, where they docked at Lake Surprise pier and Stephenson Point. Port Bolivar and High Island on Bolivar Peninsula, only a short sail across the mouth of Galveston Bay, were regular stopping points.[52]

The mosquito fleet supplied ducks not just to a city, but to a nation. One mosquito fleet schooner docked in Galveston harbor in 1893 with the remarkable total of 2,008 ducks. Vessels so packed Bolivar docks that a community spokesman in 1896 petitioned the county for a new wharf, citing its need for hunters to transport "thousands of pairs of the finest ducks and geese" they killed each winter. In 1901, both local and export merchants were "greatly supplied with canvasback and teal [that] the mosquito fleet brings in large numbers, and others come from farmers down the island."[53]

One of the larger mosquito fleet operations was run by Bolivar's James A. Crenshaw, who employed as many as nine vessels. Most, however, were one man and a boat. Smith Point's Forest McNeir was a mosquito fleet skipper who, in the 1890s, filled his sloop *Cora Dean* with oysters, fish, wildfowl, and barrels of canvasbacks destined for Houston and Galveston. Another was High Island's Henry Sullivan; Claud Kahla says that in his great-grandfather's day "they loaded up old man Sullivan's sailing boat with ducks and hauled them to Galveston." Double Bayou mosquito fleet boat captain Will Stines Sr. transported produce and game to Galveston's floating market from the late 1800s until the mid-1900s, although rabbits and squirrels replaced ducks and other waterfowl during his last few decades.[54]

Boatmen of the Galveston Bay mosquito fleet were among the victims of a norther in 1886 that brought a blizzard with temperatures that plunged below freezing. When the storm cleared, many sloops were missing, and some of their captains were later found dead. Market hunter Henry Dodge was found frozen in his sloop off Bolivar Point, his body encased in a sheet of ice. Henry Hynson lost his vessel off Smith's Point when the raging sea covered his vessel in spray that turned to ice, and the sloop sank from the weight.[55]

In addition to local city markets, buy boats and the mosquito fleet supplied Galveston's game-packing and shipping firms. In the 1870s three wholesale fish, game, and oyster dealers were listed in Galveston newspapers. One was W. G. Nelson and A. D. Sadler's store, which opened in 1875 on the Central Wharf. Nelson and Sadler sold wildfowl feathers and live fish and turtles, and, ahead of their time, they kept oysters and game chilled in Hawley's Refrigerator, a local cold storage company that used New England ice. Other dealers in the late 1870s included the Sadler and Meunier shipping company and G. B. Marsan, who filled country orders by wagon delivery.[56]

The numbers of Galveston fish, game, and oyster merchants grew to at least a dozen during the 1880s, with another half dozen or so listed as "poultry and game dealers." Among the largest were J. D. White and Company, the Gulf City Co-Operative Manufacturing Association, J. H. Lang, Colosia and Radanovich, G. B. Marsan and Company, and Theo Eggerst, a "vegetable grower and dealer" who supplied boardinghouses, hotels, and oceangoing steamers free of charge from two stalls in the Central Market. Labadie's Wharf, run by Scotsman Ebenezer Pye, embraced the latest technology in refrigerated steamers and shipped products across the Atlantic. A number of shippers also handled sea turtles, the list including Galveston Fish and Oyster Company and companies run by J. L. Belbaze and Louis Cobolini.[57]

Growth in Galveston's game-forwarding business paralleled expansion of the city's railroad network. The city in 1852 had the state's first railroad locomotive, and in 1859 a wooden trestle bridge constructed to the mainland at Virginia Point connected the city with Houston via the Galveston, Houston, and Henderson (GHH) Railroad Company. The GHH provided Galveston game merchants with an uninterrupted transportation link for more than half a century, with the exception of the Civil War and after hurricanes destroyed the bridge in 1867 and 1900. Markets to San Antonio were reached on the Galveston, Harrisburg, and

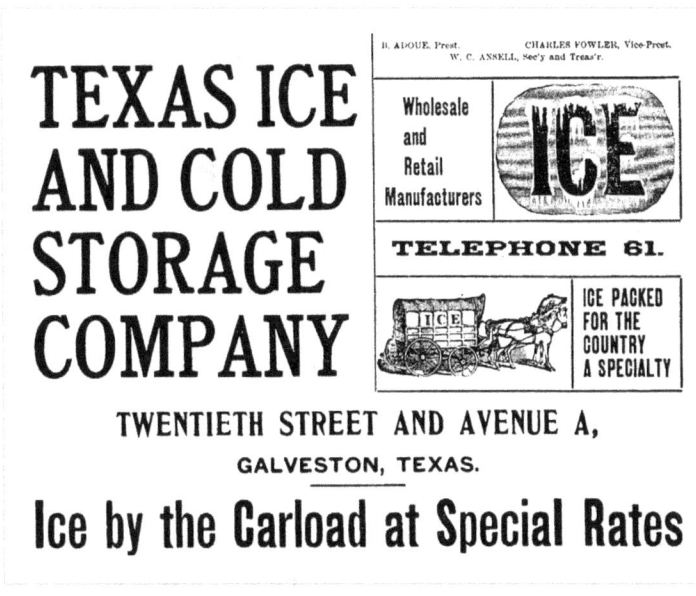

(Directory of the City of Galveston, 1899–1900 [Galveston: Morrison and Fourmy, 1899], 39, courtesy Rosenberg Library, Galveston)

San Antonio Railway by the 1870s and were quickly followed by railroad connections to the Midwest via the International–Great Northern Railroad Company.[58]

The earliest Galveston forwarding agency was Adams Express Company, in business by 1865. Houston was initially the only city Adams serviced by rail; all other destinations were by steamer. The Texas Express Company opened in the late 1860s, followed by the Wells Fargo Company Express in the 1880s. Buy boats and wagons raced to the harbor in time to make one of two scheduled daily express shipments. Market men who missed the express either shipped their birds on Mallory Line steamers or had to travel to Houston. Houston could be a long trip by sail, but if they timed it right, they caught the regular steamboat tow service from Morgan's Point up the San Jacinto River and Buffalo Bayou.[59]

Galveston merchants and express companies had access to the earliest commercial ice available in Texas. The city's first manufactured ice factory opened in the mid-1870s at 26th and H Streets, but with no fresh water on the island, its ice was made from seawater pumped from Galveston Bay. By the late 1870s C. B. Lee opened the Neptune Ice Company, capable of producing thirty tons of ice a day at its peak. In 1887, Texas Ice and Cold Storage Company dug the first artesian well on Galveston Island and with it produced Galveston's first commercial ice made with fresh water.[60]

Galveston markets were largely supplied from the prolific shooting grounds around Galveston Bay. Among the best known hunting localities, only a few miles outside the city limits, was Sweetwater Lake, known for big flocks of canvasbacks and mallards. A parade of horses, buggies, and wagons wound its way from town to the lake nearly every weekend. Offatts Bayou, right by the city and

(Directory of the City of Galveston, 1881–1882 [Houston: Morrison and Fourmy, 1881], xix, courtesy Rosenberg Library, Galveston)

only minutes from the markets, was another popular gunning destination. Market men had the entirety of the west end of Galveston Island to themselves until 1883, when ranchers strung barbed wire across it. Abruptly denied access, and no longer able to earn a living from its bounty of sandhill cranes, geese, pintails, and mottled ducks, the hunters began a bitter feud with the cattlemen, who started to find their fences cut.[61]

Prairie potholes and wetlands between Virginia Point and Clear Lake on the west side of Galveston Bay were known for concentrations of swans, sandhill cranes, geese, mallards, and shorebirds. E. A. Breitz, a news agent for the *Houston Daily Post,* worked as a market hunter along this coastal prairie corridor, making the short trip by wagon to ship his ducks on the Santa Fe line to Galveston. A visitor in 1898 recalled other market men who often shot between seventy-five and a hundred yellowlegs a day, and he wrote, "I have frequently found them so abundant that shooting them became a mere butchery."[62]

Dozens, if not hundreds, of market hunters headed east, across East Bay to the promontory of Smith Point and the famous canvasback hunting grounds of Lake Surprise, Lake Stephenson, and Wallis Lake. One was Smith Point's William G. Nelson, who got his start in the early 1870s shooting ducks for the Galveston market. He became a Galveston game dealer in 1873, and over the next twenty-five years he owned, in addition to his store with Sadler, the W. G. Nelson Fruit and Produce at the Brick Wharf and the Old Reliable Game Stand on Center Street. Nelson shot many of the birds he carried in his markets, particularly canvasbacks, which he followed as far away as Hynes Bay on San Antonio Bay. Nelson was called one of the best market hunters and marksmen in Texas, and when he died in 1903, he was fittingly buried near his favorite gunning grounds on Smith Point.[63]

Addison Whitehead, from his ranch on Smith Point, knew when the canvasbacks had arrived to the northwest shore of Lake Surprise without saddling his horse for the ride across the lower prairie. He simply watched the horizon and in the distance could see an animated sky as huge flocks rose and swirled above the lake. Addison hunted alone, riding as far into the marsh as he could before his

MOSQUITO FLEET CAPTAIN *Will Stines Sr. in his later years after a hunt at Jackson Ranch in Chambers County. (W. J. Stines Jr. Collection, courtesy Peter Stines)*

ADDISON "AD" WHITEHEAD *from Smith Point with a morning shoot of mallards. (Courtesy Joe Whitehead)*

horse bogged down. If mallards were in the sloughs and potholes between Ingleside Ridge and Lake Surprise, he snuck them, or hid in the sea cane with a couple of staked dead ducks for decoys. When canvasbacks filled the north shore of Lake Surprise, he hunted the lake edge, following alligator trails through sea cane and bulrush in waist-deep water, avoiding, when he could, the deep, slick alligator holes. Sometimes he hunted the broad water from a flat-bottomed wooden skiff.

Addison carried a ten-gauge double-barrel and thirty brass shotgun shells that he reloaded each night. Grandson Joe Whitehead says his first shot was always on the water after waiting to line up two or more birds, and he used his second barrel for a wing shot. Joe says, "I have some stories that said he killed sixty mallards a day, and others say that he killed forty mallards a day, because forty mallards was about all that he could carry out on a horse." He brought his ducks by wagon to one of the Galveston buy boats that called on Smith Point, and the dollar a pair he received paid for a new sailboat and a new house in 1898. Once, hunting snipes for the local markets, Addison and Forest McNeir were held captive for several days when an ice storm froze shut the hatch cover to the cabin of McNeir's sailboat.[64]

Mosquito fleet boat captain Will Stines Jr. was a market hunter who lived near Smith Point on Double Bayou. Grandson Peter Stines says he hunted mainly around Smith Point and, with his Remington Model 1889 ten-gauge with external hammers, "used to fill up a wagon." After a successful hunt he set sail for Galveston harbor with a cargo of ducks and produce from area farmers.[65]

Across the pass from Galveston, the peninsula of Bolivar, on the south side of East Bay, could have been a world away from urbane Galveston. With Bolivar's hardscrabble culture of seafaring, cattle, farming, fish, and fowl, most of its established families made at least part of their living from land and sea. An early market gunner was August Vogelsang, who came from Germany and settled on Bolivar Point in 1846. Vogelsang's was a small operation, his only expenses a gun and rowing skiff.[66]

Bolivar market man Edwin Hughes lived between Caplen and Rollover. When he wasn't shooting ducks, he worked as a carpenter, sewed canvas sails, made seine nets, and raised cattle, chickens, and produce. With his retriever and ponies, Hughes moved slowly from pond to pond, shooting from the saddle, his horses trained to remain steady on the shot. With two ducks lined up on the water, he killed them both before shooting a third with a second shell from his thirty-two-inch-barrel, L. C. Smith ten-gauge. Like most upper coast marsh hunters, Hughes found that his biggest challenge was not shooting enough birds, but keeping count of them, as forty mallards was as much load as his pony could carry.[67]

The Kahla family of High Island produced a long line of Bolivar market men that included Barney Edward Kahla and Fred Kahla. After the close of legal market hunting, Barney ran several duck hunting clubs while Fred farmed and raised cattle and hogs. Another from a long line of Bolivar hunters was Herman Johnson, whose aunt was born in a tent on a market gunning trip to Star Lake in Jefferson County during a snowstorm in 1898.[68]

Some of the men who shot for the Galveston market transported their birds long distances. W. A. Hughs, who moved to the Colorado County town of Eagle Lake in 1875, hunted the inland prairie west of Houston. When he killed more deer, waterfowl, and prairie chickens than local markets could bear, he traveled by wagon a hundred miles to Galveston in search of customers. He struck a deal at the Nelson and Long meat market; if Hughs could deliver his products without their spoiling, Nelson and Long would sell them.

Hughs hired a man to drive his wagons and game, but only from the middle of September until March, when the weather was coolest. Within a few years his business grew to include several upper coast cities, and the wagon deliveries were replaced by Wells Fargo Express at the Eagle Lake train depot. When Hughs died in 1917, he had become a gamesman of such reputation that his obituary touted him as "Texas' Greatest Hunter."[69]

Trinity River Delta

Huge flocks of wintering waterfowl at the mouth of the Trinity River did not go unnoticed by waterman, who built a "lucrative business" in wildfowl as early as the 1860s. The town of Wallisville was the main distribution point for Trinity River delta hunters, who, throughout the late 1800s, supplied markets in Galveston, Beaumont, Houston, and upriver settlements. Local hunters reached a

BOLIVAR PENINSULA *market hunter Fred Kahla with specklebelly, snow, and Canada geese and a few mallards. Picture is believed to be from the early 1900s. (Courtesy Melanie Wiggins, originally donated by Odessa Mouton)*

favored stand of flooded timber or marsh pond by wagon or rowing skiff, but with its maze of bayous, lakes, and shifting bars, the delta was a challenging place to hunt. It was even a difficult destination to reach; boats attempting to locate navigable passes from Trinity Bay followed a shoreline lined by the skeleton hulls of beached steamers whose captains had erred.[70]

Few names remain of the dozens of local market men from the nearby towns of Anahuac, Wallisville, Cove, Old River Winfree's, and Liberty. One was Wallisville's Emmet LaFour, who made a living fishing and gunning near the turn of the twentieth century. Civil War veteran Joe F. Maley was a cotton farmer in Cove who put down his plow each fall to make money shooting ducks.[71]

Other hunters came from farther afield, the masts of their sloops protruding above an otherwise featureless horizon. Most stayed for days at a time, others nearly year-round. A dozen hunters' shacks dotted the Trinity River delta in the late 1800s, constructed on small plots of marsh controlled by "squatter-right

A NATIONAL APPETITE

sovereignty." Their occupants scratched out a living raising marsh hogs "they sold to passing schooners for the market, shooting waterfowls for plumage, and killing alligators for their hides." Those market men were said to be a sorry lot, as "these men are not sportsmen . . . since each has his hands turned against the world and is so misanthropic as to believe the world is against him. Among them are many heart-rending stories, chapters from life in which, the human gamut is run from the highest ambitions to the saddest disappointments."[72]

Trinity River delta bogs were among the best snipe shooting grounds on the Texas coast. Loading his *Cora Dean* with a half ton of ice, a hundred pounds of No. 9 shot, and four twenty-five-pound bags of black powder, Forest McNeir made three trips a month to the delta from 1895 to 1899. McNeir's best morning shoot produced 132 birds, his best seven or eight days of shooting netting nearly 1,400. Snipes when downed were hard to spot in the marsh, and McNeir swore that his secret to retrieving the little brown birds was to shoot them so they turned one and one-half times in the air; that way they landed white, belly-side up.[73]

San Jacinto River

Thriving Houston's public market in Market Square was modernized in 1873. Derisively dubbed the "palatial butcher palace," the grand new structure housed city hall, a theater, and a large indoor-outdoor market. There, fruit, vegetables, game, and fish were hawked by a mix of vendors: "swarthy Italians," Greeks, Turks, Syrians, Germans, blacks, Chinese, and Mexicans. Fish and game stalls were located behind the meat market, where, according to historian Wayne Capooth, ducks were picked and displayed with the wingtips left intact to help customers identify their purchase. Visitors remembered hundreds of market stalls and "huckster wagons" that lined the street next to the square.[74]

When the market building burned down in 1876, former Houston mayor Thomas Scanlan built a new one, the Grand City Hall and Market House, on the same site. With its elaborate window displays of wild game, the imposing three-story building boasted a thousand-seat theater and retail shops and was "one of the most commodious market buildings in the state, and Houstonians are justly proud."[75]

Fish, oysters, and game were handled alongside farm-raised meat and fowl until the early 1880s, when, following the growing national trend in wild game consumption, many dealers began specializing only in wild game and seafood. Three fish and game retailers were listed in Houston city directories in 1889, and the number grew to as many as sixteen between 1895 and 1903. Most of fish and game dealers were located at Market Square, by then locally known as the Central Market, and on Travis Street.[76]

Shoppers in the late nineteenth century enjoyed a thoroughly modern Houston. A web of new electric lines hung from old telegraph poles and powered an electric railway, its tracks bisecting graded oystershell streets. Carbon arc street

PRODUCE WAGONS *and surreys on the edge of Houston Market Square, about the late 1800s. The Market House is located to the right. (Houston Public Library, Houston Metropolitan Research Center, File No. Mss 0187-0222)*

lamps illuminated an assortment of trolleys and surreys as well-dressed shopping patrons strolled in their white shirts, ties, and derby hats. Shoppers scrutinized selections of canvasbacks, mallards, geese, plovers, prairie chickens, Berwick Bay oysters, red snapper, turtles, fish, and shrimp at the Home Market, Eugene Artusy's Travis Street meat market, and the Congress Avenue emporium of Albert E. Cordier, who called himself the "up-to-date green grocer and butcher." Several retailers in the city's growing suburbs had side businesses; fin and fowl retailer John Caplan on Washington Avenue was also a mattress maker, and across the aisle from iced fish and game at Mertie Phillips's Main Street store were her homemade confections.[77]

Houston diners had as many wild game restaurant choices as they did retail shops. In the 1870s, oysters, fish, and game were "constantly on hand" at John Arto and Son's St. Charles Restaurant and at the Palace Coffee Saloon and Restaurant on Preston Street. Near the turn of the century, Houston's famous Rice Hotel was the place to go for "fillets of Canvas Back Duck," and at the Grand Central Hotel on Washington Avenue, fifty cents bought a ten-course dinner with larded quail and "green" goose with calf's foot jelly. By the courthouse, visitors passing the front entrance of Colby's Café enjoyed its window display of venison, ducks, geese, quail, snipes, turtles, and a tank inside that held live bullfrogs. Holidays brought out the best in local eateries, such as the 1894 Christmas dinner menu at Houston's Capitol Hotel, which featured roasted canvasback, green goose, snipes, prairie hens, quail with truffles, diamondback terrapin, and roasted opossum.[78]

A NATIONAL APPETITE

RETAIL MEAT AND SEAFOOD *dealer Eugene Artusy in downtown Houston advertised canvasbacks and mallards in 1902.*

(Modified from *Houston Daily Post*, Nov. 14, 1900).

WILD DUCKS 500 fine fat canvas back and Mallard Ducks. Berwick Bay Oysters, opened or in shell. Red Snapper and a variety of other Fish. EUGENE ARTUSY. Phones 214. 416 Travis Street.

(*Morrison and Fourmy's General Directory of the City of Houston, 1899* [Galveston: Morrison and Fourmy, 1899], 5)

J. ARTO.   J. L. ARTO.
ST. CHARLES RESTAURANT,
J. ARTO & SON, Proprietors.
Houston, ... Texas.

We have fitted up a First-Class **Dining and Oyster Saloon**, where we will insure accommodations for Ladies and the public in general. Meals can be had at all hours. OYSTERS, FISH and GAME constantly on hand. BOARD by the Week or Month. **TERMS REASONABLE.**

Houston forwarding merchants in the 1870s served mostly Galveston and Dallas, but a decade later their products were shipped to destinations throughout the United States. One of Houston's main transport arteries was the Houston and Texas Central Railroad (HTC) with Dallas connections to Saint Louis, Chicago, and the eastern seaboard. City fish, oyster, and game wholesale shippers included John H. Lang, John O'Brien, and J. P. Mohr. Lang's was established in 1866 and by the 1890s Lang had a retail and wholesale market in the 200 block of Travis Street. J. P. Mohr and John O'Brien both operated stalls in Market Square during the 1870s, and O'Brien supplied hotels across the state. As superintendent of the Texas Express Company, O'Brien had a major advantage over his competition. By the 1890s the firm of Haag and Auderer was among the city's leading fish, oyster, and game forwarding merchants and had a national following.[79]

As in Galveston, Houston game businesses were furnished by market men who often hunted long distances from the city. Large numbers of cranes, geese, and ducks from Colorado County's Eagle Lake were shipped on the Buffalo Bayou, Brazos and Colorado Railroad and later via the San Antonio and Aransas Pass (SA&AP) carrier. Hockley, northwest of the city, was headquarters for market hunting operations that delivered thousands of ducks each winter on the HTC Railroad. It was the same in El Campo, where "a great many ducks are killed . . . and shipped to Houston." At the Galveston, Harrisburg, and San Antonio Railway depot in Schulenburg, west of Columbus, loading docks in winter were piled high with "an appetizing display at the station of ducks, geese, deer, rabbits, quail, plover and other game" destined for Houston and Galveston.[80]

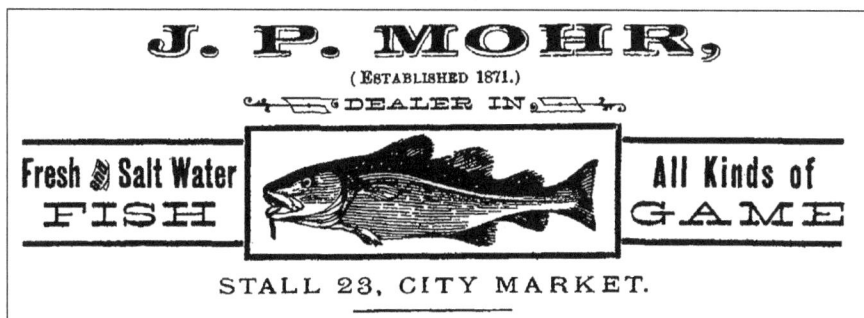

(Morrison and Fourmy's General Directory of the City of Houston, 1899 [Galveston: Morrison and Fourmy, 1899], 53)

One of the most productive gunning areas near Houston was at the mouth of the San Jacinto River, where fresh river water converged with brackish Galveston Bay. Adjacent sand shoals of Clopper's Bar and Swan Reef held rafts of pintails, canvasbacks, and swans that sometimes covered a mile or more of the water's surface. Morgan's Point, the promontory of land separating bay from river, was extremely popular with market hunters not just because of the numbers of birds, but also for its proximity to Houston and Galveston markets.

Chicago game merchant Edward T. Martin hunted ducks at Morgan's Point during the late 1800s. Over a stool of wooden decoys, he usually shot between eighty and ninety pintails and canvasbacks that, packed in barrels, he shipped back to Illinois. Decades later Martin wrote of those days as unforgettable and lamented the passing of the big flocks. But he added that his occupation was hard and thankless work, made worse by the "worry to get a price after it had gone to market."[81]

Brazos River Corridor

Situated between Galveston Bay to the east and Matagorda Bay to the west, Brazoria County offered gunners a wide diversity of hunting habitat. Mallards and wood ducks frequented flooded forest tributaries between the Brazos and San Bernard Rivers, and adjacent prairie and floodplain lakes brought Canada geese, sandhill cranes, and a variety of puddle ducks. Diver ducks and occasional swans were added to the bag from tidal and freshwater marshes near the coast.

Following collapse of Brazoria County's planter economy after the Civil War, one of the region's chief revenue sources was the harvest and marketing of fish and fowl. With its ice factory and two packing and shipping companies, the port town of Velasco, near the mouth of the Brazos River, was the area's main distribution center. Sloops and wagons carted goods from the docks to Ben Walcott's Velasco Fish and Oyster Company or the Matagorda Bay Fish and Oyster Company and from there shipped by sail to Galveston and Houston. The Velasco Terminal Railway reached the town in the early 1890s, but shippers continued to favor schooner and steamer transport that was both faster and more reliable.[82]

Among Velasco's market hunters was the "celebrated duck killer," Mr. Kellogg, who, although completely deaf, could "still see and shoot quick." A dozen commission hunters hired to supply Houston markets spent winters in Velasco during the 1890s and regularly brought "large bags to town for shipment." Watermen and market shooters working West, Chocolate, and Christmas Bays in 1892 filled the holds of three buy boats that sailed into Velasco harbor "laden with oysters, ducks, and fish."[83]

Velasco also had a vibrant local public market and several fish and game restaurants. The latter included McIlvian and Dunn's English Kitchen, which advertised the best twenty-five-cent fish, oysters, and game meals on the coast; and Charlie's Chop House, run by proprietor Charles Burridge. When Burridge closed the Chop House in 1896, he wrote his brother, explaining, "This old town has gone dead. You would be surprised to see all the vacant houses, but I hope to see things pick up again someday." He opened another restaurant in nearby Angleton.[84]

In part, Velasco's decline was due to competition from new railroads that, by the late 1890s, connected small towns all along the Brazos River corridor. In Brazoria County, depots sprouted in Angleton, Anchor, and Brazoria. Brazoria's Joe Jamison wrote that his father gave him ducks to sell to railroad men: "I would get on my pony and gallop over to the railroad to meet the train," and the brakeman "would jump off of the train to buy the ducks and then run back and jump back on." Other terminals established farther inland in Fort Bend County, with railroad connections to Houston and Galveston, provided for the distribution of birds hunted along Brazos River floodplain ponds such as Maner, Smithers, and Orchard Lakes.[85]

Matagorda Bay

Hurricanes in 1875 and 1886 saw to it that many Matagorda Bay port towns and cities once important to the early wild game trade would not see the turn of the century. That list included Decrow's Point, Saluria, and Indianola. Lack of transportation infrastructure kept others, notably Matagorda and Palacios, from realizing the full potential of their migratory resources. Only Port Lavaca both survived and thrived.

Rail did not reach the town of Matagorda until after the end of legal market hunting, so its gamesmen relied instead on maritime transport via Morgan's steamships and a dedicated schooner fleet of buy boats. For a short time in the 1880s Frank Ford and Company shipped fish, oysters, game, and sea turtles to Galveston, but Ford shuttered his doors after the 1886 hurricane and moved to Corpus Christi. The void was filled by a Galveston packing company that sent a steamboat at regular intervals to Matagorda and in 1891 the oyster steamer *Horatio*, which made runs between Matagorda and Corpus Christi.[86]

Like Matagorda, Palacios never developed a major national export business, as it was not until the last years of legal market hunting that the Southern Pacific

PALACIOS HARBOR, *with its two fish and oyster houses at the turn of the century, could not have looked more different from bustling Galveston to the east. (Collection of R. K. Sawyer)*

line reached the town. Palacios's two packing and shipping businesses, the Liberty Fish and Oyster Company and the A. R. Hillier Packing Company, opened in 1903, the last year of legal market hunting in Texas.[87]

The population of Indianola, on the southwest edge of Matagorda Bay, was second in the state only to Galveston in the 1870s. Only two years after the city got its first refrigerated packing plant in 1869, fish and fowl were shipped by more than fifteen forwarding companies. The Harris and Morgan Steamship Line and the Southern Steamship Company both called on Indianola harbor, along with sailing ships that connected the city with Gulf Coast points and eastern seaboard cities as far north as New York. The Gulf, Western Texas, and Pacific Railway Company provided the first transportation of goods by train, but only as far as Victoria.[88]

Prospects were bright for Indianola's fish and game industry in the early 1880s. At least fifty boats were engaged in the trade, and from his Indianola head-

INDIANOLA'S MORGAN PIER. *Its shipping infrastructure allowed for loading directly from Morgan steamships (rear) into cars of the Houston and Texas Central Railway (center). (Courtesy Calhoun County Museum, File No. 0306)*

quarters Frank Pauri held title as the largest fish, oyster, and game dealer between Galveston and Brownsville. The city was poised to become a major US supplier after railroad lines were linked to both the San Antonio and Mexican Gulf Railroad and the Houston and Texas Central Railway. Then came the hurricane of 1886, the second major hurricane to strike Indianola in a decade, and it destroyed the city. The *Galveston Daily News* published this from resident W. H. Crain: "We are destitute. The town is gone. Dead bodies are strewn for twenty miles along the bay. Nine-tenths of the houses are destroyed. Send us help, for God's sake."[89]

After the demise of Indianola, the future belonged to Port Lavaca. Port Lavaca had a census population of only seventy in 1884, but it grew rapidly after Indianola's surviving residents scattered to new localities. Several who reestablished their fish and game businesses in Port Lavaca got an immediate boost when the Gulf, Western Texas, and Pacific Railway Company (GWTP) pulled up their Indianola tracks and moved them to the town in 1887. Although Port Lavaca had an inland rail route to Victoria intermittently around the time of the Civil War, the new GWTP line provided shippers with direct access to inland Texas markets with connections to the nation.[90]

The town took advantage of it. Five years later, Port Lavaca grew into one of the state's largest fish, game, and oyster distribution centers, "devoted to the pursuit of supplying the big cities." At its peak, Port Lavaca merchants loaded as many as six express rail cars each day with game and seafood. The report in 1891 was that "all the market hunters have done well; during a single day last week one firm of that place shipped six hundred ducks by express to the northern markets." Some northern merchants evidently traveled to Port Lavaca to direct their businesses. In the winter of 1895, for example, "monster flocks of ducks and geese"

H. Warrach Jr.'s *export house at Port Lavaca at the turn of the twentieth century. The packing house was located just off the bay front on Guadalupe Street by the railroad. (Courtesy Calhoun County Museum, File No. A0081)*

Port Lavaca *game merchant H. Warrach Jr. (left) with greater Canada geese and sandhill cranes, Port Lavaca. To the right is a Mr. Burford, with W. H. "Will" Smith standing in the doorway of the family's ship chandlery. (Courtesy Dean Johnstone, File No. 0599)*

made their way to Calhoun County and were followed by "gamesmen [who] have arrived to make purchases for the northern markets."[91]

Port Lavaca had at least half a dozen fish and game firms in the late 1800s. Before the last track of the GWTP was laid, Galveston's William G. Nelson built "a large ice house which he fills with ice for the preservation of his fish, oysters and game." The same year, Charles Rupert, who ran a shipping business in Indianola in the 1860s, opened Port Lavaca's Rupert Company. By the 1890s other town shipping companies included the Golden Crescent Oyster Company, H. Warrach Jr., Miller Brothers Fish and Oyster Company, Matagorda Bay Fish and Oyster

A NATIONAL APPETITE

Flavius Gentry's *Port Lavaca Fish and Oyster Company on the waterfront. Visible in the picture are wooden barrels and transport wagons. (Courtesy Dean Johnstone, File No. 0371 PL)*

Company, and the Port Lavaca Fish and Oyster Company, owned by Flavius Gentry. Gentry started his shipping business in Indianola during the 1860s, and after relocating to Port Lavaca opened a waterfront warehouse with a large processing plant by the railway on Guadalupe Street. From an initial fleet of four boats in 1890, his business grew to forty sailboats and four hundred employees by the early 1900s.[92]

Most of the shipping companies maintained wharves in the Port Lavaca harbor, with the railroad depot and Wells Fargo Express Company situated less than a block from water's edge. Shippers bought barrels from the Bauer family factory located behind Melcher's Hardware Store and their ice from Port Lavaca Ice Factory. J. C. Melcher's father, Ed, recalled that at the turn of the century the ice factory could not always meet demand.[93]

Copano and Aransas Bays

The principal gunning towns of the Coastal Bend after the Civil War were Saint Mary, Fulton, Rockport, Port Aransas, and Aransas Pass. In Saint Mary, on north Copano Bay, hunting was considered one of its main industries, made up of those "who hunt for profit and visiting sportsmen." The town was burned to the ground during the Civil War, and from the ashes rose new hotels, lumberyards, a packery, and the St. Mary's Wharf and Warehouse Company. The town was destroyed again by the 1875 and 1886 hurricanes. Saint Mary, like many other Coastal Bend seaports, never regained its former prosperity and was largely abandoned by 1895. Much of its maritime trade, including the growing traffic in waterfowl, was to belong to the town where James M. Doughty and Richard H. Wood built their cattle pens in 1866: Rockport.[94]

Although Rockport was situated in an area of abundant natural resources, the lengthy and often uncertain route by schooner to the nearest railroad towns relegated it to a minor role in the export of wild game. That changed in 1888 when the SA&AP railway linked Rockport to San Antonio, and by the 1890s it connected to Chicago, Saint Louis, and New York. Watermen wasted no time in taking advantage of the opportunity. Boats of all shapes and sizes converged on Rockport, where the increasing trade volume was handled by construction of several new wharves. The main wharf was run by Capt. Robert Strachan, best remembered for his pet civet cat, which ran loose in the warehouse for years. SA&AP built a railroad wharf on pilings into the bay at North Street, where watermen loaded their wares directly into waiting refrigerated cars.[95]

Rockport's rapid growth in the market business was in a large part due to former Galveston game merchant and union leader Louis Cobolini. Cobolini, who saw the marketing possibilities of the seemingly limitless resource in fish and fowl along the middle and lower Texas coast, was the right person at the right place and time. He raised twenty-five thousand dollars in capital stock in 1893 to found the Fisherman's Union, and in its first year it attracted thirty members and a hundred boats. Cobolini quickly built the Fishermen's Union into a highly competitive coalition of watermen and market hunters from Port Lavaca, Rockport, Corpus Christi, and later Brownsville.[96]

The Fishermen's Union initially had to compete in a market dominated by upper coast market businesses, but it succeeded because it reduced competition among independent operators, provided watermen with stable wages, and earned a nationwide reputation as a reliable source for wild game and seafood. Part of Cobolini's strategy was promotion, particularly his exhibits of Fishermen Union products—fin and fowl—that he displayed in San Antonio each year. His taxidermy collections became so popular he expanded to other Texas cities.[97]

Three forwarding and shipping companies dominated the Rockport waterfront. Miller Brothers Fish and Oyster Company was the first, opened by William Miller and David Srivner in Fulton the year the SA&AP reached town, and Miller and Srivner later opened a second location down the beach in Rockport. They employed a fleet of schooners served by fast-sailing buy boats, and as a forwarding agent for Cobolini's Fishermen's Union, they purchased a "special shipping car" on the SA&AP line for direct transport to Miller's forwarding company in San Antonio. Louis Cobolini opened the Union Fish Company in Rockport behind a saloon north of Wharf Street, and by the 1890s it was considered the largest packing and shipping house in the state.[98]

Between thirty and forty market hunters were based in Rockport during the late 1800s. They included Ben Lettes, William J. Dorsett, and William Armstrong and his son Clarence, both boat captains, market men, and fishing and hunting

MILLER BROTHERS *had businesses in Port Lavaca, Fulton, Rockport, Corpus Christi, and San Antonio.*

(Modified from *Shiner* [Texas] *Gazette*, Aug. 24, 1898)

> FISH AND OYSTERS.
>
> **Miller Brothers,**
> ROCKPORT AND SAN ANTONIO,
> ..TEXAS,..
> FISH, OYSTERS, GAME,
> Etc. Sea Food of all Kinds,
> PROMPT DELIVERY
> Mail Orders given careful attention.

guides. Well-known Rockport boat builders and brothers Jim and Jed Bludworth hunted for the market. Capt. Charlie Johnson, based in Lamar, was a market man who sailed the waterways in his three-masted mail service schooner *Francis*.[99]

Local market gunner Jesus Salcedo hunted mostly along the west shoreline of Copano Bay. He was well known to workers at the Gregory SA&AP railroad depot, where he showed up every few days "with his customary sack of birds" and a bag of corn. It was said that he often exhibited a "peculiar recklessness" around trains, and in 1889 he was struck as he stepped in front of one, losing an arm and a leg. Jesus pulled himself off the track, requested that a bystander care for his horse, and then boarded the train for Corpus Christi. Passengers were horrified when he was hit by the train and then as he bled all over it on the way to Corpus Christi. But, they said, they admired his "pluck."[100]

Rockport was probably the state's second largest exporter of wildfowl behind Galveston. According to the *Galveston Daily News,* town merchants shipped over ten thousand ducks during just the first few weeks of November 1892. In 1895 the *San Antonio Daily Light* wrote that the number of ducks killed around Rockport, although not "carefully preserved," would "no doubt run close onto the twenty-five thousand mark." The *Houston Daily Post* estimated that Rockport merchants in the late 1890s shipped fifteen hundred ducks a day at peak season, with an average of six hundred per day for the five-month shooting season. The total came to seventy-five thousand ducks a year.[101]

Aransas Pass was the next major market town down the coast from Rockport. Two fish and oyster shipping establishments opened along the SA&AP route. Passengers embarking at the Aransas Pass depot shared their trips south to Corpus Christi and north to San Antonio with barrels of iced fish and game, and one remarked of "a fishy smell that pervades the whole train." Like much of the lower coast, market men in their cat-rigged scows endured a long sail to Galveston before SA&AP came to town. With rail, it was just a short run from the gunning grounds to the harbor, where waiting wagons hauled their harvests to packing houses and the rail depot. They may have also moved their wares along the Aransas Harbor Terminal Railroad, which crossed Redfish Bay in 1892 and connected with the SA&AP line.[102]

Corpus Christi Bay

CORPUS CHRISTI *Market Hall. Signs at lower right advertise city meat markets, and barely visible on the lower left is a sign advertising fish and oysters. (Courtesy Jim Moloney)*

Corpus Christi residents bought their fish and fowl from game hawkers until the 1870s, when Market Hall was built at Mesquite and Peoples Streets. The two-story building combined city hall with a dance hall upstairs and the meat market and vendor stalls in the downstairs front. Located just off the beach, the Saturday market was a collage of colors: bright green melons, oranges, the yellow of lemons, the silver of fish, and the red, black, and white of redheads against the pastels of the market building next to Corpus Christi Bay's turquoise waters. As vivid as the colors were the mixed smells of livestock, produce, meat, and salt air.[103]

Like Rockport and Aransas Pass, the export trade in wild game opened to Corpus Christi with the SA&AP railway. At least three wholesale fish and game dealers followed: the Corpus Christi branch of Miller Brothers Fish and Oyster Company; Corpus Christi Oyster, Fish, and Game Company on North Padre Island; and John Superach's Corpus Reef Fish and Oyster Company on Water Street downtown.[104]

Superach, who came to Texas from Australia in 1872, built Corpus Christi's first icehouse. His Reef Fish and Oyster Company handled fish, oysters, game, and turtles and at its peak employed over a hundred men with more than thirty boats. Historian Murphy Givens says that when the *Corpus Christi Caller* first began publication in 1883, the newspaper "would send down to Superach's for a bucket of oysters to make oyster stew for the pressmen." Superach later opened a forwarding office in San Antonio, where he shipped products across Texas as well as to Denver, Kansas City, and Saint Louis.[105]

A NATIONAL APPETITE → 77

The media closely followed the rise of Corpus Christi's market business to its peak in the late 1890s and early 1900s. The *American Angler* informed readers that "wild fowl of every description, particularly geese, canvasback and redhead ducks literally swarm [Corpus Christi Bay], and thousands of them are shipped weekly to New York City, affording an excellent living for many market shooters." So many market men, commission hunters, and sportsmen pursued the trade that it seemed, to another writer, as if there was "at least one hunter in the field from every square in town . . . supplying every table in Corpus Christi." Galvestonians cast a wary eye on their growing competitor to the south, with its large number of "hunters now following this sport as a trade" and making "a very good income."[106]

The most celebrated Corpus Christi area market gunner was John Marion Priour. Born in 1848, Priour worked as a guide, market hunter, taxidermist, and supplier of plumage for the millinery trade. History remembers him as one of the most productive ornithological collectors of Texas, with expeditions that led him from the Brazos River to Mexico. Priour's exploits live on in the colorful *A Man from Corpus Christi* (1894), written by fellow traveler A. C. Peirce. Peirce described how Priour followed the birds by horse-drawn wagon to Corpus Christi Bay, Laguna Madre, and the middle coast, often hunting for ten days at a time. His shooting trips were rough affairs of overturned wagons, spooked teams, stray horses, snapped harnesses, broken wheel spokes, wild river crossings by ferry, and spills in gullies and ravines. At night Priour slept in makeshift camps, under tarps in his wagon, or on corn husks in the corner of some farmer's corncrib.[107]

During his market hunting forays Priour rarely used decoys, preferring to crouch beside his trained horses and stalk feeding or roosting ducks and geese. With mud too deep for his horse, he got down on his belly and crawled, often killing 15 to 20 ducks with a single shot. Local newspapers kept track of Priour's prowess, remarking on hunts in 1883 that produced nearly 150 ducks and geese and an 1892 Nueces Flat hunt in which Priour and a "Mexican" killed 72 ducks with only three shots. The Mexican, though unnamed, was considered "a popular hunter in the area" who had only one arm and one leg owing to a railroad accident. He was probably Jesus Salcedo, the plucky market hunter who pulled himself up from the railroad tracks in Gregory three years earlier, leaving his horse, ducks, and an arm and leg behind.[108]

Corpus Christi waterman Robert Lee Briggs fished and caught turtles during summers and shot ducks, snipes, and geese each winter. Briggs followed the birds to Laguna Madre, Nueces Flats, and the Aransas Bay shoreline. His favorite gunning spots were on Chiltipin Dam at Gum Hollow, the mallard holes on Rincon Flats, and Mustang Island freshwater ponds near Mustang Motte. Other area market men included brothers L. D. and L. H. Berry, who in 1891 returned from a hunt with a wagonload of ducks, geese, and small birds, the lot being killed "with no trouble." Another was Robert Schallert, one of the main suppliers to John Superach's Corpus Reef Fish and Oyster Company.[109]

Plovers were a big part of the Corpus Christi market business. Local market man Neal Turner often killed 500 in a day. Another group of professional hunters in the 1890s averaged 450 plovers a day, which they shipped to Louis Cobolini's Fishermen's Union in Rockport. Yet another outfit in the early 1900s supplied an unnamed Corpus Christi shipping firm with up to 500 plovers a day that were cleaned, packed, and distributed to East Coast markets.[110]

Lower Laguna Madre

Past oak mottes and bluestem grasslands of upper Laguna Madre, and past mesquite, cactus, and Spanish daggers of lower Laguna Madre's sandy scrubland, was the verdant Rio Grande corridor. Perched on this southern edge of Texas, the towns of Brownsville and Point Isabel were both more than 150 miles from Corpus Christi, the nearest major US city. Brownsville was the largest lower coast city, and despite a population of over six thousand in 1900, it was a prohibitively long distance from almost anywhere else, not connected to the rest of the United States by rail until well after the end of legal market hunting.

The greatest demand for lower coast wildfowl was in local markets. Point Isabel, with only four hundred residents in 1894 and a "rickety hotel and some run-down hovels," still boasted a well-supplied city market "with the choicest game of all kinds." In Brownsville the ringing of the city market bell woke its residents every morning at 4:30. The two-story public market building, between 11th and 12th Streets, was surrounded by open-air meat stalls that carried wild game from September through March. Shoppers chose from more than a dozen species of ducks, three varieties of geese, and a wide range of shorebirds. In the 1870s the usual market displays of produce and meats were joined by an exhibition of dead bandits killed by McNelly's Rangers.[111]

Merchants competed with game hawkers, who gathered near the Brownsville marketplace and undersold the registered stalls. Barraged by complaints, city commissioners banned their activity in 1898. Called the "game hawker's law," the new regulation was enforced by a market stall tax of fifteen cents per deer, seven cents for each goose or fawn, and a penny on chachalacas, ducks, and rabbits.[112]

Brownsville had several wild game eateries. The city's most impressive menu graced white linen tablecloths of the Miller Hotel, where proprietor F. W. Prior's kitchen prepared recipes with ducks and geese fall through spring and shorebirds year-round. Other Brownsville restaurants that featured waterfowl included John M. Abadie's Restaurant and the Ashland Hotel, advertised by proprietor Mary Douglas as "The Only First Class Hotel in Brownsville."[113]

The huge numbers of wintering waterfowl around Brownsville, on the lush Rio Grande floodplain, and around Point Isabel, overlooking the edge of the Rio Grande delta and Laguna Madre, far outpaced the transportation infrastructure's ability to deliver them. Brownsville's only railroad, the Rio Grande Railway, went only as far as Point Isabel, and to reach the rest of Texas, Laguna Madre market

Brownsville City *Market in 1866. (University of Texas Institute of Texan Cultures at San Antonio, File No. 073 0836)*

men relied on schooners and steamships. Morgan Line steamers, for example, made port at Brazos Santiago Pass, then sailed for Galveston, where lower coast fish and fowl were distributed by Wells Fargo Express agents. Local hunters had to watch the Morgan steamer departure schedules closely so as to prevent spoilage of their harvest.[114]

Enterprising game merchants hired their own captains and vessels to reach other Texas cities. During the 1890s the Corpus Christi Oyster, Fish, and Game Company consigned the schooner *Hettie May* to transport fin and fowl from Point Isabel to their packing plant on Padre Island. Rockport's Louis Cobolini, who had his entrepreneurial eye on the game-rich Laguna Madre for years, started a schooner line between Point Isabel and his Rockport Union Wharf in 1900. One of his schooners, the *Mary Ann,* made runs with a winter cargo commonly consisting of "500 pounds of fish and 500 redhead ducks."[115]

Lack of railroads was only one barrier to the lower Laguna Madre game trade; the other was ice. When the schooner *Aransas* sailed from Brazos Santiago in 1888, it carried a cargo that included 666 hides, thirteen bales of "skins and hairs," and a sack of feathers. With no available commercial ice, the sack of feathers was worth more than the ducks that bore them.[116]

Lower coast market men developed imaginative ways to bring ducks to market before manufactured ice. Frank Garriga, who started a shipping business at Point Isabel in 1893, hauled his own ice from Galveston in insulated wooden boxes. Brownsville's Tiff Johnson solved the problem by opening a large canning factory. Tiff's cannery employed hundreds of people in the harvest, packing, and distribution of green turtles, oysters, fish, and wild game in the 1880s. Tiff's roast duck in cans, shipped by the ton, was "celebrated all over the United States."[117]

Wagons filled with thousands of pounds of ice at last rolled across wood planks of Point Isabel wharves when Frontier Fish and Oyster Company opened in 1901. In addition to supplying the lower coast maritime industry, ice from the Frontier Fish and Oyster Company was used to ship ducks on the evening train to Brownsville. Large volumes of lower Laguna Madre and Rio Grande ducks at last flowed to Texas and US cities. The glory days were, however, short-lived, curtailed two years later by Texas' first migratory bird game laws.[118]

Inland Cities

From Caddo Lake in East Texas to the Texas Panhandle, and from the upper coastal prairies north to the Red River, hunters shot a variety of wild game for local and US markets. They were opportunists, killing whatever game was most abundant or brought the best prices. For many it was game animals: deer, pronghorns, bears, squirrels, rabbits, opossums, and racoons. For others it was game birds, particularly wild turkeys, prairie chickens, quail, doves, and wild pigeons, better known as passenger pigeons. But when big flocks of waterfowl converged on lakes, in river bottoms, or over grain crops, market men aimed their guns at the available source of revenue. Like the wildfowl trade along the coast, the flow of wildfowl to and from inland points was made possible by the arrival of railroads, which allowed significant wild game export businesses to sprout in San Antonio, Dallas, Fort Worth, and Victoria.

San Antonio. San Antonio markets were supplied both by local hunters and with shipments from the coast. Typical of local hunters in the 1860s was a farmer who arrived in the city with sixty-two ducks, and what he didn't use to feed his family he sold for fourteen dollars. Mitchell Lake, on the floodplain at the juncture of the Medina and San Antonio Rivers, was the city's premier proximal fowling destination. The six-hundred-acre jungle of "man-high swamp reed," cattails, and wild coffee weeds was home to mallards, canvasbacks, teal, scaup, pintails, gadwalls, redheads, ruddy ducks, wigeons, curlews, snipes, Canada geese, and swans. In the 1870s so many hunters camped along the lake's perimeter that the night sky seemed ablaze from the light of their campfires. Each morning they hauled waterfowl by the wagonload back to town.[119]

San Antonio outgrew its public Market House after the Civil War. New markets opened throughout the growing city, including the Municipal Meat Market in Alamo Plaza, with a jail in the back, and the open-air Military Plaza, where the aroma of chili stands mixed with the smell of hay, seafood, produce, and meat. Shoppers following prices in local newspapers were advised in 1870 that the first wild ducks of the season were selling for "the rather stiff price" of a dollar a pair, but the cost dropped during Christmas that year as wagons brought full loads of

In 1886, WILD GAME, *along with oysters and fish, was "served in First-Class Style" at the Riverside Café Restaurant on Commerce and Losoya Streets in San Antonio.*

(Modified from *San Antonio Daily Light*, Jan. 12, 1886).

> F. SIMMANO.   A. HAMPEL.
> ### Oysters, Fish and Game.
> ### ❖ Riverside Cafe Restaurant ❖
> Scholz's Hall, Corner of Commerce and Losoya Streets.
>
> ☞   Lunch and Meals at all hours. Everything served in First-Class Style Polite waiters in attendance.

ducks, geese, and venison to town. Market pundits in 1896 predicted a year of good supply when a shipment of sprigtails arrived from Gregory in September, the earliest date commercial volumes of pintails had ever been available.[120]

San Antonio established a leading role in the wild game forwarding business when the SA&AP railway linked the city in 1886 to the Coastal Bend, with connecting routes that led north, east, and west. The SA&AP tracks were only a few months old when T. Talley opened Aransas Bay Fish, Oyster, and Game Depot on West Commerce Street. In addition to a wholesale shipping operation, Talley offered city residents free delivery of fish, oysters, ducks, crabs, and turtles. Several major coastal companies also opened forwarding offices in San Antonio, including Morgan City Fish, Oyster, and Game, which attached an oyster bar to its Trevino Avenue retail store; Miller Brothers on Military Plaza; and Corpus Christi's John Superach and Company. Other forwarding companies included Gus Zuercher, J. R. Scott and Company on Market Street, Mathies Brothers, and the San Antonio Ice Factory and Fish, Oyster, and Game Depot.[121]

SA&AP coastal connections that brought fresh seafood and wild game to the city were celebrated with accolades such as, "We will live well hereafter," and a large number of retail markets opened to serve residents' needs. Bellis's Market downtown featured "fresh water mallards," and the "Refrigerator Meat Market" opposite the Maverick Hotel advertised "fish, oysters and game received daily." The Silver King Market carried fish, oysters, venison, and "birds of all kinds," and Bond and Company on Houston Street had a similar line as well as a fruit distributorship. The Palace Meat and Fish Market opened in 1903.[122]

The upscale Menger Hotel's Colonial Dining Room, the city's preeminent dining establishment, was joined by a host of other restaurants with wild game on their menu. The 1880s eateries included Simmary and Hampel's Post Office Exchange Restaurant and Frank Starr's establishment on Commerce Street, which was known for greenhead mallards along with "other game birds and table delicacies." Fish and game were on the menu at John Loustenban's Elite Restaurant, the Globe Restaurant, and the Riverside Café Restaurant at Commerce and Losoya Streets, its meals "served in first-class style" with "polite waiters in attendance." Restaurant choices in the 1890s included Charles Pueschel's Short Order Restaurant and Lunch Counter opposite the Opera House, advertised as "a dining parlor for ladies and families." A similar theme was publicized at Shultz's Palm Garden at Losoya and Alamo Streets, a restaurant that catered to the "ladies and family trade."[123]

Dallas and Fort Worth. The main wild game market in Dallas was the City Market on Main and Sycamore Streets. There, shoppers inspected rows of meat stalls with strings of squirrels, rabbits, opossums, and wild ducks that hung across storefronts. City residents followed prices and availability in the "Local Notes" column of the *Dallas Morning News*, where, sandwiched between the Presbyterian Church pastor's sermon and an announcement for the ladies' circle meeting, readers in November 1899 were advised that large numbers of meadowlarks were available in the city market. In 1903, Dallas markets boasted twenty varieties of ducks, but of them, canvasbacks and redheads "stand easily first" in demand.[124]

Much as at San Antonio, coastal shipping companies arranged transport of fish and fowl to northern destinations through Dallas forwarding agents. Among the largest in the late 1800s and early 1900s were Frank Dorsa and J. J. Pitchford's Dorsa Fish, Oyster, and Produce Company and Lewis Monroe and Sons, both located on Ervay Street. In 1900, Monroe's had more demand for geese and ducks than supply and appealed in the local paper to gunners: "We want your shipments."[125]

Dallas market gunners contributed a significant amount of local game to city markets and forwarding companies. Many in the late 1800s rode horses to rolling hills and creeks of the Trinity River headlands, their approach accompanied by the roar of thousands of ducks that jumped from pecan-covered timber bottoms. One popular Dallas area haunt was Bachman's Dam on the Trinity River. In 1902 city residents were advised to avoid the dam, a dangerous place because of the numbers of Dallas market men and "nimrods shooting in all directions."[126]

In the 1950s, *Dallas Morning News* columnist Kenneth Foree interviewed a Dallas market hunter named George L. Geeo, who was fifteen when he started hunting in 1889. Armed with a twelve-gauge, a rifle, and black powder that his father kept in a lard bucket next to his ten-pound bag of shot, George once snuck a flock of Canada geese and killed six. Anticipating a three-dollar profit, he boarded the one-car Texas and Pacific train to Fort Worth. When he arrived, he found the market flooded and was lucky to make a dollar and fifty cents.

Plovers were a regular quarry for young George, who took his harvest to Dallas by wagon and peddled them to grocery stores and meat markets. When Dallas markets were glutted, George would "tie them to upright sticks and drive up a muddy Main Street" and hawk them for a nickel each. George remembered killing 111 plovers on one shoot that netted him nine dollars from Italian grocer Joe Abozo.[127]

Shoppers strolling among the offerings of Fort Worth's weekend market in 1897 cooled their palates with milkshakes, soda pop, and fresh cream and candies

> FRANK DORSA.   J. J. PITCHFORD.
> Packing and Shipping Out-of-Town Orders a Specialty.
> ## The Dorsa Fish, Oyster and Produce Co.
> DORSA & PITCHFORD, Proprietors.
> CRABS AND GAME.
> Phone 2101, 129 South Ervay St.

(Modified from *Dallas Morning News*, Oct. 11, 1903, courtesy Calhoun County Library and George Ann Cormier)

supplied by Ben U. Bell. Stalls and vendor carts carried rabbits, squirrels, quail, prairie chickens, geese, ducks, and wild turkeys. During the 1902 Christmas season, patrons were assured the holiday would be met with "increased vigilance on the part of the market man to allow nothing but the best to appear." City retail markets included Turner and Dingee on Houston Street, which advertised "big fat geese" for sixty-five cents each and mallards for forty cents in 1901, and H. N. Tanner and Company on Main Street.[128]

Much of Fort Worth's wild game trade was centered on the shipment of plovers to East Coast and midcontinent markets. J. R. Berry and Son's "refrigeration establishment," founded in 1887, dealt exclusively in the supply of plovers. The amount of birds distributed from Fort Worth was large; one merchant, for example, shipped over twelve hundred plovers in a single day to New York. In 1887, Fort Worth gun dealer Arthur Stert placed a newspaper advertisement announcing his need for a million plovers and stating that he was willing to pay fifty cents a dozen. It is not known if market gunners ever filled Stert's request, but if they had, his suppliers would have grossed nearly forty-two thousand dollars. Market hunters Lee Hughes, J. H. Taylor, and J. C. Dodd cornered the market on plovers in the late 1880s, killing an average of three hundred a day so consistently that the *Dallas Morning News* speculated they were "[commission] agents of a refrigerator outfit."[129]

Two days of wet weather in November 1893 filled prairie tanks outside of Fort Worth with ducks and geese. Hunters watched their flight patterns at night by the new "electric lights of the city," then followed them. The next morning some fifty gunners converged on Tyler's Lake, and they exhibited "such reckless marksmanship that it was really dangerous, and soon hunters were deterred by this danger." Dallas and Fort Worth meat markets were well stocked for many days.[130]

Vignettes of Other Towns. The long arm of the wild game trade eventually stretched all the way across Texas, with markets and restaurants large and small supplied by local hunters and from coastal shipments. Ducks from Caddo Lake, in East Texas, were long important to towns on its shores, but the distance to major Texas and Louisiana urban centers discouraged shipping. Rail tracks between Swanson's Landing on Caddo Lake and nearby Marshall were laid in the

1850s, but before a steam locomotive was acquired. Enterprising railroad men used oxen to pull the train uphill, then dragged the animals onto rail cars to coast back downhill.[131] After the oxen were replaced by an engine, Marshall grew into a sizable market center. Caddo Lake gunning parties returned to town in wagons filled with hundreds of ducks, and hundreds more were shipped via rail each week. At peak season, wild ducks in Marshall markets were "cheaper than beef." By the late 1870s Texas and Pacific Railway express trains connected Marshall with Dallas and Fort Worth, and later to northern markets.[132]

On the upper inland prairie north of Houston, Brenham shoppers found a ready supply of mallards and teal in local markets and no shortage of wild game restaurants. At the Exchange Restaurant on East Sandy Street, game was offered "in all styles," and special attention was promised to lady customers. Brenham's Oak Hall Restaurant served fish, oysters, and game prepared by a "splendid white cook." West of Houston, baked ducks were sold in Eagle Lake for fifty cents each in 1902, a price so high an offended diner thought the town was "becoming city-like."[133]

For a short time in the 1890s, Victoria, located about halfway between Houston and San Antonio, was probably the state's leading exporter of plovers. One of the town's shipping companies handled fifty thousand plovers for New York and Chicago markets in 1895. The next year they shipped eleven thousand to New York in just one week, with a total for that season of seventy-five thousand birds.[134]

Rolling hills and the meandering Colorado River formed the backdrop for Austin, the capital city of Texas. Austin had at least five downtown meat markets that sold fin and fowl in the 1880s and '90s; one, capitalizing on the invention of cold storage, was named the Antarctic Refrigerator Market. City diners had a choice of wild game on the menus of Simon's Restaurant and Oyster Parlor and the Popular Saloon and Chop House, both on Congress Avenue.[135]

North of Austin, Waco also had a long list of fish, oyster, and game retailers. In the public market, Wheeler and Lynham's and S. Johnson's had outdoor stalls that carried prairie chickens, curlews, "and green head ducks from Galveston." George Smith's retail market and the City Fish Market were both on Franklin Street, the latter advertising that customers could place orders using a newly installed telephone connection. Other downtown markets included J. C. Crippe, O. J. Miller, and Haun, Goebl, and Company, with three locations across town. Waco dining aficionados enjoyed fine duck dinners at the St. Charles Saloon and Restaurant.[136]

Fresh oysters and wild ducks from the coast were available to diners as far north as the Texas Panhandle in Canadian at Tex's Oyster Saloon and as far south as Laredo on the Rio Grande at Nic Constantine's restaurant, with its menu of fish, oysters, and game available night and day. Laredo residents shopped for coastal fish, oysters, and ducks at market stalls in Market Plaza, a two-story building behind City Hall. One of the city's main suppliers was Corpus Christi's Reef Fish and Oyster Company.[137]

It was a testament to how far Texas transportation had come since the Civil War that fresh fish, oysters, and wildfowl from the coast reached inland towns in the farthest corners of the state. Even more remarkable was their shipment throughout the United States and even Europe. Few could envision a time, or any reason why, it might end.

CHAPTER 4

FOWL as FAD and FASHION

The public's unrelenting desire for wild birds during the nineteenth and early twentieth centuries, and the lengths that market men went to capitalize on it, are well illustrated by examples from America's trade in canvasbacks and in bird feathers destined for the fashion industry. Canvasbacks were exalted in culinary circles as the consummate cuisine, and demand for them reached all corners of the United States and even Europe. The lofty level of the canvasback market was probably matched by the fad for use of the plumes and ornate feathers of wading birds and shorebirds to decorate ladies' hats. Both wild bird industries hold a special place in the history of market hunting and later became instrumental to America's crusade for conservation.

KING CANVASBACK

Canvasbacks were prized by epicures above all other wildfowl. The best canvasback ducking regions, the optimal diet of the big diving duck, and preferred recipes for it were debated in newspapers, sporting journals, and restaurant circles for at least a century. Demand for the white, black, and red diver exploded in the late 1880s as media and the public elevated canvasbacks to the height of culinary chic on American and European tables.

According to the *New York Times,* the "gastronomic truth" was that canvasback, along with oysters, turtle soup, and terrapin, was the only meal worth serving in wintertime New York. Early 1900s New York society, including the Astors and Vanderbilts, carefully followed the advice, featuring canvasback at all their grand balls and dinners. In 1890 the effect on East Coast and Gulf Coast oyster demand was immediate when the *New York Telegraph* advised its readers that "a fad this season in Baltimore and Washington is to take roast oysters with the [canvasback] duck instead of terrapins." Canvasbacks were so esteemed that the *Galveston Daily News* complained: "The lordly canvasback [is] not for us [Texans]: they are for our betters in New York and Washington. Rich epicures in those places do not hesitate at paying for a pair of canvasbacks a price that would buy a yearling on Texas stock ranges."[1]

Canvasbacks fetched such high prices that northern merchants and restaurateurs sometimes surreptitiously swapped them with less expensive redheads or other ducks. The deception was not well received. One outraged culinary denizen fumed, "Ten to one if you buy a canvasback from the most reputable market man you will get a redhead." Diners, too, disparaged the practice. "The restaurant man knows the value in the name so he serves up teal, wood duck, and black duck for canvasback. [But] the flavor of the canvasback is unmistakable to anyone who has knowingly eaten it." Texas redheads, far more abundant than canvasbacks, almost certainly played an important part in the ruse.[2]

Great Resorts of the Canvasback

The affinity between canvasbacks and bodies of water with *Valisneria spiralis*—eelgrass or wild celery—was well known to market hunters, game merchants, restaurateurs, and epicures. Wherever wild celery grew, it brought huge flocks of canvasbacks to feed on its tender bulbs and roots, and it imparted a flavor to the bird's flesh unmatched by any other natural food source.

Throughout the United States, exceptional wild celery habitats were known as the "great resorts" of canvasbacks, and their geographic names still resonate in hunting and culinary lore. Early famed gunning grounds on the northeastern Atlantic seaboard were at Pollepel's Island and Fishkill Landing on the Hudson River in New York. On the upper Chesapeake Bay they were the Susquehanna Flats and adjacent Gunpowder, Sassafras, Bush, Elk, and Middle Rivers. Tucked behind coastal barrier islands were the renowned gunning waters of Back Bay in tidewater Virginia and North Carolina's Currituck, Albemarle, and Pamlico Sounds. In Wisconsin, it was where Rock River drained into Koshkonong Lake. Far to the south, it was Lake Stephenson and Lake Surprise in Texas.[3]

During the late 1700s until the 1820s, demand for canvasbacks in northeastern markets was met by local hunters. One of the first large cities in which demand outstripped local supply was New York, and when it did, market men quickly headed south to the extensive wild celery flats of upper Chesapeake Bay. There, groups of hunters lived aboard large sailing sloops during winter, and it sometimes took them only two to three days to fill their boats with ducks that they sent north by schooners and steamers.

By the 1830s the canvasback trade on the eastern seaboard grew so competitive that every piece of water rich in wild celery between Connecticut and Virginia was tightly controlled by hunting syndicates. A decade later, shooters and shippers expanded their range further south to Virginia's Back Bay and North

Carolina's Currituck Sound. Hunters delivered their ducks to Norfolk, and from there small steamships transported them to New York.[4]

In search of new supplies after the Civil War, market gunners again pushed farther south, to North Carolina's Albemarle and Pamlico Sounds. One reason for the move was a marked decline in wintering canvasbacks on Chesapeake Bay, caused by the market hunter's pervasive, "unrelenting greed." Ornithologists at the same time noted that canvasback numbers "have greatly increased along the short rivers in North Carolina." Much of the remaining Atlantic Flyway canvasback population shifted to the North Carolina coast by the beginning of the twentieth century.[5]

Declining canvasback resources also impacted the north central US markets. Canvasbacks in Chicago markets, for example, traditionally came from Minnesota's Heron Lake and Wisconsin's Koshkonong Lake, but with greater competition, game merchants were forced to increase the radius of their search. Chicago in the early 1880s was likely the first city to cast its net over Texas, to canvasbacks from Lake Stephenson in Chambers County, and it lit the fuse of the wild duck business in the Lone Star State. America had discovered a new source for its prized canvasbacks.[6]

Texas Canvasbacks

Before the Civil War, Texas canvasbacks were primarily sold in local markets. By the 1880s, America's seemingly insatiable appetite for the bird, combined with the infrastructure to supply it, provided Texas with the opportunity to become a major player in the market hunting and shipping business. Express railroad cars began moving barrels of Texas canvasbacks to all points on the compass, particularly to Washington, Baltimore, Philadelphia, New York, Chicago, Saint Louis, New Orleans, Kansas City, and Denver. Typically, Texas game houses only shipped birds out of state that weighed over two pounds. Those that weighed less were shipped to "Texas points."[7]

While rail transported Lone Star State birds within the continental United States, steamers provided for the trans-Atlantic trade. When commission agent P. A. Lang consigned "four sacks ducks" on the steamer *Charles Fowler* for shipment down Buffalo Bayou in 1872, it might have been hard for him to fathom that, only fifteen years later, ducks would cross the Atlantic. The first direct consignment of Texas meat to Europe was delivered by the ocean steamer *Rowena*, which sailed from Galveston to London's Leadenhall market in 1887. Among the cargo held in the *Rowena*'s refrigerated storage were "48 fowls" and seventy canvasbacks that sold "like wildfire" and were "eagerly bought up by London householders." The wake of the *Rowena* was followed by many more trans-Atlantic steamers.[8]

Wild celery–fed canvasbacks from the Chesapeake Bay's Susquehanna Flats set the culinary, and price, standard. Because Chesapeake Bay dealers resented competition from other regions many did their best to convince the buying

> Game—Ducks by the hundred pairs 40 to 65c; canvass back, in lots of 50 pairs 75 to 85c. per pair. Geese $9.00 to 12.00 per dozen. Partridges $1.50 per dozen. Squirrels $1.50 per dozen. Rabbits $3.00 per dozen. Wild pigeons $1.00 per dozen. Snipe and other small game 90c to $1.00 per dozen.

THE CANVASBACK *was always listed separately in market reports. In this 1872 Galveston market listing, all species of ducks were grouped together and sold in lots of two hundred. Canvasbacks were sold by the hundred. Partridges were either quail or prairie chickens, and wild pigeon was the name commonly used for the now extinct passenger pigeon.*

(Modified from *Galveston Tri-Weekly*, Dec. 27, 1872)

public that birds harvested from anywhere else were inferior. Despite proximity to ready markets, for example, canvasbacks from Long Island did not bring premium prices, as "their flesh is not distinguishable from the ordinary duck's because, in the absence of the wild celery, they demean themselves by feeding upon fish." Canvasbacks in the markets of Charleston and Savannah were reputedly "very poor, insipid, and at times fishy." It was the same with canvasbacks shot on the Hudson River, Great South Bay, and parts of coastal North Carolina. Some shippers even went to great lengths to substitute second-rate canvasbacks for prized Susquehanna Flats birds, such as shipping their birds first to the Chesapeake Bay and then to New York.[9]

It was no surprise that the appearance of Texas canvasbacks brought out the worst in East Coast market syndicates. The *Baltimore Sun* informed readers that the Texas canvasback grounds were "not in the same class with Maryland." Another article quoted an East Coast dealer: "[When] we get an order from a hotel or restaurant which will pay first class price we send first class birds from Chesapeake Bay . . . [but] if they don't care to pay more than $4 a pair we send them birds from other places." Many of those second-rate canvasbacks, the article opined, were from Texas. A New York game dealer wrote: "If the market hunters of Texas wish to make a name, and consequently a price, for their canvasbacks and redheads, let them plant wild celery in their deep lakes."[10]

Perception affected price, and although Texas canvasbacks fetched higher prices than any other duck within the state, they did not receive top dollar in northern cities. From Orange to Corpus Christi, canvasbacks brought the market hunter about eight dollars a dozen from local game merchants, who in turn received about two to five dollars a pair from northern wholesalers. These dealers usually listed the birds as "common canvasbacks"—the name used for birds from anywhere other than Chesapeake Bay—and sold them in northern markets for up to seven dollars a pair. The exception was Texas canvasbacks that crossed the Atlantic to London and Liverpool, where they commanded the remarkable price of twenty-five dollars a pair in the late 1890s.[11]

Canvasbacks once frequented the entirety of the Texas coast and inland rivers and lakes. But there were places, many with growths of wild celery, that stood above all others. The most celebrated canvasback grounds were a chain of three lakes deep in the East Bay marshes of Chambers County on the corner of land between Smith Point and East Bay. The lakes, located on Eliza Stephenson's East Bay land grant, included Lake Surprise, Saint Claire Lake, and White's Lake. In later years Lake Saint Claire was called Blue, Little, or Wallis Lake, while White's Lake began to appear on maps as Lake Stephenson.[12]

Canvasback concentrations on Lake Stephenson and Lake Surprise were unparalleled, their fresh water in the middle of an otherwise extensive saltwater marsh home to more canvasbacks than any other place in Texas. The big divers came each year on the first clear, cold November night, dropping from the darkness until, silhouetted against the moonlight, huge concentrations covered the water. It was hard to imagine room for more, but still they came. Celebrated writer Emerson Hough visited Lake Stephenson in the early 1890s, and in an 1893 *Forest and Stream* article he wrote of so many canvasbacks that, at a distance of a quarter-mile from the lake, he could hear them splashing and feeding on wild celery. Lake Surprise was a mile and a half long, with aquatic vegetation and eelgrass that covered a thousand acres. The lake held so many canvasbacks that when they were flushed, their ascent "shook the air, sounding like the roar of a freight train crossing a wooden trestle."[13]

The market hunting history of the chain of three lakes can only be traced back to the 1870s, when as many as twelve professional hunters killed so many birds for Galveston and Houston markets that they emptied hundreds of kegs of powder each gunning season. Smith Point resident and fish, oyster, and game merchant William G. Nelson was one of those gunners. Nelson, who procured his own canvasbacks for his Galveston wholesale and retail markets, knew the East Bay marshes so well he could launch a pirogue on East Bay at Saint Claire (Wallis) Lake, paddle through its linked, winding bayous without following a false waterway, and come out at Double Bayou on Galveston Bay some ten miles away.[14]

By the late 1880s, George "Bud" Stephenson controlled hunting rights on the chain of lakes, hiring Illinois market gunners to shoot ducks for Chicago markets. One was professional hunter Billy Griggs, who followed the birds down their migratory flyway to the Gulf Coast each winter. Griggs's market gunning career was described by historian Wayne Capooth, who wrote in *Waterfowling America*: "When Billy Griggs goes anywhere, he doesn't tell anybody where he is, or how to find him." In the early 1890s Griggs hunted Lake Stephenson and shipped his birds from Galveston to Chicago through the Bond and Whitcomb Commission Company. Typical of his prowess was weeklong hunts in which he killed a thousand snipes and more than five hundred canvasbacks.[15]

In the winter of 1892, Bud Stephenson's gunners shipped between one and four barrels—about fifty to two hundred birds—each day to Chicago and Saint Louis. Stephenson's was a tightly controlled family business, and not without detractors. He made more money shipping birds north than selling them in Texas and raised the ire of Galveston residents when he stopped sending prized canvasbacks from the chain of lakes to local markets. Stephenson also banned outside sportsmen and other market gunners and dealt with usurpers harshly. Boats and decoys were stolen, and rifle bullets passed uncomfortably close to those who trespassed. Boatmen of the upper coast mosquito fleet were said to have avoided the place.[16]

Wealthy San Antonians were among the livid when, accustomed to winter sporting shoots on Lake Surprise, Stephenson also denied them access. They took their grievances to the national periodical *Forest and Stream,* penning an unflattering but anonymous commentary that was probably written by San Antonio's Oscar Guessaz, at the time a contributing editor to *Forest and Stream* and president of the Texas State Sportsmen's Association. The article portrayed Bud Stephenson as the head of a "gang" of market hunters and accused him of shooting an Austin sportsman with a load of BB shot. The disdain that Texas gunners developed for Bud Stephenson, however, would pale in their contempt for the next market man to control the chain of three lakes: Col. William Moody.[17]

Virginian William Lewis Moody came to Texas in 1852 to practice law, and after the Civil War he dominated the Galveston mercantile and cotton business. Waterfowling history best remembers Colonel Moody for his gunning resort on Lake Surprise, "the finest private hunting preserve in Texas, and maybe the best canvasback duck preserve in the United States." Moody purchased the lake in 1892 and the next year he added Eliza Stephenson's Lake Stephenson and Wallis Lake to his holdings.[18]

Smith Point's Forest McNeir, with his brother Pascal, was hired by Colonel Moody in 1897 to guide, cook, pilot Moody's coal-fired steam launch *Pherobe,* and handle the packing and shipping of Lake Surprise canvasbacks. McNeir put those years to pen in *Forest McNeir of Texas* (1956), bringing Lake Surprise market hunting to life for generations of waterfowlers. The McNeirs' was an era when the cold and rain were simply ignored, and travel to the shooting grounds was by horse and wagon. On the return trip the wagon was loaded to the top with ducks "nearly every day of the season." Nights were spent plucking, packing, and icing birds, forty-five to fifty to a barrel. By sail or steam launch, the McNeirs hauled full barrels to Galveston harbor, where they met the American Express wagon for shipment by steamers or express rail.[19]

The McNeirs were only a couple of the market hunters Moody hired during the 1890s to early 1900s. Most were contract hunters who paid the colonel with a portion of their profits. Both the volume of their kill and the money they made were considerable. Moody retained Billy Griggs from his earlier days with Bud Stephenson, and during the winter of 1893–94, Griggs shot more than five thousand canvasbacks. The next year Moody made nearly eight thousand dollars' profit from eight hired gunners. One cold morning in the late 1890s, Forest and Pascal McNeir fired three hundred black-powder shells in a span of only forty-five minutes, their harvest of nearly two hundred fat canvasbacks "worth $835

COLONEL MOODY *at Lake Surprise, early 1900s. (Courtesy Doug McLeod, Moody Foundation)*

in the New York market for the Christmas holidays." In the last year of legal market gunning, Moody's market hunters shipped an average of three hundred ducks a day.[20]

Like Bud Stephenson before him, Moody barred access to Lake Surprise, Wallis Lake, and Lake Stephenson to all outside gunners. Moody went a step further, building a fence around the property, and he hired a watchman for enforcement. The creation of what some viewed as a personal canvasback kingdom generated widespread resentment and became the subject of bitter media attacks.

One of the main topics of malevolence was controversy over Moody's title to the land. The *San Antonio Daily Express* took a peculiar interest in this theme, railing against Moody in strongly worded editorials that called his Lake Surprise purchase a "fraudulent patent." For years a story circulated that Moody paid only one dollar to the State of Texas for Lake Surprise, ostensibly as an experimental rice farm. San Antonio's Oscar Guessaz took a vocal position in the fray, charging that Moody's rice farm was merely a cover for "the whole business of duck killing." That Moody's regular hunting guest was Texas governor Hogg was seen as further proof, and a January 1894 *San Antonio Express* editorial titled "The Nimrod's Grievance" inferred that shipments of ducks made to the governor influenced the state's decision making.[21]

The issue of land title was still a topic of debate fifteen years later when Emerson Hough brought the tale to a national audience in the 1908 *Saturday Evening Post*. Hough's unfavorable article elicited a vigorous denial by Colonel Moody, published in the *Galveston Daily News*. The *News* added its own editorial, siding with Moody, who, they wrote, had "been the subject of many fake stories and the object of bitter attacks. He has even been investigated by the Bureau of Biological Survey [and] Department of Agriculture, while suffering in silence while slanderous stories were being circulated." The story continued to circulate long after Moody died.[22]

More controversy dogged Moody and his canvasback kingdom when, in 1894, it was reported that the amount of lead shot poured into his chain of lakes was so great that birds died from it. The saga started when a Galveston city inspector "condemned as unfit for food a lot of ducks offered for sale by a hunter from the vicinity of the lake [Stephenson]." The writer speculated that "at the time they departed this life they were either victims of lead-poisoning or were suffering from its effects," and continued: "In the gizzard of each one of the rejected ducks were found from half a dozen to forty shots of various sizes."[23]

Oscar Guessaz quickly took up the cause, with: "Assuredly; a great many ducks are found daily on that lake stone dead, and without shot marks, and if one takes the trouble of investigating further it will be found that the gizzards of the birds are filled with shot, which they have picked up on the bottom of the lake while feeding."[24]

Forest and Stream weighed in with what they called "self-poisoning of ducks" and noted that at both Lake Stephenson and Lake Surprise, gizzards contained not only lead shot, but also old percussion caps. Readers were assured that ducks that died in this manner were not sold by reputable game dealers, although Billy Griggs slyly remarked that he knew of at least one shipment that had been gathered up dead and sold to Chicago markets.[25]

Lake Surprise was in the eye of the public storm again in 1900 when Moody replaced the McNeir brothers with caretakers William and Lee Kennedy and Robert Heiman. The new custodians brashly asserted themselves as sovereign, rightful property owners and declared that anyone—including Colonel Moody—they found on the property would be dealt with as a trespasser. Sheriff John L. Frost, who was dispatched to evict them, borrowed a fresh horse at Whitehead Ranch and headed to Lake Surprise. He was never seen again. According to Joe Whitehead, the riderless horse made its way back to the barn, its bridle reins cut and bloodied. The Kennedys and Heiman were summarily rounded up, and they denied murdering the sheriff. Then they confessed. Then they recanted the confession. The district attorney dismissed the case.[26]

The beginning of the end for Lake Surprise market hunting was not a result of overshooting, lead poisoning, game laws, or even murders. It was salt water, which came in from the Gulf of Mexico with a roar during the great hurricane of 1900, killing most of the wild celery. That autumn some of the vegetation returned, and with it some canvasbacks, although the *Galveston Daily News* noted that the birds were not as fat as in previous years. Galveston shoppers seemed to prefer to buy, instead, puddle ducks that had "attack[ed] the rice fields." Wild celery returned the following year but was destroyed again during storms in 1908 and 1915. Both wild celery and canvasbacks disappeared for good from fabled Lake Surprise by the mid-1900s.[27]

While Lake Stephenson and Lake Surprise rose above all other Texas canvasback resorts, there were other reputable localities. On the upper coast they included Lost and Keith Lakes, located in a maze of coastal wetlands that paralleled the Gulf of Mexico for nearly thirty miles west of Sabine Lake. The 267-acre Lost Lake, with its wild celery, sago pondweed, and banana water lily, was probably second only to the chain of lakes for numbers of wintering canvasbacks. Another celebrated shooting ground, only a short wagon ride from Galveston, was Sweetwater Lake, with growths of wild celery that made it a "fine feeding ground for canvasbacks."[28]

There were two prominent localities in the middle coast and Coastal Bend: Hynes Bay and Harbor Island. Hynes Bay, at the north end of San Antonio Bay, was tucked between the Guadalupe delta and the curving shoreline bordered to the southwest by Blackjack Peninsula. The small body of water with a big reputation for canvasbacks was a major destination for gunners who set sail from Seadrift, Rockport, Port Lavaca, and as far away as Galveston.

Galveston's W. G. Nelson likely discovered Hynes Bay when he, like other gunners, was barred from the chain of three lakes in his native Chambers County. Nelson was probably the first market hunter to commercialize Hynes Bay canvasbacks, in the late 1880s opening a shipping business in nearby Port Lavaca that almost exclusively handled area canvasbacks. Rockport's Ben Lettes followed canvasbacks to Hynes Bay, and on one shoot in 1891 he killed nearly five hundred birds. The next year William J. Dorsett, also from Rockport, netted $320 from a harvest of four hundred canvasbacks. Several Seadrift hunters made the short crossing to Hynes Bay. One man and his three sons, who hunted for New York markets, shot three hundred canvasbacks in an hour and a half. They would have brought in more had they not "killed many that they could not get." Another Seadrift market gunner killed and shipped sixteen hundred ducks in just a few weeks in 1901.[29]

Harbor Island, known by hunters as the Big Flats, was located between St. Joseph's and Mustang Islands at the convergence of Aransas, South, Redfish, and Corpus Christi Bays. Harbor Island was lauded in the late 1890s as "the best canvasback water left open to the public in the United States," and its huge wintering concentrations of canvasbacks and redheads brought market men from Aransas Pass, Port Aransas, Rockport, and Corpus Christi. Some of the best hunters averaged seventy-five to a hundred ducks a day and earned up to fifteen hundred dollars a season. According to one market man, the largest Harbor Island commercial operation used sink boxes supported by a small fleet of sloops and schooners. With their schooners filled with over half a ton of ice, they remained on the hunting grounds for four or five days at a time.[30]

Harbor Island was one of the places hunted by the Spears family, who remain there today as operators of South Bay Hunting Club, started by Gordon "Pop" Spears. The story is passed down of Pop's great-uncle Edward, who shot ducks, mostly canvasback, for Corpus Christi markets. Edward piled ducks high in a horse-drawn cart, then headed to Portland, where he waited for low tide to ford the narrow oyster reef at the mouth of Nueces Bay as he made his way to Corpus Christi.[31]

Canvasbacks were Texas' most extensive wild game industry, and some of the numbers killed for market are part of the public record. In 1903 Colonel Moody's Lake Surprise operation shipped an average of three hundred ducks a day, with a total for the four-month shooting season of more than thirty thousand ducks. Tallies from the Coastal Bend are similar. Louis Cobolini's Union Fish Company shipped 418 barrels of ducks, nearly all canvasbacks and redheads, from Rockport in 1897. With about sixty-two ducks to the barrel, Cobolini's total that year was approximately twenty-six thousand ducks. The peak for all Rockport merchants combined reached about thirty thousand canvasbacks in the late 1890s. About the same time, Corpus Christi game merchants shipped more than twenty thousand canvasbacks in just two months.[32]

At their peak, then, Lake Surprise, Rockport, and Corpus Christi shipped about eighty thousand birds a year. The numbers do not take into account the other large coastal centers of Orange, Beaumont, Port Arthur, Houston, Port Lavaca, and Aransas Pass, and they do not include ducks sold in local markets. The Lone Star State had a remarkable reign in canvasbacks.

FEATHER MERCHANTS—PLUMES, SKINS, AND QUILLS

Americans in the late nineteenth century did not limit their wild game passion to just the culinary; they found ways, as well, to bring it to fashion, primarily in ladies' hats. In the rigorous culture of style that defined the late 1800s, hats were a mandated accessory. Women did not leave home without top wear, their choice of style, fabric, and adornments a reflection of social standing. Feathers were one of the main trimmings, and the rarer the feathered accessories, the better. The millinery trade in ladies' hats, along with secondary markets in bird skins, eggs, and wing feathers for quill pens, cut a large hole in America's plume-bearing and ornately feathered birds.

A THOROUGHLY FASHIONABLE *1890s ensemble with a feather boa, feathered hat crown, trailing plumes front and back, and stuffed bird. (Courtesy University of Texas Institute of Texan Cultures at San Antonio, File No. 068 3085)*

The list of waterbirds targeted for the plumage and skin market was long, made up of several egret species, roseate spoonbills, whooping and sandhill cranes, terns, herons, ibises, pelicans, seagulls, grebes, avocets, skimmers, and a host of smaller shore and wading birds. In order not to offend delicate feminine fashion senses, the business of bird killing, plucking, and skinning was cloaked in euphemisms. Feather hunters went by the stylish name of plumassiers; procurers of skins and those who thieved eggs from springtime nests amongst screaming and squawking hen birds were merely collectors.[33]

Feathered hat adornments were popular in US fashion as early as the 1840s, but demand was small. Even as late as the 1870s the "artistic milliner . . . was something of a rare bird." With the late 1800s came an explosion in European and American taste for feathers, and the millinery industry grew from a half-million-dollar business to five million dollars a year nearly overnight. New York was the center of America's fashionable millinery, and at its peak, ten thousand women and children worked in the city's hat factories.[34]

Making hats from velvet, silk, satin, straw, wool, tulle, and crepe, fashion houses designed a dizzying array of styles: touring hats, top hats, flat-crowned boaters or canotiers, "fascinators," Connelly turbans, wide-brimmed Gainsboros, church hats, bowlers or derbies, bonnets, and "Juliet" hats. Their adornments included netting, lace, ruffles, bows, tailings, brooches, and, most important, feathers. Short feathers circled hat crowns, while longer plume-feather aigrettes

FOWL AS FAD AND FASHION

stuck up or hung down from the back as a tailing. Ladies' top wear displayed not only plumes, but also bird wings, stuffed bird heads, and sometimes whole birds that peered out from a mélange of feathers. Hat fads included dyed bird feathers formed into the shape of butterflies that, suspended on wires, flitted in the air. The rage in the fall of 1887 was a silk beaver hat trimmed with feather tips. Other styles that year were a bonnet of glacé velvet with whole birds and wings in shades to match, and a hat accented with parrot throat feathers, a plume rising from its crown of Irish lace. The fashion highlight of the 1896 season was osprey feathers that dropped down over the wearer's ears.[35]

Bird parts migrated from hats to entire wardrobes. Grebe breasts, for example, were very popular for trimming "muffs, colarettes, and capes." European and American society pages followed the most spectacular feathered fashions, such as the gown of a London woman adorned with six hundred Brazilian hummingbirds. The evening dress of one young girl was trimmed with fifty canaries, while another wore a dress accented with dove wings.[36]

Dozens of Texas milliners and department stores carried the latest in feathered hats and accessories, their inventories imported mostly from Paris or New York. The number of Texas milliners who designed their own feathered creations was probably small. One was Moke's Millinery Parlor in San Antonio, which in 1890 advertised an inventory of six thousand "fancy birds" for its line of hats. In Laredo, F. Lozano owned a large fashion business that specialized in bird mounts and wings.[37]

At the front end of the feather business were the gunners. At first most shooters were local, but after Atlantic Coast plume birds were largely eradicated during the 1880s, commercial hunters discovered the Texas Gulf Coast. Hunters aimed their guns toward spring nesting sites, or rookeries, and dozens of these avian oases dotted Texas bays. Among the largest were Bird Island in Galveston Bay, the black mangroves behind Port Aransas, Big Bird and Little Bird Islands in Upper Laguna Madre, and Green Island near Point Isabel. Rookeries were easy to locate, as huge flocks with swirling colors and raucous cries invariably gave away their location. Some of the smaller, more inaccessible nesting sites were a secret closely guarded by hunters.[38]

Half a century before rookeries succumbed to the feather hunter's gun, a traveler to appropriately named Bird Island, in the Galveston Bay chain of Vingt'-une Islands, found the roost covered in so many snowy egrets that it appeared to him like a bank of snow. Discharging his "heavy loaded old gun into the midst of them . . . thousands of birds instantly flew up, with such a fluttering, and screaming, and yelling, that no scene of noise and hubbub I ever witnessed could be at all compared with it." The writer had never before seen a snowy egret and described them as "generally birds of considerable size, though some of them possessed only superior longitude, for among those I picked up were bodies not bigger than a small duck's, mounted on legs measuring a foot and a half below the knee.

F. LOZANO, TAXIDERMIST.

Dealer in Southern and Mexican Birds, Natural History specimens, Birds and Wings for ladies hats a specialty.

Spanish and English spoken.
No. 1107 Lincoln St., Just west of Laredo National Bank.

(Modified from *Laredo Times*, May 21, 1901)

Almost all of them had plumage abundant and white, or bordering on pink, and neck long enough to keep up a connection with the earth."[39]

Soon the world knew about the long, delicate plumes of the snowy egret. They became the jewels in feathered crowns, in such demand that the bird was sometimes dubbed the "bonnet martyr." Snowy egret plumes cost the most and numbered the fewest, between fifteen and twenty from each bird. Billy Griggs, who hunted in Texas for the millinery trade each spring, received prices that ranged from a low of $140 to as high as $640 a pound. Forest McNeir hunted for the spring feather market and usually received $3 a plume. Plumes rarely fetched less than $400 a pound in city markets during the late 1880s. It was big money, and it created a big industry. A New York merchant in the 1880s ordered plumes from Texas hunters in lots of ten thousand each; another merchant shipped two hundred pounds to France during a single year.[40]

Another part of the feather industry was the trade in bird skins destined for milliners, museums, and collectors. Corpus Christi's distributors Henry Palmer and Capt. William Anderson shipped two thousand bird skins from North Padre Island to New York in eleven months during the 1870s. Frank B. Armstrong, in Brownsville, established a national following as a dealer in "Mexican and Southern birds, Mammal Skin, Bird Eggs, and Specimens of Natural History." Armstrong's listing of available skins was four hundred birds long, and included in his inventory were whooping crane skins priced at eighteen dollars each. Robin Doughty wrote that, in the cargo of the fifteen-ton schooner *Flower of France*, which capsized near Saluria during the hurricane of 1886, were six hundred seagull skins. In parts of the United States, brightly colored wood duck skins sold for as much as four dollars at the turn of the century.[41]

Ornithologist Florence Merriam Bailey visited Corpus Christi in 1900 with her husband, a field agent for the US Biological Survey. She wrote of two local hunters who, in one week, shipped a thousand bird skins, mainly terns, yellowlegs, avocets, and willets. In her writings Bailey sympathized with the Texas gunners, who, she said, were "mainly poor settlers in a country where it is hard to make a living, and they shoot the birds merely to add a little to the meager support they can give their families."[42]

Demand for skins even included grackles, called jackdaws in Texas. Rockport dealers paid between six and ten cents per bird, the venture profitable enough that several market hunters gave up shooting waterfowl to concentrate on the black birds. Killed by the thousands in the 1890s, jackdaws were skinned, rolled in plaster of paris and arsenic, then stuffed with cotton and placed in a paper cone to dry.[43]

Profitable, too, were wing feathers from pelicans, geese, and swans used to manufacture quill pens. Quality quills were much in vogue; as early as the 1850s, merchants publicized their shipments of swan and goose quill pens along with other northern and European "seasonable and fashionable goods." During the 1870s the "latest conceit" was swan quill pens with painted scenes on their feathered backs. Swan quills fetched the highest price and sold for as much as twenty dollars per hundred. The quills with the highest durability were said to come from an unnamed species of goose "found in the Hudson Bay territory."[44]

The eggs of wading birds and shorebirds were also sold, both for local consumption and to collectors. Naturalist George B. Sennett wrote that along the Texas coast nests were robbed of tens of thousands of eggs each spring and summer. "Egging" was practiced in every Texas port town, he said, and boats sometimes traveled over a hundred miles in search of nesting sites. Eggers filled tubs and barrels, then peddled their harvest locally to shop owners or had them shipped to collectors. One group of entrepreneurs plucked thousands of pelican chicks from their nests and boiled them to make cooking oil. With its strong taste, the rendered pelican product never caught on in the marketplace.[45]

As they steadily disappeared along America's shores, wading birds and shorebirds became one of the symbols of the things gone astray in man's relationship with nature. They helped, in part, to bring about the crusade for wildlife conservation, a battle that would pit powerful shooting, shipping, millinery, and restaurant interests against sportsmen, naturalists, and conservationists. Theirs would be a contest played out first in the media and waged finally in the legislative halls of state and national politics.

CHAPTER 5

THE WINDOW CLOSES

Wildlife in the late 1800s and early 1900s was caught in an eddy by crosscurrents of competing interests. Birds and animals were sustenance in rural communities, income to market men, valued on the table by upper-class gourmands, and shot by all classes of society for sport. Farmers killed wildlife when it destroyed crops or attacked livestock but embraced those animals and birds that ate insects or otherwise contributed in some way to crops and produce. An increasing number of people came to enjoy wildlife for its own sake. America had once been unsettled enough that diverging wildlife interests did not often overlap. By the approach of the twentieth century they were destined to collide.

Game animals, resident game birds, wildfowl, and other migratory birds were eliminated from large areas around East Coast settlements as early as the 1700s. Well-intended county and state game laws did little to stem the damage. The wave of destruction continued to push across the frontier as the ax, plow, and gun crossed the Appalachians. The prospect of empty skies, forests, and fields motivated some of America's sportsmen, naturalists, farmers, and other concerned citizens to form alliances dedicated to wildlife preservation. By the late nineteenth century these groups were successful in an almost quixotic effort to protect wildlife through passage of state laws and, later, groundbreaking federal legislation.

At first, while many recognized the effect of habitat destruction on game animals and birds, it was not part of the battle cry. The environment was a price, it seemed, America was willing to pay for progress. Instead, focus was on the market hunter, whose gun was considered one of the main culprits in the downward spiral of America's wild game. Not wealthy and poorly represented in the halls of business and politics, the market hunter was an easy target. Too, he had blood on his hands. For the men who made a living by procuring game, time—legally, at least—was about up.

TOO MANY GUNS

The killing, transportation, and sale of migratory waterfowl made up one of the largest pieces of America's trade in wild game. Few people counted the commercial gunners who supplied America's wild birds, but if they had, the number would have been in the thousands. The duck shooting business on the upper Chesapeake Bay before the Civil War employed hundreds of men from New York to Virginia. Some four hundred commercial market men hunted North Carolina's Currituck Sound near the turn of the century. As many as five hundred gunners made a living from wildfowl on the outskirts of New Orleans during the late 1800s, and they were close enough to the city that the sound of their guns resonated through its streets, reminding one visitor of a battlefield. Numbers like these examples were repeated across America's wetlands.[1]

There were hundreds of market hunters among Texas' "poor citizens living along the waterfronts." The spoils of their occupation were largely celebrated by society until the late 1800s, when, as in much of America, the number of men making a living from guns came to be viewed as cause of declining bird resources. The warning flag was first raised in Texas by sportsmen, who saw the market man as a competitor for dwindling numbers of birds. Houston sport hunters at the turn of the century who found only empty skies in the once game-rich prairie south of the city complained of market hunters "so thick that they were a nuisance [and that] have pretty well shot it out." It was the same in Refugio County, where "Sportsmen acquainted with Hynes Bay will remember how it used to be the favorite spot [for waterfowl] of any place along the coast, but some four or five years ago a number of market hunters took possession of the bay, shooting these wildfowl for the market and since then they have not been so numerous."[2]

The dogged, year-round pursuit and harvest of wild game by one category of market hunter—the commission hunter—brought them immediate notoriety by not just sportsmen, but also the public. Commission hunters, employed by game merchants and shipping companies, were paid with a percentage of the kill. They arrived late to Texas, largely as a consequence of decreasing resources in formerly prolific regions such as the East Coast, and did not appear in any great numbers until the 1890s. In an open letter to Texas sportsmen, reprinted in *Recreation* (1901), publisher George Shields wrote of Currituck Sound commission men who moved to Texas because they had "succeeded in practically exterminating the great clouds of wild fowl that formerly wintered there." Of their new shooting grounds, he said: "The most notorious butchers of the lot have gone to Corpus Christi, or Aransas Pass, to continue their slaughter. They have prospected the coast, have found the place they were looking for, and have written back to certain of their kind in North Carolina to come to Texas at once. They report millions of ducks there, and say the Texas shooters know little about how to slaughter or ship them; so the thoroughbreds from Currituck sound are likely to have a walk-over."[3]

Texans hardly knew how to come to grips with the new breed of market man. One uneasy portrayal described them as men with swivel guns who "travel in wagons or boats, wear grass suits and slaughter waterfowl in car load lots." Another wrote that they "hire help in slaughtering game [and] divide the country into districts and operate like soldiers." An 1895 editorial in the *Dallas Morning News* noted the impact that commission hunters had on that city's rail industry, as carloads of "fat geese and ducks" arrived from across Texas, then shipped on to Saint Louis and Chicago.[4]

The commission market man in America is perhaps best exemplified by Saint Louis's Nat Wetzel, proclaimed "King of the Market Hunters" and one of the "world's biggest commercial agents in wildlife." Looking back on his career in 1950, Wetzel recalled, "During the time I employed 125 professional hunters for my wild game business, we killed more game than anyone else in the United States." He was probably not exaggerating. Wetzel hired hunters from Canada to the Gulf Coast to supply his Western Commission and Western Poultry and Game companies, which, with offices in Saint Louis, Kansas City, and Houston, shipped game worldwide.[5]

Wetzel provided his hired hands with five-shot pumps and ammunition shipped by the railroad boxcar. His was a state-of-the-art operation that watched migration patterns, weather, and the competition and communicated the information to his army of hunters by telegraph. According to author Wayne Capooth, rather than barrels, he shipped his ducks in refrigerated boxes that he stored for up to two years, timing their arrival in the market at peak prices. Only a few names of Nat Wetzel's hired guns remain for posterity. One was Tom Ray, who worked for Wetzel's Western Commission Company. Ray traveled to Beaumont from Missouri each winter, living in a tent and shooting ducks on Taylor's Bayou west of Port Arthur.[6]

After the turn of the century, commission men such as Wetzel were denounced by a progressively more agitated public and its growing opposition to market gunning. In a letter to the editor of *Western Field* in 1903, a game law proponent called Wetzel "a market hunter whose unparalleled nastiness unquestionably classifies him as the biggest and altogether most unconscionable game hog in the whole abominable sty."[7]

NUMBERS OF BIRDS

No one may have been counting the hunters, but some certainly counted their score. By the turn of the twentieth century the phenomenal numbers of birds harvested for market assured either their extermination or a backlash. America chose the latter. On Maryland's Susquehanna Flats, a Havre de Grace market man in the 1840s killed a remarkable 7,000 canvasbacks in a single winter. In the 1880s the Havre de Grace sink box fleet returned from a one day's shoot with 1,500 canvasbacks; one gunner alone killed 540. Guns from about fifty sink box operations bristled from upper Chesapeake shores, and combined with another estimated 150 professional gunners who shot from punting skiffs or blinds, they marketed up to 35,000 ducks a year.[8]

South of the Chesapeake, William Temple Hornaday documented two Currituck Sound market men who, in a week, killed 1,400 bluebills for East Coast markets. In the winter of 1911, 135,000 ducks and fifteen hundred geese were killed and shipped to market from Virginia's Back Bay and North Carolina's Pamlico Sound. Another 100,000 were marketed from Currituck Sound. In South Carolina, Georgetown markets handled as many as 5,000 black ducks and mallards in a day.[9]

West of New Orleans, between Lac des Allemands and Lake Salvador, a group of six or seven market men delivered 4,800 ducks to the French Market after just a few days afield in the 1880s. Wayne Capooth wrote of three northwestern Louisiana gunners who, in 1888, killed nearly 1,300 ducks, mostly mallards, in a span of seven hours. At the time, it was considered a world record. In 1911 the Louisiana State Game Commission reported that the state's waterfowl harvest came to a staggering 3,176,000 "sea and river" ducks, almost a quarter million geese, and more than six hundred thousand snipes, sandpipers, and plovers.[10]

In western Tennessee's Reelfoot Lake, an average of a thousand ducks a day were killed each winter between the mid-1800s and 1915, with most shipped to Chicago, Memphis, Nashville, and Saint Louis. Swans were often a part of the tally until they "were burnt out with powder and lead," mostly disappearing by the 1870s. Chicago markets were the main destination for millions of birds killed each summer in Iowa, Nebraska, Minnesota, and Illinois. In four days in 1894, three Detroit market men killed about 720 ducks, mostly redheads, for midcontinent markets.[11]

On the Pacific Coast, a California commercial hunter claimed he supplied city markets in 1877 with more than twelve thousand ducks and geese, more than three hundred sandhill cranes, and sixty swans. In its "Game Shipments" section, the *Woodland Daily Democrat* wrote of three Sutter County market hunters who, after one excursion, shipped forty-five sacks—nearly three thousand ducks—to San Francisco markets. Two brothers from Lake Elsinore killed and shipped more than five thousand in a season. Los Angeles markets alone handled some fifty thousand geese in 1885-86. During a single year in the 1890s, California markets sold nearly eighty thousand teal and four hundred sandhill cranes. Markets at the turn of the century received "a hundred tons" of ducks a year from just one Oregon location.[12]

In Texas, a reliable estimate of the number of annually exported waterfowl is available only from Rockport and Corpus Christi. At its peak in the late 1890s,

Rockport merchants shipped an average of six hundred ducks a day for a five-month shooting season, the town's total each year about seventy-five thousand ducks. In the last year of legal Texas market hunting, Chief Warden S. W. Stanfield of the Texas division of the League of American Sportsmen (LAS) estimated sixty thousand ducks and geese were shipped from Corpus Christi. The amount of waterfowl killed in Texas is incalculable if one considers not only other coastal and inland cities involved in the game trade, but also the volume of birds killed for local markets. It couldn't last.[13]

THE KILL

Much of nineteenth- and early-twentieth-century society favorably embraced the image of a duck hunter, his shotgun at the ready as flocks of ducks made their way to wooden decoys floating on a windswept bay, the sun rising in the background. This was not, however, the picture of the late-nineteenth- and early twentieth-century market hunter, whose killing methods became entirely unpalatable to an increasingly informed public.

Leading the list of insidious killing devices were swivel and punt guns, used to shoot into large flocks of waterfowl on the water. America waged a long war on the big guns, and Texas sportsmen joined the battle. One decried the unsportsmanlike conduct of the "market-hunter butcher at work with his swivel gun" in which, with only "two or three discharges . . . three or four hundred fowl will be killed." Almost as disdained were extended magazine tubes, available on some semiautomatic shotgun models, which allowed shooters to discharge up to eleven rounds without reloading.[14]

Night shooting was another grievance. For rural and small-town residents across the United States, winter nights at times sounded like a battle zone as professional gunners snuck birds, shot from blinds, or used sculling boats fitted with big guns. Sportsmen who followed in the wake of the night hunter often found that most birds were driven from roosting and feeding grounds. One Texas sport hunter greeted with empty morning marshes advised: "When waterfowl hear guns roaring and the fire flash in the dark, they take wing and never return." Dismay turned to anger when Galveston sportsmen, on a four-day excursion in 1901, never saw a duck. Blaming the "ravages of night pot-hunters," they took their complaints to the press.[15]

Large bags were sometimes made by gunners who raked shot across feeding and resting flocks from behind slow-moving steers. This was called bull-hunting in California, where a Central Valley market man was said to have killed four hundred ducks with only ten shots. In the Lone Star State the Texas Game, Fish, and Oyster Commission reported that some professional hunters made kills of about three hundred to four hundred ducks and geese a day behind trained oxen.[16]

Ducks were baited to the gun with corn, sorghum, barley, wheat, rice, tomato seeds, and even sugar beet pulp. It could be hard to keep flocks of hungry birds off of bait. A Havre de Grace, Maryland, gunner remembered a hunt over corn in the 1890s in which ducks kept coming despite a continual barrage of some thirteen hundred rounds, and 360 ducks were retrieved at the end of the day.[17]

Market men traditionally baited an area for several consecutive days. They knew that if bait was scattered, ducks tended to "feed promiscuously," reducing the numbers that could be killed. Instead, they spread the bait in a narrow line, as it concentrated birds for the shot. Harry Walsh, in *Outlaw Gunner*, professed that two bushels of corn could sustain a thousand ducks. For puddle ducks, bait was simply broadcast in shallow water. It was more labor-intensive to bait diving ducks, because they frequented deeper water. Upper Chesapeake Bay hunters attached corncobs to wires that they weighted down below the surface of the water, or they made holes in burlap sacks that they filled with corn kernels and stones.[18]

Some Texas market men spiked their bait. An account from an 1874 *Forest and Stream* told of an innovative hunter near Goliad who soaked corn in alcohol and opium. With the concoction spread on the ground, in three days he caught fifteen hundred geese, which were destined for the feather market. In 1886 a group of market hunters soaked half a barrel of corn in opium for two weeks. They, too, caught their geese by hand, wringing the neck of enough to earn over four thousand dollars.[19]

Ducks were netted and trapped. Market men used dozens of different net and trapping configurations, from staked fishing nets to elaborate wild duck nets, as well as snares and wooden cages. Another common but effective means was to string baited hooks to a harness secured to the ground by pegs and typically placed on the edge of a "beach at low water." The success of this "painful mode of capture" was considered "equal to its cruelty." Another notoriously efficient device popularized on the Chesapeake Bay was called the net trap; it was a funnel-shaped net supported by hoops that led to a baited, rectangular enclosure. Trapped ducks were dispatched by wringing their neck. It was easier to deal with netted ducks—they drowned.[20]

During the late 1880s, eight groups of trappers ran some twenty duck nets on the Susquehanna Flats. They made hauls of 800 ducks a day using nets as long as two hundred yards. California duck netters at the turn of the century set simple, staked fishing nets baited with corn and often caught 50 to 75 ducks from a single setting. An operation in Colorado netted 840 ducks and nearly fifty Canada geese using just one net. The fact that netting and trapping waterfowl was outlawed in Texas in the early 1900s suggests it was practiced, but few easily found references exist.[21]

There were some unusual killing methods. With the arrival of the petroleum industry in California, new refineries began discharging large volumes of crude oil into San Francisco Bay. Hundreds of wild ducks "made perfectly helpless by a coating of petroleum on their wing feathers" were clubbed for Oakland and San Francisco markets.[22]

A LIST OF THE MISSING

With the latter half of the nineteenth century came an alarming decrease in America's game animals, game birds, and migratory birds and wildfowl. The cause, in part, was the gun. In part, too, was destruction of habitat. Robin Doughty, in *Wildlife and Man in Texas,* paints a vivid picture of America's transformation as wilderness became cities, prairie grasses were converted to grazing land and farmland, wetlands were drained, trees were felled, and streams and rivers "ran red and brown with runoff."[23]

In Texas, declines in the great buffalo herds, deer, pronghorns, wild turkeys, prairie chickens, quail, mourning doves, and passenger pigeons were evident by the late 1800s. Many of the vanquished or vanishing birds were, only a short time before, found in astonishing numbers. Passenger pigeons had migrated to Texas in "countless millions" and covered miles of inland forests. They fed on "bitter mast" of first-year acorns with such voracity, and in such large numbers, that their weight broke tree limbs. By the first decade of the twentieth century, destruction of nesting habitat and overhunting led to their extinction.[24]

Eskimo curlews were hunted for the market from Canada to Argentina, and the flocks that migrated through the Lone Star State were similar in size to those of passenger pigeons. By a few accounts they were uncommon after 1875. Some of the last sightings were in Lampasas and in Calhoun and Victoria Counties between 1886 and 1905 and around Galveston Bay as late as the 1960s. Texas market hunters were given the dubious distinction of being listed as a major contributor to their demise.[25]

The milliner's trade in plume-bearing fowl took a terrific toll on shorebirds and wading birds, particularly the fashionable snowy egret, which, along with several other species, was entirely annihilated along the eastern seaboard by the 1870s. Plume hunters next moved south to Florida rookeries, where they virtually exterminated snowy egrets by the 1880s. Masses of shooters then moved to the Texas coast, with methods so efficient that, within a decade, snowy egrets were uncommon in Matagorda Bay, and by 1905 the white bird was "very rare on the Gulf Coast."[26]

The snowy egret was joined by a host of other birds. One was the wood duck, with its explosion of every color of the spectrum, which was targeted by feather merchants, milliners, and manufacturers of artificial fishing flies. Wood duck numbers declined fairly early, and the bird was considered in Texas at the turn of the century as "formerly abundant, now exceedingly rare."[27]

Individual states had the sole authority to govern their game birds, animals, migratory birds, and songbirds until the twentieth century, and they did so with varying degrees of success. According to Theodore Sherman Palmer, who followed the ebb and flow of game protection in a series of landmark publications in the early 1900s, the first game laws in America were enacted along the Atlantic seaboard during the late 1700s. Most dealt with protection of deer, particularly the use of uncontrolled fire to drive them to waiting guns. Massachusetts in 1818 passed the first protective nonmigratory game bird legislation, and by 1864 twelve states east of the Mississippi River had enacted some form of bird protection.[28]

The first law in the United States to protect waterfowl was passed by Virginia in 1832, and it prohibited shooting ducks and geese at night as well as the use of big guns for any birds destined for market. Many early protective measures foresaw the future, such as the 1836 Massachusetts law that forbade sale of "marshbirds" and Rhode Island's 1846 measure that outlawed migratory bird shooting during spring nesting season. By the time the first shots of the Civil War were fired, approximately twenty migratory waterfowl and shorebird laws had been passed in twelve states. Between 1861 and the end of the nineteenth century, another nine states and the District of Columbia adopted some form of waterfowl legislation.[29]

Although it was well intentioned, game protection under the auspices of individual states was wildly inconsistent. Virginia, for example, prohibited skiff hunting in 1838, but only in two counties. An 1839 Delaware law made it illegal for nonresidents to kill or capture wildfowl, but it included just parts of Delaware Bay and the Delaware River. Louisiana's 1852 law prohibited shooting ducks and snipes only on state-owned lands in Saint Bernard Parish. A California regulation the same year provided for a closed season on wood ducks and mallards but covered just twelve counties. New Jersey outlawed night hunting in 1859, but only on Barnegat Bay.

It is curious how long it took for some states, particularly those with a prominent place in the chronicles of big-volume market hunting, to embrace game laws. North Carolina passed its first law in 1869, but it dealt only with "fire hunting"—the use of lamps on skiffs for night hunting—and outlawed the practice in just six counties. It was not until 1872 that Maryland took any legislative action to protect the dwindling stock of canvasbacks on Susquehanna Flats. Maryland went on to build a respectable slate of regulations that included a waterfowl hunting season, allowed shooting only three days a week, and limited big guns and night shooting. Most important, monies were allocated for enforcement, with formation of a Board of Special Ducking Police, locally called the duck policemen. Illinois lawmakers, always outlobbied by Chicago market interests, did not pass their first waterfowl legislation until 1903. Even then, it had little effect; the sale of wild game within the state was outlawed, but because it was legal to sell game from other states, the law was impossible to enforce.[30]

Concerned citizens and hunters were the first to promote organized game protection groups, but as with early game laws, their effectiveness was limited to the states in which they were chartered. Likely America's first conservation group was the New York Association for the Protection of Game, organized in 1844 as a trap shooting club that, ironically, used passenger pigeons as targets. State conservation groups grew quickly in popularity; by the mid-1870s there were nearly a hundred chartered organizations in the United States.[31]

Nature found a powerful ally as the theme of conservation crossed state boundaries with protective organizations founded at the national level. A major catalyst to the nationwide movement was small birds, and they had a big impact. The harvest of songbirds and other nongame species struck a chord with a segment of society new to game protection—the nonhunters—who proved crucial to the coming fight.

Blame for America's "fearful decrease of our small migratory birds" was placed on the "millions of all kinds of birds killed to satisfy the palate of the gourmands." Sold in markets and restaurants, the culinary list included robins, cardinals, blackbirds, bobolinks, meadowlarks, both yellow-shafted and red-shafted flickers, called pigeon woodpeckers, sparrows, swallows, gray catbirds, wood thrushes, red-eyed vireos, flycatchers such as the eastern kingbird, cedar waxwings, mockingbirds, and tanagers. An 1891 account by Mrs. M. E. W. Sherwood even offered advice on how to prepare owls and hummingbirds, in which the latter were "daintily served in nutshells."[32]

Among the most heavily harvested nongame birds in America were robins, bobolinks, and meadowlarks. The most popular small bird on the table in the South was the robin, and millions were killed each year. One Texas market hunter organized parties of men and boys on nightly roost shoots; during the winter of 1903 they supplied 120,000 of the orange-breasted birds to local restaurants. Bobolinks went by the names rice bird or reed bird and were more common east of the Mississippi River than in Texas. Considered a "delicious morsel," especially prized were "buttery reed-birds" from Delaware marshes. Some East Coast markets handled nearly a million of the birds each fall. Meadowlarks were popular in markets because of a flavor that "in some respects resembles that of quail."[33]

Protective awareness at last encompassed the gamut from the sparrow to the buffalo, its advocates a union of sportsmen, naturalists, conservationists, farmers, and concerned citizens, the nonhunters. Together, they changed the face of conservation in America, educating a nation and its lawmakers and crafting legal language that governed the killing of plumage, game, and nongame bird species. The first national coalition was probably the International Association for the Protection of Game, founded in 1874. Over the next thirty-seven years it was followed by the American Ornithologists' Union (AOU), the National Association of Audubon Societies (NAAS), the Boone and Crockett Club, the LAS, and the American Game Protective and Propagation Association.

The International Association for the Protection of Game was the product of author and journalist Charles Hallock. Only a year after its founding, Hallock organized a convention attended by representatives from thirty-eight states and Canada, their goal to prepare a code of cooperative laws for presentation to state legislatures. Within the code's language was formulation of uniform game laws by "zones." With conservation a concept still in its infancy, few states took notice of the proposal.[34]

Hallock's crusade for education was more successful. Along with naturalist and early conservation pioneer George Bird Grinnell, he used his publication *Forest and Stream* to inform and cajole a national readership on the need for game protection. Hallock's partner Grinnell became a founding member of three other organizations that shaped America's conservation awareness: the AOU, the NAAS, and the Boone and Crockett Club.[35]

George B. Sennett, with Grinnell and other influential leaders, founded the AOU in 1883. In addition to contributions to natural science, the AOU in 1886 ambitiously authored a legal framework—a "model law"—to assist states in their efforts to protect songbirds and birds targeted in the millinery trade. Texas was one of the many states that later adopted its legal language.[36]

The AOU was aided in its efforts by the NAAS and its state affiliates. The mission of the NAAS—to provide the public with "a more lively appreciation of the value of preserving the wild bird and animal life of America"—struck a nerve, and by the late 1880s the association was represented in twenty-three states. NAAS's William Dutcher was given credit for passage of the model law in thirty-two states.[37]

Theodore Roosevelt founded the Boone and Crockett Club in 1887 and filled his organization with distinguished sporting and conservationists. Boone and Crockett Club themes included game protection, an end to market hunting, and protection of wilderness lands; the latter became the basis for the US national park system.[38]

The influence of America's conservation groups was readily apparent in state legislation passed in the last two decades of the nineteenth century. A number of states did away with spring shooting, restricted the sale of game, and provided protective measures for plumage-bearing birds and their eggs. Many states also adopted the AOU model law to control the killing of nongame bird species. Another outcome was an emphasis on enforcement, and it came in all shapes and sizes. Rhode Island required town and city councils to hire a special constable to enforce its game laws as early 1875. By the 1880s, game protection in the United States was most often under the auspices of county or state fish and game commissions and game protective societies or associations. Officials with the authority to arrest law violators were called fish and game protectors or duck policemen, and in North Carolina they were gamekeepers. Increasingly, however, they were called game wardens.[39]

By the turn of the century, conservation groups focused their migratory bird protection efforts less on individual states and more toward the choppy waters of federal jurisdiction. The LAS was instrumental in shepherding public and legislative opinion toward federal auspices. Founded by George O. Shields in 1898, the group also promoted bag limits, hunting seasons, and gun licenses and opposed sale of all wild game. They hired their own game wardens, paying a reward to any warden who secured a conviction.[40]

The LAS and its supporters found a new and powerful ally in the White House with Theodore Roosevelt. One of the messages delivered by Roosevelt in his first address to Congress in 1901 was the importance of conserving America's natural resources. Two years later, acting on recommendations from Frank Chapman of the AOU and NAAS's William Dutcher, the president set aside a three-acre rookery in Florida to protect its remaining birds from plume and egg hunters. Named Pelican Island, it was America's first national wildlife refuge.[41]

THE FIGHT FOR GAME LAWS IN TEXAS

If accounts from the first half of the nineteenth century were a celebration of the numbers and diversity of wild game in Texas, in the second half they mostly documented its decline. The first to embrace the theme of wild game conservation, and protective laws to attempt to ensure it, were hunters—mostly educated, wealthy, urban men who wielded considerable political and business influence. While their success in taking the first steps toward preservation of the state's natural resources was a legislative triumph, their motivations were self-serving. Sport hunters saw the market man as a competitor for a limited resource, and they set out to eliminate him.

The first Texas game law, passed in 1860, provided protection for bobwhite quail on Galveston Island for a period of two years, with a closed season between March and September. The local Galveston law was passed because Texas, like many states, left game protection up to individual counties, although it "resulted in considerable confusion."[42]

Sportsmen attempted to pass a statewide game law as early as 1874. Titled House Bill No. 328, it contained language that provided some protection to all game, fowl, and "insectivorous and singing birds." It was a peek into the future, however, when the bill was gutted by amendments that made a mockery of it. One of the most damning struck out the name of every animal, fowl, or fish referenced in the document. Austin's Mark Byrd expressed his disgust in a letter to *Turf, Field, and Farm* in 1876. Legislators, he said, were intimidated by innovation and even more afraid of angering railroad interests. The bill was dropped.[43]

Hunter-conservation groups were founded across Texas between 1881 and the first decade of the twentieth century, with most under the auspices of either the Texas State Sportsmen's Association (TSSA) or the Texas Game Protective Association (TGPA). Theirs was a quarter-century or more of passionate, tireless effort, despite repeated legislative failures and an almost total absence of support for law enforcement. Every legislative year brought renewed attempts to chip away at the barriers to game protection.

Two of those widely credited for early Texas initiatives are Oscar Charles Guessaz and Mervyn Bathurst Davis. Guessaz, of San Antonio, was a boisterous, brawling force to be reckoned with in media and sporting circles. He ran the *San Antonio Daily Times,* the *Weekly Times, Texas Field* and *Texas Field and Sportsman* monthly magazines, and the nationally circulated *Forest and Stream,* and he used a pointed pen to advocate an end to market hunting and garner support for game laws in all his publications. With like-minded sportsmen, Guessaz founded the TSSA in 1877 for the purpose of framing bills for the state legislature and to promote game laws. It was the first conservation organization in the state.[44]

Mervyn Bathurst Davis left the Civil War battlefields of Virginia and headed to Texas in the late 1860s. By the 1870s he was a newspaper correspondent for the *Waco Daily Reporter,* a Texas Ranger, and later Waco correspondent for the *Dallas News.* Davis, who along with Champe Carter McCulloch and Herman E. Ambolt in 1881 formed the TGPA, based in Waco, also headed the Texas branch of the NAAS. Combining his skill as a journalist with a passion for natural history, Davis and Guessaz created the first rumblings of what would eventually become the storm of public opinion and legislative action to protect migratory game birds in Texas.[45]

Made up of urban sportsmen from San Antonio, Waco, Dallas, Galveston, and Houston, Guessaz's TSSA was only a year old when, at the second annual convention in Waco, its founders announced that "steps will be taken in regard to a game law for the next legislature to consider." The TSSA succeeded; the first Texas statewide game law was drafted and passed in 1881. Although it did not address migratory birds, the law provided for a season on deer and game birds and protection of various songbirds. The 1881 law was, however, without teeth. It was said to have been "violated day after day and year after year" with no known instances "wherein parties have been prosecuted." Too, counties could still petition for exemption from the new law, and many did.[46]

Ten years later, Mervyn Davis, with his NAAS Texas contingency, led the first successful effort to protect plumage birds. Largely based on an 1877 Florida law designed to preserve that state's "sea birds and plume birds," Texas' 1891 legislation made it a misdemeanor to kill seagulls, terns, shearwaters, egrets, herons, and pelicans and protected the eggs of those birds. As with the 1881 TSSA legislation, however, there was little notice of the 1891 bill. The *Galveston Daily News* wrote that in many counties "a man is laughed at who would urge its enforcement." The

Oscar Guessaz, *bottom right, with members of the Texas Shooting Club in 1902. (Courtesy University of Texas Institute of Texan Cultures at San Antonio, File No. 075 1121)*

Dallas Morning News noted that twelve years later "not a single prosecution [had] been made." Too, like earlier laws, counties could file a petition for exemption, and by 1895 fifty-six counties were excluded from the Texas 1891 game law.[47]

Oscar Guessaz and the Harris County Game Protective Association, with the backing of Waco's TGPA, in 1893 introduced the first Texas game bill that included language to protect waterfowl. Brought to the legislature as a series of amendments to Davis's 1891 law, the bill proposed to outlaw transportation of migratory birds by railway and express companies outside of the state and made it illegal to shoot migratory birds at night. Supporters explained to the press: "If the tonnage of game killed in Texas for account of northern caterers was computed it would startle the people into promoting measures of suppression." The measure was defeated in the legislature by seven votes.[48]

A second game bill sponsored two years later passed the Texas house. Although it received a majority vote in the senate, it was defeated at the last hour. Lawmakers remember that, with time to debate the bill running out and the legislative session drawing to a close, supporters had the senate clock turned back one hour. When another thirty minutes was requested to finish debate, it was declined by Lieutenant Governor Jester with, "[I] do not think the bill of sufficient importance to the people of Texas to warrant such procedure."[49]

Texas game law proponents plotted vigorously for another run at the 1897 legislative session. Newspapers throughout the state rallied to raise public awareness, and Guessaz's editorials in the *San Antonio Daily Light* at times reached a fever pitch. In his editorial titled "Bold Attempt to Steal Somebody's Thunder," he aimed his pen at the inaction of the prominent San Antonio Gun Club, of which he was a member, for "not [having] done one solitary thing" to influence Austin legislators "to annihilate, at one fell swoop every market hunting individual in the state." The *Dallas Morning News* offered: "It is a well known and existing fact that millions of birds . . . are annually hauled out of the state of Texas by professional market hunters," and "it will only be but a few years when this wholesale slaughter will have destroyed all the game worthy of that name within the borders of the state of Texas." Citizens throughout the state were asked to supply any evidence of the "wholesale destruction of our state game" by market hunters to the assistant attorney general.[50]

R. R. Lockett and Waco's Turner Hubby with the TGPA played a critical role in drafting the game laws for the 1897 legislative session. State House Bill No. 221 ambitiously declared that all game, fish, birds, wild animals, and wildfowl were the property of the state and that the hunting, killing, and catching of same was to be a privilege as distinguished from a right. The bill carried an amendment making it a penalty for any carrier to ship, transport, or haul game outside of Texas. In an effort to end the legal era of swivel and punt guns, the only legal weapons were guns that could be put to the shoulder. Another measure protected waterfowl from slaughter at night. A minor amendment prohibited destruction of prairie chickens for the "space of three years." The last was not a conservation move; the logic was that, if the birds were given a chance, they would increase to such an extent "as to provide unlimited sport." The original draft included language to expand existing protection to all plumage birds, but that never made the final bill.[51]

The game law was passed and went into effect August 20, 1897. But for its supporters, it was a pyrrhic victory. Pressure from representatives of coastal counties, many of whose constituents made their living from market gunning, successfully lobbied for an amendment that read: "Nothing herein contained shall be construed to prohibit the sale or shipment of wild ducks and geese." Further, the amendment that made it unlawful for railway companies to transport wild game was challenged on the basis that it interfered with personal liberty, "amounting to destruction of the right of property without due process of law."[52]

Laws outlawing the sale of wild game were again drafted for the twenty-sixth legislative session of 1899, this time making it illegal to sell game birds except in the county in which they were killed. The result was the same: in the twenty-sixth legislature the House adopted it only after a provision was added exempting the sale and shipment of ducks and geese.[53]

Texas, like most states before the 1900s, was forced to try to bring law and order to the killing of wild game because the federal government was nearly powerless to do so. According to Rudy Rosen of the Texas Rivers Institute, a series of 1840s-era decisions by the US Supreme Court designated that wildlife was to be held in trust by the states for the benefit of all the people. The first challenge to states' rights in the matter of game protection came with watershed legislation introduced in the late 1890s, and it marked the beginning of more than twenty combative years as the fight for federal authority wound its "troublesome course through Congress."[54]

The federal government's foray into wildlife law started with three pieces of somewhat overlapping legislation. One was the Teller bill, introduced by Senator Henry M. Teller in 1897, with its language that prohibited "interstate traffic in game killed in violation of local laws from any state." Although it originally covered only big game, the clause was later extended to include game birds and "other waterfowl." Iowa's John F. Lacey sponsored the Lacey bill the same year, and the Hoar bill, aimed at the feather trade, was introduced in 1898.

Amendments from the Teller, Hoar, and Lacey bills were combined into the Lacey Act, signed into law by the 56th Congress in 1900. The Lacey Act provided a legal framework for those states without game laws, upheld existing laws for states that had them, and, most critically, prohibited interstate bird traffic in violation of any state law. In its summary report, the House committee optimistically concluded that "where States are powerless to protect themselves, the National Government has ample power." Despite that professed power, the Lacey Act largely failed. It was challenged, as expected, on the constitutionality of federal authority over matters of the states and did not provide funding or enforcement.[55]

Recognizing that both existing state and newly promulgated federal legislation were ineffective, Texas game law proponents intensified their efforts, enlisting support from Henry Philemon Attwater. Attwater had the perfect pedigree: he was director of the NAAS, was a recognized "scientist and authority on Texas birds and animals" in his role as "general industrial agent" of the Southern Pacific Railway, and had served on the AOU committee. Attwater, Guessaz, and Davis, with continued support from the TSSA and TGPA organizations and the Texas branch of the Audubon Society, prepared for the 1901 Texas legislative session. Their efforts suffered a major setback when Galveston's Cecile Seixas, secretary of the first chapter of the Texas Audubon Society, was killed along with her mother and two sisters in the hurricane of 1900.[56]

Still, progress was made. In 1901 they succeeded in adding an amendment to the existing game law that made it illegal to shoot waterfowl using artificial lights of any kind, although the law applied to just thirteen Texas counties. Game law advocates failed, however, in their efforts to outlaw night hunting and to restrict the sale of waterfowl. Once again the tide of prevailing sentiment was too powerful to swim against. Their victorious opponents explained the outcome: "The law against shipping game does not apply to that which is not produced in the state. Ducks are migratory and come from the Great Lakes."[57]

Support came from an increasing number of fronts before the 1903 session. The reformed Audubon Society and newspapermen continued their vocal rally, and a new ally was found in agriculture, the latter a result of "an awakening to the important fact that the birds have some value in destroying insects" and not because of a "sudden increase in the habits of feathered animals." Attwater, Guessaz, and Davis and their supporters at last prevailed when the twenty-eighth legislature passed the Model Game Law in 1903. It almost didn't happen. Senator Terrell of McClellan described how close they came to failing again: "It was the closing day of the 28th Legislature, when many members were standing over their bills in the committee room, rushing them to completion before the Speaker's gavel fell for the last time. . . . A wild rush was made for the Speaker's signature, then across to the other end of the hall for the lieutenant governor's signature. It was the last bill signed."[58]

The Texas Model Game Law was structured on the AOU and NAAS model law, and its language contained two critical, and controversial, passages: a reaffirmation that all wild birds and game animals were to be declared property of the state, and an amendment prohibiting the sale and shipment of all game in or out of the state for a period of five years. In a nod to sport hunters, no restrictions were placed on the number of "birds or fowls" they could kill, but the maximum that could be shipped by rail was limited to twenty-five. Enforcement became the responsibility of railroad companies, which were required by law to possess a signed affidavit accompanying any waterfowl transported by rail. On paper, the door was shut on the market hunter.[59]

The Texas Model Game Law also included language to eliminate the trade in wild bird feathers, with an amendment that outlawed the sale of any part of the plumage, skin, or body of any nongame bird. In a move to curtail the egg trade during nesting season, it was illegal to take or destroy eggs of some species of shore and wading birds.[60]

For game law supporters, 1903 was a legislative triumph, though hardly complete. The senate, again bowing to pressure from legislators whose constituents made their living from the commercial sale of migratory birds, placed a five-year moratorium on the bill. The Model Game Law would expire in 1908.[61]

Efforts to repeal the 1903 regulations were immediate. The *Calhoun County News* railed against the laws as an "intolerable injustice" that would rob hundreds of coastal citizens of their livelihood. The editor advised, "The *News* has started an agitation that, we believe, will convince [the legislature] of its mistake and result in amending the game law." Rockport businessmen claimed the law, in its first year, cost the region forty thousand dollars. One Rockport market man, angry when his main source of income was taken away, complained that "any

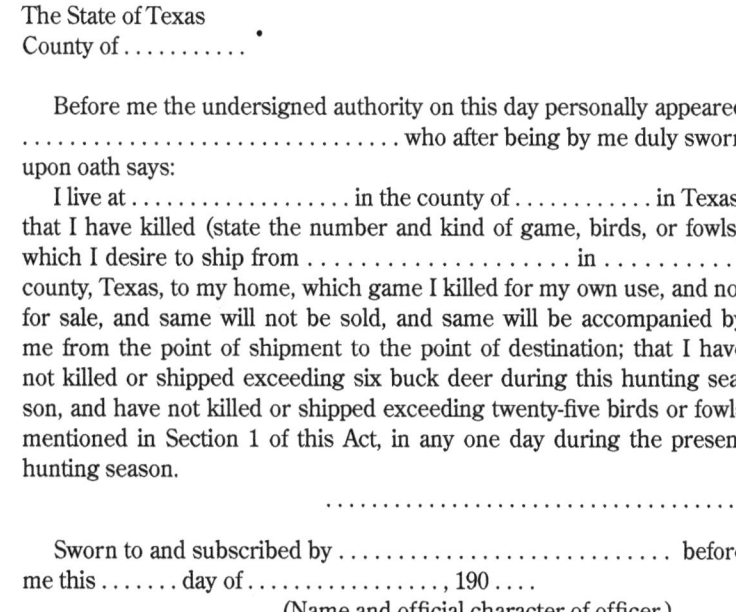

The State of Texas
County of ....

Before me the undersigned authority on this day personally appeared .... who after being by me duly sworn upon oath says:

I live at .... in the county of .... in Texas; that I have killed (state the number and kind of game, birds, or fowls) which I desire to ship from .... in .... county, Texas, to my home, which game I killed for my own use, and not for sale, and same will not be sold, and same will be accompanied by me from the point of shipment to the point of destination; that I have not killed or shipped exceeding six buck deer during this hunting season, and have not killed or shipped exceeding twenty-five birds or fowls mentioned in Section 1 of this Act, in any one day during the present hunting season.

....

Sworn to and subscribed by .... before me this .... day of ...., 190 ....
(Name and official character of officer.)

THE AFFIDAVIT *that ended the era of legal market hunting. Railroads could no longer ship wild game without the hunter present to accompany his or her legal limit.*

(Modified from H. P. N. Gammel, comp., *The Laws of Texas: Supplement Volume to the Original Ten Volumes, 1822–1897*, Vol. 12 [Austin: Von Boeckmann-Jones Company, State Printers, 1904, and Gammel Book Company, Austin, Texas, 1906], 225, 1967).

sportsman could come here and kill all the ducks he is able to kill so long as he only brings them to his boarding house." He observed a party of visiting sportsmen who killed five hundred ducks and, not wanting to risk transporting them, fed most to a farmer's hogs.[62]

Texas hoteliers and restaurateurs organized a bill to repeal the game law in 1904, but when they failed, most of the state's restaurants begrudgingly relented; wildfowl on menus simple or fancy disappeared, although some were just moved to "confidential menus." A ray of hope reappeared in 1906 when upper coast county judges, led by Beaumont's J. P. Wheat, ruled the Model Law unconstitutional. As a result, courts dismissed all existing indictments against Galveston County and Jefferson County restaurants and market men. Judge Wheat didn't worry much about the finer points of his legal position in his ruling. After all, he said, in much of Texas "there has never been any notice taken of the law whatever."[63]

Davis, Guessaz, and Attwater continued their crusade, pushing for a permanent game law. Attwater and Davis organized a lecture campaign at local clubs and state organizations. In an address at College Station in 1905, Attwater advised that "wholesale slaughter of what remains of our game birds and animals must cease," and if hunting them were not regulated, "more of them will soon be exterminated." He accurately predicted that one of the birds likely to disappear would be the prairie chicken, and it was later to bear his name. Guessaz still relied on his ability to persuade through pen and press, with newspaper editorials, pamphlets, and posters explaining the law in English, German, and Spanish. Attwater

MARKET GUNNERS *thought it was unfair that sportsmen were allowed to kill large numbers of birds as long as they did not sell them. This photo of mainly pintails and redheads is from a Rockport hunting club, 1907. Note the wooden shipping barrel on the right. (Courtesy Jim Moloney, File No. 2657)*

arranged distribution of the posters in Southern Pacific Railroad depots throughout the state.[64]

Support came yet again from big-city newspapers. The *Dallas Morning News*, in what was perhaps wishful thinking, wrote that the 1903 Model Game Law was "generally observed by the people without efforts on the part of the authorities to enforce it [as] Texas is too poor to provide a fund with which to prosecute offenders." The article went on to speculate: "The great increase in the number of geese and ducks and all other kinds of game . . . is due directly to the observance of the game law of the state during the past year. By reason of the law, hundreds of thousands of ducks and geese escaped destruction in Texas last winter. These birds, after a flight often of 24 hours without lighting for food and rest, at last reach the Gulf Coast where they fall, exhausted, and at once go to sleep on the water, in which condition they are easily slaughtered in large numbers."[65]

With expiration of the Model Game Law at stake, tension ran high in Austin before the 1907 legislative session. Market hunters and game merchants established a lobby in the capitol to influence lawmakers on their behalf, while Attwater, Guessaz, and Davis huddled with the Game Law Committee to draft revisions to the existing law. Introduced as House Bill No. 345 of the thirtieth legislature, the measures included the first limit on the number of ducks that could be killed per day—a total of twenty-five—with a possession limit of seventy-five. Regulations for a hunting season were proposed, but they excluded waterfowl. The issue of law enforcement, largely ignored in the 1903 legislation, was addressed by Senator Terrell's Game Warden Act, which proposed allocation of funds for a chief deputy commissioner and deputy commissioners, or game wardens.[66]

Supporters were jubilant when the Permanent Game Law passed the regular session, but their euphoria was short-lived when Governor Campbell vetoed it. Resurrected at a second special session, it passed again, but the governor still refused to sign it. For all the effort, for all the passion, it was not a particularly striking finish for either side when the bill was quietly filed with the secretary of state and became law without the governor's signature.[67]

The ink was hardly dry on the Permanent Game Law when, as with the 1903 Model Game Law before it, detractors circled their wagons. District Judge Pope of Beaumont fired the first volley in 1908 when he ruled it unconstitutional to forbid the sale of wild ducks. The *Galveston Daily News* reported that, because of his ruling, ducks were available again in Galveston city markets, and the *Victoria Daily Advocate* made it known that ducks were also being sold all over the state. Charles Bryant, deputy game warden for Jefferson and Orange Counties, told the press that "the action of the courts in permitting the sale of ducks has practically nullified or emancipated the law," and now "little attention is paid to the wardens by those after game." Then he resigned. He asked his deputies to do the same "until such time as the status of the game law in Texas is definitely determined by the action and review of the higher courts."[68]

The legal wrangling that followed Judge Pope's ruling was closely watched throughout the state. As the Texas attorney general explored the merits of Judge Pope's decision, Pope stiffened in his position, strengthening his language from "unconstitutional" to "absurd, ridiculous and violative of the bill of rights." In January 1909 the higher court made its long-awaited ruling. The case involved Bard Bladeone, found guilty of selling ducks and geese in Port Lavaca, who appealed his conviction to the Court of Criminal Appeals in Dallas. He lost.[69]

THE FINAL ACT

It was another thirteen years after passage of the Lacey Act before the federal government successfully waded back into game law waters. It was not for lack of effort. As early as 1904, Pennsylvania naturalist George Shiras III introduced "A Bill to Protect the Migratory Game Birds of the United States," which advocated use of federal government "police powers" to protect and enforce migratory bird laws. Shiras's draft was used as the foundation for the Weeks-McLean Law, or the Federal Migratory Bird Act (FMBA), which, with the energetic support of the three-thousand-member American Game Protective and Propagation Association, became law in 1913.[70]

The 1913 FMBA had far-reaching implications. In contrast to the Lacey Act, which still acknowledged state sovereignty over migratory birds, the FMBA boldly transferred that authority to the federal government. Commercial market hunting, and the shipment of migratory birds across state lines, was made a federal offense. The law established a hunting season for migratory birds in every state in the union and prohibited killing swans, curlews, and cranes. Although violently opposed in the Midwest, a treaty with Canada that outlawed spring shooting of migratory birds was adopted in 1916.[71]

Like the Lacey Act before it, the FMBA never reached its full potential. Only a small number of wardens were authorized to enforce it, and they made few arrests. Too, the law was challenged on the issue, again, of states' rights. As it mired in the mud of legal finagling all the way to the Supreme Court, the guns kept blazing.[72]

Passage of the Migratory Bird Treaty Act (MBTA) in 1918 included a commitment from Canada, Japan, Mexico, and Russia for the protection of a shared migratory bird resource. Legally, the most important part of the MBTA was its Enabling Act, which strengthened government jurisdiction over migratory waterfowl, songbirds, insectivorous birds, and plume birds. Practically, however, the most essential piece of the MBTA was allocation of federal funds for enforcement. While the 1918 MBTA did not go unchallenged, the American justice system had at last taken notice of progressively empty skies.[73]

Oscar Guessaz and Henry Attwater lived to see the US government protect not just birds within the state but entire waterfowl flyways. Guessaz died in 1925 and Attwater in 1931. Mervyn Bathurst Davis died in 1912 and did not live to see the results of his efforts to end the nation's trade in wild bird feathers. But by then it hardly mattered. Plumage birds had been largely exterminated in much of the United States, and according to Henry Attwater, most of the feather hunters had, by the early 1900s, moved their operations to Mexico, Central America, and the Amazon.[74]

It was a quiet day in the Jefferson County marshes. Against a dark purple sky, the groundskeeper of the Lost Lake Preserve saw a pink bird and shot it. The year was 1913, and it was the first roseate spoonbill—once one of the most popular of the milliner's targets—that had been seen in the area for a long time. It was by then so uncommon that he donated it to a museum.[75]

CHAPTER 6

THE LAW AND THE OUTLAW

The early 1900s were a time of transition between old ways and new, the latter fueled by industrial and technological progress. Railroads connected all major Texas cities, whose night skylines were illuminated by newfangled electric lights. Urbanites traded latest gossip by "automatic" telephones that didn't require the assistance of an operator. Horseless carriages had made their appearance, always drawing a crowd of spectators but frightening horses.

Many Texans strode boldly into the future, while others steadfastly kept both feet firmly planted in the past. A sizable segment of shooting society could still not accept that natural resources were anything other than unlimited, or grasp a need for their regulation. They could choose to comply, or not, with each new piece of state and federal legislation. If they chose not to, they were now on the wrong side of the law. The presence and mandate of the custodians of those laws—game wardens—were anathema to every tenet that a man who lived off the land embraced.

FIRST BADGES

The roots of Texas' game wardens, today assigned to the Texas Parks and Wildlife Department (TPWD), dates back to 1879 with the Texas Fish Commission. Abolished in 1885 due to lack of funds, it resurfaced in 1895 as the Fish and Oyster Commission (FOC) under the auspices of Commissioner Isaac P. Kibbe. First based in Rockport, then Port Lavaca, the office was responsible for overseeing harvest and trade in coastal fish, oysters, green turtles, and terrapins.[1]

Neither the Texas Fish Commission nor the FOC had authority to enforce the first statewide 1881 Texas game law. More than twenty years later, when the Model Game Law was passed, there was still nothing in FOC's charter that

GAME PROTECTIVE *associations were responsible for many of the arrests between the 1903 Model Game Law and passage of the Permanent Game Law in 1907.*

(Modified from *Galveston Daily News*, Nov. 10, 1905)

NOTICE to sportsmen and all other law abiding persons in Texas, especially in Galveston: Wild ducks, wild geese, snipe, quail and other wild game birds are being killed in Galveston County in large numbers and are being openly sold in the market and in the restaurants in this city in violation of the game laws of Texas. All sportsmen and all citizens who believe in the enforcement of the law are requested to send their names to the undersigned to the end that a Game Protective Association be formed and a Game Warden or Wardens be appointed for Galveston County, as is the case in Harris County and many other counties of the State. Do not delay. Address BALLISTITE, Box K, care Galveston News.

---

included migratory wildfowl enforcement. But it would not have mattered; FOC had only five deputy commissioners in 1903, and their jurisdiction covered the entirety of Texas' fish and oyster industry. The issue of enforcement remained entirely up in the air until passage of the Permanent Game Law in 1907.[2]

Both hunters and politicians believed that the only way to enforce game laws before 1907, rather than by state mandate, was to enlist sportsmen's clubs. As early as 1885 the Houston Gun Club prosecuted hunters who killed deer and prairie chickens out of season near Arcola. By the 1890s, several clubs were involved in protective game enforcement, including the Harris County Sportsmen's Association, the San Antonio Gun Club, and the Canadian (River) Sportsmen's Club. Several hired their own game wardens, as did the Harris County Fish and Game Protective Association, which in 1905 kept the identity of their lawman a closely guarded secret. The Galveston Game Protective Association actively solicited funds to hire their own game warden the same year.[3]

Two years later, a game division was added to the renamed Texas Game, Fish, and Oyster Commission (GFOC) when Senator Terrell's Game Warden Act was passed in 1907. The program was to be administered by a chief deputy commissioner for a salary of eighteen hundred dollars a year, with game wardens, called deputy commissioners, paid three dollars a day plus expenses. A game warden was to reside in every Texas county and be given the same level of authority as a sheriff. Nonresident hunting license monies and fines from game law violations were to support the new department, with the caveat that revenue was not to be used for "protecting the birds and beasts."[4]

If the late 1800s to early 1900s was a period of legal wrangling to pass game laws, the same was certainly true for their enforcement. The entirety of the six--hundred-dollar budget appropriated for the FOC office in 1903, for example, was recalled by the legislature that year. There were more gyrations in 1907 when, immediately after it was passed, the game warden bill was repealed and then resurrected. Sportsmen had such little faith in the state's commitment to game law enforcement that Galveston County hunters organized a fund-raising drive in 1907 to pay the salary of their new game warden, George W. Stevens, in the event the state did not. Part of Stevens's remuneration was to be collected from fines, and the hunters had even less reason to believe a local judicial system would ever levy penalties for game law violations.[5]

After serving eleven years under three governors, GFOC Commissioner Isaac Kibbe was replaced in 1907 by Richard Wood. Commissioner Wood appointed former newspaperman R. W. "Bob" Lorance as chief deputy commissioner, with his first duty to sort through the pile of 400 game warden applications for 133 positions statewide. That year, Texas newspapers carried the names of the newly nominated GFOC wardens, their position treated with both prestige and deference.[6]

Several early game wardens were former market gunners and waterfowl hunting guides. They included, on the upper coast, Charles T. Cade, who was proprietor of the Sea View Hotel hunting and fishing resort near High Island. On the middle coast, Port Lavaca's Capt. Frank Bauer was a guide before he became Calhoun County's first game warden. In Coastal Bend, Capt. William Armstrong was one of Rockport's best-known market men and sporting guides. Andrew "Pop" Sorenson, who served for forty-one years in various capacities with the GFOC, was an early hunting guide and founder of Rockport's Port Bay Hunting Club.[7]

Despite the good intentions, game law enforcement advocates found their expectations dashed when Chief Deputy Commissioner Lorance issued his first report at the end of 1907. That year only seventy-five hunting licenses were sold, with the GFOC collecting just $180 in fines for all fish, oyster, and game law violations. Of those, only one case was prosecuted that was related in any way to migratory bird transgressions. By 1909 the number of game law violations jumped to nine, but the gross revenue from fines totaled only $90. The National Audubon Society was so incensed with what they viewed as an indefensible lack of Texas game law enforcement that the next year they assigned field agent C. E. Brewster to investigate. Brewster's findings confirmed their suspicions.[8]

During GFOC's four years under the auspices of Commissioner Wood, the department remained almost entirely focused on fish and oysters. In Wood's annual reports to the governor, for example, he still used the old Fish and Oyster Commission letterhead rather than the one of the Game, Fish, and Oyster Commission, and none of his reports ever mentioned wild game or migratory birds. Wood was replaced in 1911 by newspaperman Col. William G. Sterrett, who, in contrast to his predecessor, never avoided the topic of game laws. Huge sections of his first annual report, and every one after it, were packed with passionate passages on preservation of Texas game and migratory bird resources.[9]

IT WAS LEGAL *to sell ducks for a short time in 1908 and came close to being legalized again in 1911. Shown is part of a hundred-duck legal limit for four gunners in the early 1900s. (John Winter Collection, courtesy Cliff Fisher)*

Sterrett came out of the gate swinging. A spirited supporter of game laws, he was on the job only two months when, during the 1911 legislative sessions, Liberty County representative Stevens proposed a bill allowing duck hunters to sell their daily limit of twenty-five ducks. A vocal opponent of the Stevens bill, Sterrett worked feverishly to sway the vote, his fervor so high that he was charged by Stevens, and formally rebuked by the House, for lobbying on the floor. Opposed as well to the seventy-five-bird possession law, Sterrett stumped to convince legislators that it was too high and was abused by "northern hunters who kill during the season just for the sport of it." He proposed that surplus birds be collected by GFOC deputies, placed in cold storage, and shipped to orphanages.[10]

Sterrett in 1912 pointed out that the number of game wardens on the books was misleading. Many, he said, were drifting back to more profitable occupations. Instead of a three-dollar salary paid only on days they were in service, Sterrett advocated a fixed salary. He cited his success with two experimental "special deputies," hired at a salary of two hundred dollars a year, who had prosecuted more game law violators than the rest of the force combined. Called state rangers by the press, they were W. C. Stephenson and Robert Goodfellow, and they were first assigned to Jefferson County. Goodfellow during the next three years made cases from Caddo Lake to Del Rio.[11]

The battle over wild game transported surreptitiously by rail continued to rage during Sterrett's tenure, and in 1913 he oversaw an innovative but controversial program in which train conductors were given the authority of deputy game wardens. Additionally, he authorized both "express train and boat employees" to

A Canada goose *and between seventy-five and one hundred ducks, mostly redheads, killed by northern sportsmen in Port Lavaca about the 1910s. Large legal hauls of birds like these often made their way to the outlaw market. (Courtesy Gary Chambers)*

witness signature of the state's mandatory twenty-five-bird limit affidavit and to charge hunters twenty-five cents for the service.[12]

William Sterrett was replaced in 1915 by William W. Wood. Wood was GFOC commissioner at another critical juncture in the history of game law enforcement: passage of the 1918 Migratory Bird Treaty Act (MBTA). Although the federal government had a role in game regulation after the turn of the century, it was not until the MBTA that the gates to the federal government swung wide, and federal game wardens passed through it. Federal game wardens, assigned to the Bureau of Biological Survey in Washington, were at first as understaffed as state law enforcement officers. In 1919 there were only twenty salaried federal wardens assigned to migratory bird protection in the whole of the United States. To leverage their small staff and budget, the first federal wardens in Texas were deputy state game commissioners—state game wardens—who carried dual titles.[13]

OUTLAW HUNTERS

The relationship between game warden and the outlaw hunter was to be a delicate dance for many decades, with some of its legal and ethical boundaries in black-and-white and others blurred. At first, the laws the wardens enforced were primarily aimed at the men and businesses that profited from the killing and sale of wild game. Many market hunters simply quit. They fished. They trapped. Some became guides for the burgeoning business of sport hunting.

On the surface, most businesses involved in the wild game trade appeared to comply with the new regulations. Soon after the 1903 Model Game Law was passed, Texas fish, oyster, and game shippers dropped the word *game* from their business monikers. Migratory birds were not featured as prominently in Texas marketplaces, and reports that carried waterfowl prices went silent. Dallas meat markets in 1903 reported wild game as "very scarce" and "not freely offered." The great markets of Galveston also relented, although Point Isabel markets continued to advertise wild ducks at six cents each until 1904.[14]

Still, it took time for cultural reform to sprout after the first regulatory seeds were sown. The tradition of harvesting nature's bounty ran deep for many in Texas. Ducks at the turn of the century fed the wave of workers that arrived for oil field jobs; communities of cooking tents lined the edge of the forest of derricks, the smell of duck gumbo mingling with that of oil. Each fall, as scores of men headed off to work the rice harvest, a cooking shack was kept busy feeding crews on the ducks they killed. Ducks and geese were supplied at every small-town church social and community affair. Housewives fed their families on wild ducks, and for years many purchased ducks from peddlers who traveled door-to-door. In 1912, Special Deputy W. C. Stephenson circulated a bill "directed to ladies and calling their attention to the law which makes it an offense to buy wild ducks." Rather than fine them, he gave them a warning "so as not to make the prosecutions more harsh than necessary."[15]

Although the culture of wild game involved a large number of people, they individually accounted for the destruction of only a small amount of wild game. At the other end of the spectrum was the small number of people responsible for very large volumes. They were the outlaw market hunters and made at least part of their living supplying illegal wild game to Texas residents and restaurants and to well-to-do epicures in northern cities. Outlaw market hunting got its start because, despite laws on paper, there was very little law enforcement in the years between the Model and Permanent Game Laws and even up to the 1918 MBTA. Too, while the law forbidding sale of wild game was clear in Texas, such sale was legal in many other states. The opportunity for profit was not lost to Texas market hunters, merchants, and shippers who enjoyed a fifteen-year period of near impunity.

The men behind the guns after 1903 were outlaws, a harsh word they would not have used to describe themselves. Maryland historian Harry Walsh's description of Chesapeake Bay outlaw hunters could be said for Texans as well: they were poor but essentially honest men who followed long-established customs and recognized "few laws but their own." Walsh wrote that the men who had fed a nation through fishing and hunting were "the last of a group that had laid the foundation for a society, only to see it rise above them."[16]

Third-generation Port Lavacan J. C. Melcher says of Texas' outlaw market men: "Even though it was illegal, that's how they earned their living. Somebody in

Austin can write laws and the locals weren't gonna abide by them. Austin was two hundred miles away. There weren't that many game wardens." But like a number of people who understand coastal communities, he adds: "It's very hard to put modern values on things that occurred back then. Market hunters did it to make money and feed their families. They lived off the land." Hockley rancher Jim Warren adds: "It was a mentality of harvesting what belonged to you. For the previous generation, [the laws] were thrown on 'em, and there was just so much game."[17]

One of the first arrests for shipment of Texas waterfowl did not occur in the Lone Star State, but in Missouri. Missouri enacted a game law in 1906, and that year state game wardens intercepted ninety barrels, containing as many as five thousand wild ducks, that left Waco bound for a Chicago restaurant. The contraband was shipped in barrels marked seafood, a common ruse in which waterfowl were hidden beneath fish and ice.[18]

Texas' first roster of game wardens began targeting game dealers and market men in 1907. Galveston County deputy game warden George W. Stevens had been on the job just one week when he seized 127 wild ducks from seafood and produce dealer Charles Demack and Company. In another raid that year, 170 ducks destined by rail for El Paso were confiscated.[19]

In 1908 a Rockport cold storage plant was shuttered after shipping thousands of birds by express trains to Houston and northern markets. Fifteen hundred geese stored for the Christmas season were seized, putting an unnamed Houston man out of business. In Bay City, an unnamed game warden broke a ring of market hunters and shippers that employed boys all under nine years old to do their shooting. The game warden who made the arrest said he could do nothing with them "on account of their tender age."[20]

With a tripod-mounted eight-gauge shotgun, Granville Elias "Bill" Minter shot ducks for the market on freshwater ponds north of the town of Aransas Pass. He opened Minter's Fish House in Aransas Pass in 1909, and from there he shipped ducks along with fish to Saint Louis. Although he was never caught, Bill was keenly aware that he faced the same predicament as that of many other Texans during the time period: sale of wild ducks had been outlawed in the Lone Star State but was, until 1918, still legal in other parts of the country. He, like other market men, made good money whenever he could get his birds across state lines.[21]

While Bill Minter shipped his illicit consignments by rail, others used schooners and steamers. One enterprising shipper circumvented the law by transporting "his cargoes of ducks out to the high seas, without the three-mile limit of Texas jurisdiction on the Texas shore, where, by pre-arrangement they are transferred to an ocean-going vessel" and on to other states.[22]

Galveston harbor did a steady illegal business in the early 1900s. For several weeks in 1910, boats from Chambers County and High Island docked at Galveston's Pier 26, where waiting wagons hauled piles of burlap tow sacks filled with ducks to the express railway depot. Deputy Game Warden J. McNamara managed to arrest only one, J. A. Kozick of Galveston, with ninety ducks. That year NAAS field agent C. E. Brewster met a "half-breed market hunter" in a Galveston County rail depot as he was shipping his kill of over two hundred birds. The hunter told Brewster he had shipped ducks every day, fall through spring, for the past sixteen years except on Sundays. Brewster also uncovered a group of professional hunters that worked for a Chicago consignment firm. The operation provided its local hunters with an entire fleet of sailing skiffs, and each boat was fitted with an ice box that held a thousand ducks.[23]

In 1911, Galveston County game warden J. W. Campbell arrested produce dealers Charles Demack and Louis Schember for selling 134 ducks. Campbell quickly learned that it did not matter if outlaws sold one duck or a thousand, Texas courts treated them the same. In Campbell's case, the judge refused to recognize that each bird was a separate offense and set the total fine at ten dollars. It was Demack's second offense in four years. The next year Campbell boarded Henry Sullivan's schooner *Stella*, part of the High Island mosquito fleet, and confiscated 440 ducks. In another 1912 raid, John M. Gieselman and Barney Tiller were arrested with two barrels of ducks they sold quietly to trusted customers of their Gieselman and Company meat market on Travis Street in Houston.[24]

In 1919, George C. Shupee, who carried the titles of both state and federal warden, made a sweep of Fort Worth department and millinery stores, confiscating hundreds of dollars' worth of heron plumes. When he seized wild ducks from a Waco cold storage outfit the same year, the judge pronounced that the case was "the first complaint of this nature ever filed in [a Texas] Federal Court." Shupee once arrested a Tulia man who was illegally shipping sandhill cranes to zoos across the United States, procuring each live bird by "a crippling shot to the wing." In one of the last big illegal trafficking hauls of the 1910s, acting Texas game, fish, and oyster commissioner William Sterrett netted eleven hundred ducks from a Houston cold storage facility.[25]

CONFIDENTIAL MENUS

The 1903 Model Game Law was only a few months old when a Houston restaurant posted the sign, "Boys, the legislature fixed us on the game question. Eat liver." A Fort Worth restaurateur who kept stuffed wild duck on his menu was like many who explained to patrons that they were tame. Likely the first indictment for the sale of wild ducks in Texas restaurants was brought against Beaumont's Holmes Duke, A. L. Kilber, and Tom C. Fuller in 1905. The next year the Galveston Game Protective League filed complaints on the same charge against five Galveston restaurant owners and a game merchant. When game warden Harbernacher sat down for a meal at the venerable Tremont Hotel in 1907, his wild duck dinner led to the arrest of hotel proprietor Otto Sens, a leading member of the Harris County Fish and Game Protective Association.[26]

In what was supposed to be a surprise sweep of Beaumont hotels and restaurants by J. D. Cox and Special Deputy Robert Goodfellow in 1911, advance warning assured that, when their net was cast, it caught only one proprietor. The case against him was dismissed, although, in a sign of the racial times, the establishment's "negro waiter" was fined ten dollars for serving the illegal birds to restaurant customers. The next year Special Deputy W. C. Stephenson arrested Beaumont's Tom Fuller for the sale of wild ducks. It was Fuller's third offense in seven years, and he was fined ten dollars.[27]

Raids in Brownsville in 1914 netted several dining establishments, including the famous Miller Hotel. When Barney Morton, manager of Houston's Rice Hotel, served wildfowl at a banquet for the Galveston mayor in 1920, he never suspected that the mayor's guest list included law enforcement officials. A suspicious game warden removed himself from the table and, prowling the hotel kitchen, found a barrel of ducks in the refrigerator. In 1921 a joint investigation by federal wardens and state game warden J. J. Broussard led to confiscation of 146 ducks from an unnamed Galveston seafood business, after which the illegal bounty was distributed to area orphanages.[28]

UNEVEN JUSTICE

Outlaw hunters found they sometimes had an ally in the Texas judicial system— one that often refused to prosecute cases involving harvest of nature's bounty, as their dockets were filled with items far less "trifling." Throughout the early 1900s, wildfowl cases were commonly dismissed, or if prosecuted at all, fines rarely amounted to more than twenty-five dollars. Facing a judge in 1905, an Eagle Lake hunter explained the forty-two ducks he killed as an accident, the result of firing both barrels at a flock on the water. He said he could have left them to rot but didn't like to waste. His defense was good enough for the judge. The same thing happened when a Wharton man killed thirty-one with one shot. Explaining that he wanted only to feed family and friends, he too was acquitted.[29]

The prevailing attitude was summarized by the *Eagle Lake Headlight* with: "If ducks are so numerous on a pond that a few more than the limit are killed by a single bombardment by hunters, there's no jury that will convict them for exceeding the bag limit." The editor went on to declare: "If the magistrate in one of our courts [were] to actually charge [an] alleged culprit and fine him, on the next election day that magistrate would be soundly defeated at the polls." According to Robin Doughty, Commissioner Richard Wood was so disgusted with the lack of public and judicial support that he dubbed his job the "wild theory of enforcement.[30]

Sometimes judges conjured up imaginative ways to protect their constituents. Before 1913, only one case of selling wild ducks ever went to trial in Orange County. The defendants were acquitted when the court decided it was legal to sell ducks in Texas that the hunters claimed were killed in Louisiana. A Galveston judge thought that one hour in federal custody taught enough of a lesson to S. J. Gaido, proprietor of Gaido's Café, and J. M. David, who were arrested for selling ducks in 1925. Game wardens were pretty sure charges would stick when they caught Jerome Stone shooting ducks from his speeding power boat, but the case was dismissed when the wardens could not prove the ducks were wild.[31]

1929 TO 1940S

The number of illicit businesses and shipping operations overtly bringing wild ducks across state lines decreased dramatically during the 1920s. That decline was in part due to the 1918 MBTA, which brought national regulation, funding, and federal game wardens. Too, cultural mores were advancing across the nation. GFOC Commissioner J. R. Jefferson, who took the helm in 1920, was probably fairly accurate when he reported: "The Department has at last put out of business or minimized the activities of the market hunter." Then came the Great Depression.[32]

Progress made in the attitudes of Texans with respect to wild game took a giant step backward during the Great Depression, a time when many were forced to turn their guns on nature as means to survive. Texas lawmen and courts both largely looked the other way. In Houston, Alex Wolff remembered seeing ducks and geese advertised for sale on the hoods of cars parked on Main Street. James Smock has memories of cars driving slowly through the city's neighborhoods, ducks and geese strung all across the vehicle. It was the same throughout Texas.[33]

Randy Chatagnier is the keeper of family stories from the Depression's lean years in Port Arthur. He tells of his grandfather Rene Chatagnier, an orphan with a third-grade education who learned carpentry and shot ducks to feed his family. Of his nine children, two—Roland and Murphy—followed in his footsteps to the marsh. In 1929, when Rene was an unemployed carpenter and son Murphy an unemployed baker, they turned to outlaw market hunting as a way to make ends meet.

The two men hunted at Lighthouse Bayou across from Sabine Pass, with the local community helping to keep the law at bay. Randy says, "The story Dad always told me was if the big boathouse doors were open, they hunted. If the doors were closed, then the caretakers had seen a game warden." With ammunition expensive, Rene and Murphy were like most who held their shots until a large group of mostly mallards and pintails was on the water in front of them, then whistled to get the ducks' heads up before the volley. At the end of a hunt,

OUTLAW HUNTERS *near Sabine Pass, 1920s, with part of the results from a hunt that yielded 650 ducks, mostly mallards, destined for an illegal game shipper. (Courtesy Jack Holland)*

GEESE FOR SALE *in 1927 Houston. It was common for hunters, particularly during the Depression, to return from the field and drive through Houston neighborhoods to sell their kill. (Courtesy James Smock)*

"they took their ducks to Houston Avenue in Port Arthur, where local black families would pick them in exchange for a portion of the kill. The rest they sold."[34]

Rene's younger son, Roland Chatagnier, also hunted ducks, and his wife, Lillian Richards, remembers that "ducks were meat during the Depression. That was our main meat supply." She recalls, "Mr. Chatagnier would go duck hunting out of season. He'd come back and sell the ducks in the courthouse. That would tickle me—the people who knew it was against the law to do it would be buying the ducks."[35]

Linnie Evelyn Stephenson Standley, who turned ninety in 2012, remembers some of the outlaw hunting on Smith Point in Chambers County. Until the 1930s, only thirteen families resided at Smith Point, and most were poor. Evelyn's family, like most, lived without electricity and indoor plumbing. In 1940 Evelyn married Morris Standley, who over his lifetime worked as a cowboy, fisherman, trapper, and builder of boats and made extra cash selling game.[36]

Ducks were Standley's biggest moneymaker, and in the 1940s he sold them to two large restaurants in Houston and Beaumont. The family cleaned the birds before they were transported and kept all the feathers, which they used at home or sold. Rather than the more common ten- and twelve-gauge guns, Morris instead used a .410, figuring that the small gun would be more difficult for game wardens to hear. As Evelyn looked back on what she called "bootleg hunting," she never considered it was wrong. For her, and many other rural Texans, it was a necessity.[37]

Eagle Lake hunting guide Louis Schorlemmer tells of his father, L. C., who shot for the outlaw market around Tivoli during the 1920s and '30s. L. C. hunted Refugio County agricultural fields, moving bundled milo shocks around to create large openings with fresh grain where the shocks had been. Ducks poured into the natural bait. A buyer from Houston distributed all his birds.[38]

Rick Pratt of the Port Aransas Museum collected shooting stories from several longtime Port Aransas waterman families. Lloyd Dreyers, who worked as a fishing guide for Bill Ellis at the Tarpon Inn, told Rick that his father "and the men would shoot all the ducks they could," then hang the cleaned birds on clotheslines in their backyard to drain and dry. Dreyers gutted and hung countless ducks, so many that as an adult "he hated the things." Dreyers never asked where the ducks were sold; he only knew they went to a hotel. Port Aransas fishing and hunting guide Henry Studeman also remembered how locals sold ducks to hotels "outside of Port Aransas" during the Depression. Rick says that when fishing guide Bill Hart was a boy in the 1930s, his father sent him out every day with a bucket that he and his brothers were expected to fill with fish and game. His father, Bill said, was busy scratching out a living with "the men [who] shot ducks and then sold them."[39]

In Corpus Christi, fishing guide Billy Shika grew up listening to market hunting stories from Jimmy Futch, who shot ducks with a Browning A5 autoloader during the 1920s and '30s. Jimmy's son, Ed, became a heart surgeon in Galveston and a member of the Port Bay Hunting Club in Rockport and established a fellowship grant to Ducks Unlimited's Institute for Wetland and Waterfowl Research.[40]

On East Texas' Caddo Lake, writer Fred Dahmer told of watermen who "celebrated more in . . . breaking the limits than in keeping the limits." He could not name a single person who hunted legally. The outlaw hunting culture was so pervasive that, anxious for the state to assign game wardens to the lake, citizens of nearby Marshall donated land and a house, locally called the State House, to the GFOC in 1912. The next year, when GFOC Commissioner Sterrett moved special rangers W. C. Stephenson and Robert Goodfellow into it, they did not receive a warm welcome. When outlaw duck hunter Joe Dixon spotted game warden Goodfellow snooping around his property, he shot him. His gun, loaded with bird shot, didn't kill the lawman, but Joe was sure he'd think twice before prowling around his property again. The two wardens had not been on the lake for more than a few months when their boat was stolen.[41]

Caddo Lake historian Wyatt Moore in 1983 told Thad Sitton how, as a young man, he sold ducks locally and to gambling houses near Shreveport. The $1.50 he received for mallards and pintails, and fifty cents for mottled ducks and teal, was good money in 1920s East Texas. Moore spun tales of the Galbraith brothers, another group involved in the Caddo Lake outlaw market trade. The Galbraiths, he said, killed ducks and geese "by the hundreds" from cypress tanks they sank to the waterline and surrounded with two or three hundred decoys.[42]

Moore went on to describe a creative method that the Galbraiths developed to harvest geese. Watching where the big birds roosted, the brothers found a suitable hollow tree stump from which they stretched four trotlines several hundred yards into the lake, the trotlines floated by wooden "perchneck" corks attached every ten feet. One brother hid in the stump, while the other circled the outside of the flock in a bateau, slowly moving closer to the birds. Wyatt said the geese wouldn't cross the floating lines but instead swam parallel to them, funneling right toward the stump and the waiting brother with a nine-shot Model 11 Remington autoloader.[43]

TOOLS OF THE TRADE

Pump and semiautomatic shotguns were the preferred choice for most twentieth-century outlaw market men, but they were by no means the only weapons. A US Army Corps of Engineers dredge operator in the early 1930s was using dynamite to dig the Intracoastal Canal across Bolivar Peninsula. After spotting big flights of mallards over a pond east of High Island, he loaded a bucket with number 6 shot, rigged up his charge and blasting cap, then positioned the apparatus in the pond. The detonation resulted in more than a hundred dead and dying ducks on the water. He had plans to sell them to Galveston and Houston restau-

A HUNDRED DUCKS *and two pump shotguns (second from left and on right) at Matagorda Bay, 1922. (John Winter Collection, courtesy Cliff Fisher)*

THE BROWNING A5 *autoloader, stock-in-trade for sportsmen as well as outlaw hunters for many decades. (Courtesy Palmer and Talley Melton)*

rants, but his morning profit was lost when he inadvertently blew up his skiff and gun.[44]

Inland prairie and coastal marsh outlaw market men still used trained oxen, walking unnoticed alongside the grazing animal and into resting waterfowl until close enough to fire. The lawbreaking hunters were extremely hard to catch, as a "lookout would be posted atop a windmill and would warn the stalkers of the approach of a game warden." Hunting over steers was outlawed in 1941, but despite the fact that the big animals were difficult to hide, the practice remained popular in Texas for several more years.[45]

Punt and swivel guns, mounted to a gunning skiff, were relatively common in Texas during the Depression. The Womack family remembers a market hunter who sculled Maner Lake in Brazoria County at night with a four-gauge swivel gun

Plovers remained a favorite target of outlaw hunters. Shown is a harvest of sixty illegal birds confiscated by federal game warden Frank Clarkson. (Courtesy US Fish and Wildlife Service, USFWS/Elkins, WV, Neg. No. B-48461)

affixed to his flat-stern cypress skiff and a lantern on the bow. He sold his ducks to Houston hotels, including the glamorous Shamrock Hotel, in the 1940s.[46]

On the middle coast, Ed Melcher told his son, J. C., of the days when punting skiffs slipped into the darkness of shallow bays around Port Lavaca. At nearby Seadrift, Leonard Moss Fisher, later the "first flying sheriff of Texas," fed the town from a punting rig during the Depression. Grandson Steve Fisher says he "had a punt gun on the bow of the boat. He rowed out at night, and made his first shot at daylight unless it was a moonlit night. He carried wooden kegs, and loaded up three or four kegs with ducks from one shot. Then he'd go back to town and deliver them to families." Steve says the right amount of shot to load the big gun was "just about a filled bucket," and adds, "They didn't need to shoot but once, then spent the rest of the day pickin' ducks."[47]

To the south on Aransas Bay, the father of Rockport's Johnny Atwood told him of local punt gunners who "used skiffs, and drifted into them." Port Aransas taxidermist Ancel Brundrett hunted ducks for the illegal markets, and the hull of his old sneak boat, with the four-gauge punt gun still mounted to it, sat next to his taxidermy building for years. The boat, according to Rick Pratt, had an arched top and a cockpit with coaming to act as a splashboard. In addition to his punt gun, Ancel shot two Model 97 twelve-gauge Winchesters with extended magazines. His son, Jeb, remembered he sold the pintails he killed for thirty-five cents a pair, and redheads for fifty cents.[48]

Texas hunting guide Forrest West was raised on a Caddo Lake with his uncle, Boyd Buford "B. B." MacMullan, who used a punting rig on the lake before the

THE LAW AND THE OUTLAW

A federal game warden snapped this photo of the Gingham Inn nightclub, which was given the caption "Closed after Jack Hornor sent to Leavenworth for 13 months for serving wild duck dinner, Mar. 26, 1938." (Courtesy US Fish and Wildlife Service, USFWS/Elkins, WV, Neg. No. B-50801)

1940s. Forrest remembers the big gun was made from oil field pipe and mounted to a cypress skiff. As with most of the Depression-era gunning stories, the family never discussed where B. B. sold his ducks.[49]

The iron grip of the Great Depression was loosened in parts of Texas by the late 1930s. With its end came the first bite out of Texas outlaw market hunting from the teeth of the federal government, when lawmen assigned to the US Biological Survey, located in Washington, DC, launched a covert sting in 1938. The operation led to the indictment of ten Dallas and Fort Worth restaurateurs and over fifty charges involving thousands of wild ducks, doves, plovers, and quail. Jack Horner, who offered migratory birds almost year-round on the menu of his Gingham Inn in Fort Worth, was dealt the stiffest sentence with thirteen months in the Leavenworth penitentiary.[50]

If the federal government thought Leavenworth delivered a message of reform to Texas outlaw market hunters, they were wrong. The message came in 1956.

1956: THE FEDS COME TO TOWN

One of the two men huddled along the edge of the wooden bridge over Oyster Bayou in Chambers County later remembered that the night was quiet, the sky black as ink. He was an outlaw buyer, and the other was a market man who assured him that, any time now, his 'rat trappers would come along and deliver the order for a hundred ducks. The only reason they wouldn't show, he said, was if they suspected the buyer was a federal agent. On that cold night in 1955 the muskrat trappers never came, and a year later the outlaw buyer proved indeed to be an undercover agent, Anthony Stefano, of the US Fish and Wildlife Service (USFWS).

In the predawn hours of April 18, 1956, more than a hundred law enforcement officials from eight states converged on southeast Texas. In three hours, fifty-three Texans, from a total of fifty-six issued warrants, were rounded up and charged with violation of federal game laws, ending two years of undercover work. It was the most extensive raid in the history of the USFWS up to that time, and it netted businessmen, ranchers, watermen, hunting guides, and even law enforcement officials. The list included men from Port Arthur, Beaumont, China, Winnie, Liberty, Dayton, Cove, Wallisville, Anahuac, High Island, Galveston, Houston, Katy, and as far south as Corpus Christi.[51]

The arrests, mostly for illegal possession, transportation, and sale of wild ducks and geese, were vigorously followed in newspapers and periodicals throughout country. Writer Hart Stilwell sat in the courtroom nearly every day to cover the trials for Texas papers, Ed Zern and Tom Lineaweaver provided an investigative account for *Sports Illustrated,* and Houston's Bob Brister with Ben East wrote a version for *Outdoor Life.* For a state that historically relegated game law violations to the back pages of newspapers, if they received mention at all, Texas was suddenly at the center of a frenzy of state and national press.[52]

The covert operation was born when the USFWS received reports from field agents who believed that as many as two hundred thousand birds had been illegally killed and sold locally or shipped to other parts of the country. In 1954, lawyer and undercover agent Anthony Marc Stefano volunteered for the investigation, posing undercover as a jewelry salesman and part-time trader in the sale of wild game.[53]

Freddie Abshier recalls how Stefano infiltrated the local community:

> In the mid-1950s, Bob Singleton [biologist for the Texas Game and Fish Commission] told me to watch out for a guy peddling jewelry who wanted to trade things for ducks and geese. Well, about three weeks into the [1955 or '56] season I was drivin' a rice truck in the evenings. When I'd get off work I stopped at a little beer joint in Raywood on the way back. There was a red Cherokee, and when I walked by it I could see little palettes of beads, watches and rings. So when I got inside I got me a beer, and this gentleman, he was in a little suit, he was about five foot six or seven, weighed about 140 pounds, and had a little old felt hat on. He had these cards of jewelry and stuff on a big palette. He wandered over to me and wanted to know if I wanted to buy any jewelry or a wristwatch. He asked us if we duck hunted. When I said I did, he said his wife sure could use a pair of greenhead mallards, and he'd be willing to trade something for them. I run into him maybe a half a dozen more times, and it was always in these little beer joints. I never sold a duck, but I gave away a ton of 'em. A lot of it wasn't really legal I guess.[54]

Stefano's immersion into the culture of the Texas outlaw hunter for two intense years started in November 1954 on a hunt with a High Island guide who offered to sell the ducks he killed. Stefano, the buyer with the cash, quickly won the confidence of the community and expanded his circle of sellers. According to Bob Brister and Ben East (1956), he made purchases from Roy Hudspeth of 238 ducks in two transactions. High Island's Vernon Kahla sold 115. The Royer brothers, Clovis and Nelson, handed over 200 ducks in three months, with Nelson volunteering that he had killed birds for the market for thirty-seven years. Some in the group operated with seeming impunity, informing Stefano that local law enforcement officials would alert them to any game wardens in the area. The ducks and dollars kept flowing.[55]

There were leaks, there was intrigue, and at times Stefano faced very real dangers. His cover at the start nearly collapsed. The story goes that Stefano paid Sam Hargraves Sr. an advance of $125 for a hundred ducks, but instead, Hargraves kept the money. In a game of cat and mouse, Hargraves figured if he turned Stefano in as an illegal buyer, he wouldn't have to pay him back. So he reported him to federal agent Garth Christopher in Beaumont. For the next two years Hargraves was led along as his "case" was built against Stefano, while in fact it was being built around Hargraves. On that cold night on the bridge over Oyster Bayou it was Sam Hargraves's hired apprentices that never delivered the hundred ducks. He allegedly raised the stakes when he told Stefano, "If I sold a man 100 ducks and found out he was a wrong guy, I'd kill him. I'd get off easier for murder than for selling that many ducks."[56]

Federal game warden Frank Clarkson worked the case behind the scenes. At one point during the investigation, Clarkson's phone rang in the middle of the night, and the caller told him it would be wise to move his federal agent out of the state—a Katy outlaw hunter was planning to kill him. Stefano continued to press on.[57]

Another time Stefano was allegedly challenged by a suspicious Johnny Boortz, owner of the Top Hat restaurant and nightclub, in Alvin, the dinner menu of which, if you were trusted, included wild duck. Boortz wanted Stefano to prove he was a jeweler and not an agent. In Stefano's version of the story, Boortz flashed his diamond ring and demanded, "What about it? You're supposed to be an expert." Stefano pulled out his jeweler's eyepiece and studied the ring. "I told him the stone was one carat and 32 points, but that it probably wasn't too valuable because it had a tiny fissure and a carbon deposit on it. Boortz just laughed and told me I was right, that he'd been told the same thing by another jeweler."[58]

Galveston County constable Ike Franks had heard reports of a pending raid and suspected Stefano. It was pouring rain when, accompanied by Johnny Boortz, he confronted Stefano late one night at his home. Stefano's defense—"If I was an agent, I'd have arrested you a year ago"—as well as Boortz's reminder that Stefano provided an impressive assessment of his diamond mollified him. Franks left, and Stefano's tenuous cover remained intact.[59]

During the roundup on that spring morning in April 1956, the shell game that Sam Hargraves Sr. had been playing with the law ended with his arrest by

Some of the players in the 1956 sting. Pictured are both state and federal game wardens. Left to right, Joe Matlock, M. H. Boone, Bob Cross, Frank Clarkson, Assistant Division Chief Lawrence, unidentified state game warden, Regional Supervisor Dugger, W. E. Ritter, and Don Krieble. (Courtesy US Fish and Wildlife Service, USFWS/Elkins, WV)

federal game warden Garth Christopher. He received five months in jail and a five-hundred-dollar fine. With his son Sam Hargraves Jr., who pleaded guilty to the sale of nineteen ducks, he later returned to his guided day-hunting operation on Turtle Bay near Anahuac.[60]

Vernon Kahla served six months in federal prison. High Island's Luther Berwick served time for the sale of six ducks and five geese, as did his brother, Walter Berwick, for selling twenty-five ducks. The Berwicks later ran a hunting camp on High Island and fished commercially. High Island Justice of the Peace Richard Black also served a jail sentence. Ike Franks, a father of five and well-respected Galveston County businessman, served ninety days in the Houston federal penitentiary for sale of sixty ducks. Franks had been a deputy constable since 1940, and during his incarceration his wife completed his term. He ran for reelection from jail and won. Franks remained a constable until 1964 and continued to run his Hall's Bayou duck hunting lodge.[61]

Katy's William "Bill" Freeman stood before Federal Judge Ben C. Connally in Houston as the assistant district attorney described him as "one of the worst offenders and a man who didn't need the money." Stefano told the judge Freeman had killed sixteen hundred ducks in one season. Freeman's side of the story was very different. He said he took Stefano hunting and gave the undercover agent all the birds but wouldn't take money for them. Stefano instead stuffed a fistful of shotgun shells in Freeman's pocket and walked away. State game warden Joe Briers was supposed to testify against Freeman that day in Judge Connally's court, but when his car radio crackled to life with a dispatcher's message that it was his time to appear, Briers flipped it off and kept driving. Freeman pled guilty to the sale of 115 birds. He was dealt a four-month jail sentence and a five-hundred-dollar fine that was waived under the condition he not hunt for three years.[62]

Nelson and Clovis Royer, Roy Hudspeth, and former Beaumont policeman Jim Fergusen avoided jail and paid fines of between four hundred and five hundred dollars. The Top Hat's Johnny Boortz was fined for selling twenty ducks at his nightclub. Gerald "Buddy" LaFour was charged with sale of waterfowl after he traded two boxes of shotgun shells for four ducks. His father, Morgan LaFour, was charged with the sale of ten ducks. According to the family, Morgan traded the ducks for a watch. Sylvia Lamb, Morgan's niece, remembers the man with the watch who called himself a wholesale jeweler. "He was like one of the family. He used to be at the house, and Aunt Clara [LaFour's wife] used to make 'im these big ol' breakfasts. He told Morgan, 'You know I have these nice Bulova watches. You ought to give your wife one for Christmas.' Aunt Clara was so proud of that watch." Morgan pleaded guilty and was fined. He remained a commercial fishermen and duck hunter for the rest of his life.[63]

Cove's Manson Clark was another hunting guide targeted by Anthony Stefano. Historian Kendon Clark never spoke publicly about the 1956 raid that netted his father, but he wrote it down. In his unpublished manuscript, "Memoirs, or Fulfilling My Obligation," he begins, "The arrest weighed heavily on the minds of our family." Stefano, he wrote, insisted that Manson sell him ducks, but "Daddy told him repeatedly it was illegal to sell wild ducks, that he would give him some, but Stefano wouldn't take them unless he was allowed to pay for them." On one hunt Stefano explained how he badly needed ducks for a weekend dinner party. Manson offered him two ducks and told him if he needed more to visit his brother-in-law, Harley Maley. Maley gave him two or three, and when he wouldn't take money for them, Stefano stuffed two dollars in his pocket and walked away.[64]

On that April morning, Maley was charged with the sale of the ducks he had tried to give away. Manson Clark was charged with conspiracy, the charges stemming from advising Stefano that Harley might have a couple of ducks to give him. "Daddy," Kendon wrote, "didn't even know what the word conspiracy meant." Manson was fined a hundred dollars. Harley Maley was fined two hundred dollars and spent a month in jail.

"When it was all over," Kendon continues, "Daddy felt he would be regarded as a common criminal. He did not even go to church the following Sunday, saying he did not think 'good' people would want anything to do with him anymore." He did go to church the next Sunday, and most after that. The local community never lost faith in Manson Clark, who returned to the marsh and was later the subject of a book, television documentaries, and numerous articles that followed his prowess as an alligator hunter, trapper, and outdoorsman.[65]

The arrests drew a justifiable bead on coastal Texas from within the state and throughout the nation. But the record shows the press played very freely with the story, often with puzzling contradictions. Many newspapers carried the headline that Texas outlaws slaughtered more than two hundred thousand birds, overlooking that the number introduced as evidence was actually three thousand. Zern and Lineaweaver, in their *Sports Illustrated* account, attributed parts of the Sam Hargraves story, as told by Brister and East in *Outdoor Life*, instead to Luther Berwick. Similarly, there are very different published versions of the Franks and Boortz confrontation. Too, it is curious that the Top Hat's Johnny Boortz, an alleged ringleader of the operation, was only charged with the sale of twenty ducks.[66]

One of those charged in the 1956 sting, who remains anonymous, says, "We deserved to be arrested—we broke the law. But all the lies that came out afterwards, that's what I object to." Cove's Kendon Clark agrees: "These were common men who had no recourse with the press. It was a helpless feeling, and it left so much hard feeling."[67]

There are others, however, who believe that Stefano only scratched the surface of the illegal activity. Smith Point's Joe Whitehead says that after "they came in here and did the sting operation, the High Island trash dump filled up with picked pairs of mallard ducks, thousands of them, 'cause everybody was getting rid of 'em." One of those arrested in 1956, who prefers to remain anonymous, remembers it, too: "The next day the dumping grounds out here was full of ducks. If there were big market hunters here, they didn't get them. The ones they got were the easy mullets."[68]

In the end, Texans received a black eye for the 2,410 ducks and 474 geese collected by Anthony Stefano and the US Fish and Wildlife Service. Former TPWD biologist Charles Stutzenbaker says: "Nineteen fifty-six was kind of the end. It was harder to find ducks on the confidential menus in Texas after that." The following fall, it seemed that newspapers across Texas were full of advertisements for new hunting guide services. Men who had never thought about making money from ducks in any other way than from the market had begun to turn to sport hunting.[69]

CHAPTER 7

EPILOGUE: THE LAST BIG STING

As Greg Keddy pulled out of the dirt road leading from O. D. LaBove's Shooting Resort in Jefferson County, he saw "all these little Chryslers flying into the club with [men wearing] dark suits." With all the traffic, Greg figured the next day would be busy with a big corporate hunt. He was wrong. It was December 12, 1988, and what Keddy saw were some of the one hundred USFWS agents who, converging on Texas, marked the end of a three-year investigation that targeted mostly day-hunting outfits. By the time it was over, a total of two hundred club owners, guides, and clients from forty hunting clubs had logged more than thirteen hundred violations of the Migratory Bird Treaty Act.[1]

The covert federal operation had started in 1985. Chambers County guide Gene Campbell remembers that his guiding service along with LaBove's Shooting Resort at Sabine Pass were the first targets. Gene says, "They were doing so good with us, they said, 'We can get in with all of these operations and make a hell of big fanfare about this thing.'" They did. Between 1985 and 1988 the undercover operation, involving about half a dozen USFWS special operations agents posing as day hunters, had crisscrossed the coast. Jamie Spears remembers they had the best of every kind of outdoor gear, including new Browning Citori shotguns. Gene Campbell adds, "There were always two of them, and they were good tippers. Always a hundred-dollar tip."[2]

Most of the charges leveled against sport hunters by USFWS agents were for shooting over the limit, after dark, or out of season, baiting, using electronic recorders called "Willie Nelsons," and wanton waste. Several agents, who claimed to be outdoor painters or art collectors, also netted a couple of enterprising hunters willing to procure protected bird species. As Gilchrist's Boots Faggard puts it, "Some of the boys fell for the 'I'll pay you twenty-five dollars for a protected bird' story." The most flagrant of these outlaws was charged with possession and sale of a northern flicker, a kingfisher, an ibis, two Caspian terns, three species of herons, songbirds, ducks, and various protected shorebirds. The shooter faced nine felony counts.[3]

The lawmen's prize, however, was LaBove's Shooting Resort. Founded in the late 1950s by third-generation outdoorsman O. D. LaBove, and run by the extended family during the 1980s, LaBove's had been in state and federal lawmen's sights several times before. Charles R. "Doc" McCallum, state game warden in 1953 and later a special agent for the USFWS, arrested O. D. LaBove twice for baiting in the late 1960s and early '70s. Convinced he was unfairly targeted by the lawman, LaBove wrote to President Nixon complaining that Doc McCallum was a man "going much too far in his duties." Nixon didn't reply, but the Department of Interior did, and supported their agent.[4]

O. D. LaBove died six years before the LaBove's Shooting Resort name was splashed across television, magazines, and newspapers throughout the United States for its involvement in gross violations of federal game laws. In the years between LaBove's death and 1988, his Sabine Pass guiding service continued to provide client hunts over baited or "sugared" duck ponds, and at the legendary pit blind near Keith Lake as many as twenty gun barrels poked out of its oleander cover, raking huge flocks of snow geese as they sat on the water. Undercover agents videotaped a hunt—ironically at the request of LaBove's guides—in which thirteen shooters killed 139 geese above the legal limit. LaBove's Shooting Resort faced nine felonies and fifteen misdemeanors with maximum fines that could have totaled over 4.5 million dollars, and those numbers excluded charges meted out to dozens of individual hunters and LaBove guides. Proprietor Jeanette LaBove, O. D.'s widow, was charged with another eight felonies.[5]

LaBove's Shooting Resort, Gene Campbell, and thirty-eight other guiding operations accumulated an impressive list of violations during the 1988 sting, one applauded by most of Texas' law-abiding sportsmen. *Houston Chronicle*'s Bob Brister spoke for many when he wrote: "This sting needed to be done." But there was a second list, and it hung in the craws of public sentiment and later the courtroom. It was a very long list of hunters with comparatively trivial charges.[6]

A litany of indictments, for example, was filed for transportation of illegal waterfowl. The law, originally intended to put an end to the surreptitious trafficking in ducks by outlaws who smuggled barrels of waterfowl labeled as seafood or produce into railroad cars, was instead tacked onto offenses for killing more than the allowable daily limit. More than a few guides, their stories remarkably consistent a quarter of a century later, are adamant that it was the undercover agents, not they, who shot those over-the-limit ducks. Violation of the Lacey Act, another tool in the arsenal against market hunters, was supposedly added to one hunter's tally when, with too many birds, he crossed into the federal sovereignty of Anahuac National Wildlife Refuge.

Dozens of citations were issued for tagging and documentation violations—a bookkeeping infraction. Agents who swept into John Glen's Corpus Christi taxidermy shop confiscated a pair of wood ducks from his desk because they weren't tagged. Forrest West, of Los Patos Guide Service, was cited for duck tags that fell off of clients' ducks in the cleaning shack. Allegedly an invoice for cleaning ducks was used instead as proof that another hunter was selling ducks. According to Rockport guide James Fox, hunters were also charged with harassing waterfowl when they used airboats to run to and from duck blinds. Fox was watching the arrests unfold on television, and as images of the snow goose slaughter at LaBove's Shooting Resort splashed on the screen, the knock on his door was a court summons, the charge conspiracy. Fox was depicted as the ringleader of a group of outlaw shooters that did not exist, and the indictment was later dropped.[7]

As might be expected, many of those charged in the 1988 sting remain adamant that they were victims—not breakers—of the law. Their versions would be less believable if, in the end, the level of prosecutions had matched the initial hyperbole. When the government dismissed eighty-four felonies and almost as many misdemeanors, federal prosecutors were among the biggest and most vocal supporters for leniency.[8]

The 1988 sting was the third time in fifty years that federal law enforcement laid a Texas-sized trap for migratory bird violations. But with its mix of blatant outlaws and the hardly guilty, 1988 was divisive, and remains so to this day. It was a defining moment in Texas hunting for many reasons, not the least of which was that the excesses were not by market hunters' guns but by sportsmen's. Few could deny that, somewhere between 1956 and 1988, the era of the market hunter had ended.

Market men and their exploits are now relegated to a few widely scattered pages of history. No longer are their kills of shorebirds, ducks, geese, swans, and cranes bartered at the edge of the town square by game hawkers or hung across market stalls or in the windows of big-city markets. The sails of the market hunter's schooners and sloops have all been furled, and his guns are now silent. Quiet, too, is the Texas skyline, once animated with wildfowl over the coast, inland rivers, lakes, and prairies. The great skeins of birds are gone, probably for good, and it has been too many years to blame that on the market hunter.

*Summer turned to winter, and the schooner's big sails gave way
to smaller ones, better suited to heavy winds. In place of seats and awnings
that made it comfortable for summer visitors are ice and ammunition chests.
The ducks are in, and it is time to gun.*

NOTES

CHAPTER 1

1. Matilda C. Houstoun, "Texas and the Gulf of Mexico; or, Yachting in the New World," in *Home and Travellers Library, American Culture Series* 1 (1845): 137.

2. Light Townsend Cummins, *Emily Austin of Texas, 1795–1851*, Texas Biography Series, No. 1 (Fort Worth: TCU Press, 2009), 194; Frank W. Flack, *A Hunter's Experiences in the Southern States of America* (London: Longmans, Green, and Co., 1866), 278.

3. Kathleen Huson Maxwell, ed., *Hobart Huson: A Texas Coastal Bend Trilogy* (Austin: Eakin Press, 1994), 73; Murphy Givens, "Murphy Givens' Radio Column for April 25, 2003," *Corpus Christi Caller-Times*, Apr. 25, 2003, http://www.caller.com/news/2003/apr/25/murphy-givens-radio-column-for-april-25-2003/.

4. *Galveston Daily News,* Mar. 3, 1887.

5. Frederic William Simonds, *The Geography of Texas* (Boston: Athenaeum Press, 1905), 71.

6. *Galveston Daily News,* Nov. 16, 1876; Rudolph Rosen, "The North American Model of Wildlife Conservation: A Century of Species and Habitat Management in America," presented at the Environmental Studies Colloquium, Whittier College, Whittier, CA, Mar. 17, 2010, 1–8.

7. Mike Bradshaw, *Texas Game Warden Chronicles* (Carrizo Springs, TX: Mesquite Bean Press, 2009), 6–8.

CHAPTER 2

1. Francis Parkman, *La Salle and the Discovery of the Great West*, The Works of Francis Parkman, Vol. 3 (Boston: Little, Brown and Co., 1878), 141.

2. Ann Vileisis, *Discovering the Unknown Landscape* (Washington, DC: Island Press, 1997), 163.

3. Charles Stutzenbaker interview, Oct. 24, 2008, Port Arthur, TX; David Lobpries, pers. comm., Mar. 19, 2010.

4. Melanie Wiggins, *They Made Their Own Law* (Houston: Rice University Press, 1990), 47; J. C. Clopper, "J. C. Clopper's Journal and Book of Memoranda for 1828," *Texas Historical Association Quarterly* 13, no. 1 (1909): 44–80, digital images, The

Portal to Texas History, University of North Texas Libraries, , http://texashistory.unt.edu/ark:/67531/metapth101051/m1/52/, crediting Texas State Historical Association, Denton.

5. "A Week's Sport in Texas," *New Monthly Magazine* 145 (1869): 20-31.

6. Ann Macklin Peel, ed., *To Become A Texian—The Letters and Journeys of Caroline Cox Morgan and Her Family, 1839-1857* (Frankfort, KY: privately printed, 1997), 2. The Portal to Texas History, University of North Texas Libraries, http://texashistory.unt.edu/ark:/67531/metapth26718/; *Telegraph and Texas Register,* Oct. 22, 1845; B. R. Brunson and Andrew Forest Muir, "Morgan, James," *Handbook of Texas Online,* http://www.tshaonline.org/handbook/online/articles/fm050.

7. *Dallas Morning News,* Sept. 13. 1902.

8. William Preston Johnston, *The Life of Gen. Albert Sidney Johnston: Embracing His Services in the Armies of the United States, the Republic of Texas, and the Confederate States* (New York: D. Appleton Publisher, 1878), 146.

9. Benjamin Harris Neal, "Recollections of Dr. Benjamin Harris Neal: Pioneer Days When Sturdy Men Laid Strong Foundations," *Nesbitt Memorial Library Journal* 1, no. 3 (1990): 97.

10. *Galveston Daily News,* Sept. 24, 1910; H. T. Fretelliere, "San Antonio De Bexar, Half a Century Ago," *Texas Magazine* 5, no. 5 (1912): 55.

11. Percy B. St. John, "Wild Sports in the Far West," *New Sporting Magazine* 10, no. 50 (1845): 384-87.

12. Jeremiah Hughes, ed., *Niles' National Register* 69-70 (1846): 371; William A. McClintock, "Journals of a Trip through Texas and Northern Mexico in 1846-1847," *Southwestern Historical Quarterly* 34, no. 1 (1931): 20-37.

13. Frank W. Flack, *A Hunter's Experiences in the Southern States of America* (London: Longmans, Green and Co., 1866), 30.

14. Wiggins, *They Made Their Own Law,* 13-39.

15. Jean L. Epperson, *Filibusters, Pirates, and Privateers of the Early Texas Coast* (Houston: Kemp and Co., 2010), 41; E. Littell, ed., "Life of Jean Lafitte," *Littell's Living Age* 32, no. 407 (1852): 442.

16. Littell, "Life of Jean Lafitte," 445.

17. Gary Cartwright, *Galveston, A History of the Island* (New York: Atheneum, 1991), 57.

18. Mattie Austin Hatcher, *Letters of an Early American Traveller, Mary Austin Holley: Her Life and Works, 1784-1846* (Dallas: Southwest Press, 1933), 119.

19. Jean L. Epperson, *Historical Vignettes of Galveston Bay,* 4th ed. (Houston: Kemp and Co., 2011), 43-53.

20. Flack, *A Hunter's Experiences,* 26; Charles H. Stevenson, "Report on the Coast Fisheries of Texas," in *United States Commission of Fish and Fisheries, Part XVII, Report of the Commissioner for 1889 to 1891* (Washington, DC: Govt. Printing Office, 1893), 375.

21. "A Week's Sport in Texas," 27; Flack, *A Hunter's Experiences,* 281; "Texas Historical Marker Application," n. 11, Sept. 1988, 1, courtesy Port Arthur Public Library; Forest McNeir, *Forest McNeir of Texas* (San Antonio: Naylor, 1956), 11; Freddie Abshier interview, July 10, 2009, Anahuac, TX; Stevenson, "Report on the Coast Fisheries," 375.

22. "Texas Historical Marker Application," n. 11, Sept. 1988, 1, courtesy Port Arthur Public Library; Needmore Ranch foreman Robert Chesson to Gerry Cordts, Gerry Cordts pers. comm., June 29, 2009.

23. Flack, *A Hunter's Experiences*, 278; *Galveston Tri-Weekly News*, Dec. 8, 1871; J. R. Singleton, *Texas Coastal Waterfowl Survey*, FA Report Series No. 11 (Austin: Texas Game and Fish Commission, 1953), 49.

24. John K. Strecker Jr., "The Birds of Texas," *Baylor University Bulletin* 15, no. 1 (1912): 13.

25. Ibid.; Oliver Davie, *Nest and Eggs of North American Birds* (Philadelphia: David McKay, 1898), 103; Elliot Coues, *Key to North American Birds* (Cambridge: Cambridge University Press, 1896), 689.

26. "The Feathered Game of Texas," *Bailey's Magazine of Sports and Pastimes* 6 (1863): 195; C. R. Tinan, "The Wild Goose," in *Shooting on Upland, Marsh, and Stream*, ed. William Bruce Leffingwell (New York: Rand McNally, 1890), 341.

27. Flack, *A Hunter's Experiences*, 274.

28. Strecker, "Birds of Texas," 13; *Galveston Daily News*, Dec. 25, 1902; Daniel Giraud Elliot, *Wild Fowl of North America* (New York: Francis R. Harper, 1898), 19; William Harrison Ainsworth, ed., "A Week's Sport in Texas," 31; *Galveston Daily News*, Sept. 26, 1880; Flack, *A Hunter's Experiences*, 274.

29. Lois W. Burkhalter, *Gideon Lincecum, 1773–1874: A Biography* (Austin: University of Texas Press, 1965), 40.

30. *Galveston Daily News*, Dec. 5, 1887; Mar. 9, 1894; Sept. 24, 1910; Kenneth Foree, "Geese, Smart Men Alter Town's Life," *Dallas Morning News*, Nov. 3, 1964; *Brownsville Daily Herald*, Nov. 30, 1892, Chronicling America, Library of Congress and National Endowment for the Humanities, http://www.loc.gov/chroniclingamerica/lccn/sn86089174/1892-11-30/ed-1/seq-3; *Proceedings of the United States National Museum* 1, no. 17 (1878): 169.

31. Robin W. Doughty, *Return of the Whooping Crane* (Austin: University of Texas Press, 1989), 18; Vernon Bailey, *Biological Survey of Texas*, North American Fauna, No. 25 (Washington, DC: Govt. Printing Office, 1905), 24; Charles B. Cory, "The Birds of Illinois and Wisconsin," *Field Museum of Natural History, Zoological Series* 9 (1909): 3; Russell Clapper oral history by David Todd and Joan Walker, June 20, 1998, Anahuac, TX, Conservation History Association of Texas, Texas Legacy Project, Reel No. 1018, http://www.texaslegacy.org/bb/transcripts/clapperrusstxt.html; "Feathered Game of Texas," 195.

32. "Feathered Game of Texas," 195; George J. Durham, "Game in Texas," in *A Texas Scrap-Book* (New York: A. S. Barnes and Co., 1875), 482–83; Henry Hall, ed., *The Tribune Book of Open-Air Sports* (New York: Tribune Association, 1887), 423; Roger Reed, "The Yellow-Legs or 'Telltale,'" *Sports Afield*, January 1898, 35; "Resorts of Game: When and Where It Can Be Found in Season," *A Compilation of the Game Laws of the Principal States and Provinces of the United States and Canada* (New York: M. B. Brown & Co., 1872), 242; *Fort Worth Morning Register*, Aug. 27, 1899.

33. Neltje Blanchan, *Birds That Hunt and Are Hunted* (New York: Doubleday & McClure, 1899), 229; H. E. Dresser, "Notes on the Birds of Southern Texas," *The Ibis: Quarterly Journal of Ornithology* 2 (1866): 39, Internet Archive, http://www.archive.org/stream/ibiso2brit/ibiso2brit_djvu.txt; "Resorts of Game," 229, 242; Emerson Hough, "Plover-Shooting," in *Shooting on Upland, Marsh, and Stream*, 208; *Dallas Morning News*, Nov. 22, 1903; *Fort Worth Morning Register*, Aug. 27, 1899; *Galveston Daily News*, Nov. 20, 1880; Thomas C. Abbott, "Snipe and Snipe-Shooting," in *Shooting on Upland, Marsh, and Stream*, 257; Hall, *Tribune Book of Open-Air Sports*, 423.

34. McNeir, *Forest McNeir of Texas*, 31; *Civilian and Galveston City Gazette,* Jan. 28, 1843; "Shot Tower," *Wikipedia*, http://en.wikipedia.org/wiki/Shot_tower.

35. In collection of Chesapeake Bay Maritime Museum, Saint Michaels, MD.

36. Robin W. Doughty, *Wildlife and Man in Texas: Environmental Change and Conservation* (College Station: Texas A&M University Press, 1983), 94; Ed Holder, "Market Hunters Took Their Toll," *Brazosport Facts,* Sept. 26, 1994; Joe Whitehead interviews, June 14, 2008, and Aug. 9, 2008, Smith Point, TX.

37. "Feathered Game of Texas," 195; Blanchan, *Birds That Hunt and Are Hunted*, 230; *Galveston Daily News,* June 4, 1880.

38. Doughty, *Wildlife and Man in Texas*, 94.

39. Charles Stutzenbaker, pers. comm., Feb. 18, 2010; Flack, *A Hunter's Experiences*, 274.

40. Stevenson, "Report on the Coast Fisheries," 376; Wayne Capooth, *Waterfowling America*, Vol. 2 (Memphis: privately printed, 2008), 425; Rick Pratt interview, Sept. 24, 2009, Port Aransas, TX.

41. Flack, *A Hunter's Experiences*, 280–86.

42. William Jarvis, "The Woodcock," in *Shooting on Upland, Marsh, and Stream*, 55; "Feathered Game of Texas," 195.

43. McNeir, *Forest McNeir of Texas*, 31; Harry M. Walsh, *The Outlaw Gunner* (Cambridge, MD: Tidewater Publishers, 1971), 77.

44. Walsh, *Outlaw Gunner*, 65.

45. *Galveston Daily News,* Feb. 10, 1895; *Corpus Christi Caller-Times,* Jan. 18, 1959; Jesse Burnam, "Reminiscences of Capt. Jesse Burnham," *Southwestern Historical Quarterly* 5, no. 1 (1902): 12–18, digital images, The Portal to Texas History, University of North Texas Libraries, http://texashistory.unt.edu/ark:/67531/metapth101021/; Kathleen Huson Maxwell, ed., *Hobart Huson, A Texas Coastal Bend Trilogy* (Austin: Eakin Press, 1994), 19.

46. William Allen and Sue Allen Taylor, *Aransas: The Life of a Texas Coastal Community* (Austin: Eakin Press, 1997), 94; Murphy Givens, "Pieces of String Too Short to Save," *Corpus Christi Caller-Times,* June 18, 2008, http://www.caller.com/news/2008/jun/18/pieces-of-string-too-short-to-save/.

47. Alex H. Halff, *St. Charles Bay Hunting Club: Sport, Tradition, and Camaraderie* (Houston: Gulfstream Graphics, 2003), 3; *Brazosport Facts,* July 24, 1966; *San Luis Advocate,* Feb. 22, 1834, reel no. 1320048509, Brazoria County Historical Museum; Ducroz family file, no. 112, notes from Charles Ducroz, Sept. 29, 1975, Brazoria County Historical Museum; Keith Guthrie, *Texas Forgotten Ports*, Vol. 1, *Mid–Gulf Coast Ports from Corpus Christi to Matagorda Bay* (Austin: Eakin Press, 1988), 128; Hobart Huson, *Refugio: A Comprehensive History of Refugio County from Aboriginal Times* (Houston: Guardsman Publishing, 1953), 2, 13; Maxwell, *Hobart Huson*, 19.

48. "Ice Making in Lakeville," *Holmes County Historical Society Newsletter,* http://holmeshistory.com/nletter/?page_id=26; Brownston Malsch, *Indianola, the Mother of Western Texas* (Abilene: State House Press, 1988), 66, 189; Guthrie, *Texas Forgotten Ports*, Vol. 1, 167; *Houston Weekly Telegraph,* Apr. 20, 1859; *Civilian and Galveston Gazette,* July 19, 1845.

49. *Flake's Bulletin* (Galveston), Apr. 21, 1867; *Galveston Tri-Weekly News,* Apr. 21, 1871.

50. Rockport Maritime Museum Collection, Rockport, TX; Abigail Curlee, "His-

tory of a Texas Slave Plantation, 1831–63," *Southwestern Historical Quarterly* 26, no. 2 (1922): 79–127, digital images, Portal to Texas History, University of North Texas Libraries, http://texashistory.unt.edu/ark:/67531/metapth101084/, crediting Texas State Historical Association, Denton, Texas; W. T. Block, "A History of Jefferson County, Texas, from Wilderness to Reconstruction," http://www.wtblock.com/wtblockjr/History%20of%20Jefferson%20County/chapter%207.htm; *Dallas Morning News*, Feb. 27, 1893; W. S. Adair, "Early Days in Texas," *Dallas Morning News*, Jan. 29, 1933.

51. *Dallas Morning News*, Feb. 27, 1893.

52. Curlee, "History of a Texas Slave Plantation," 79–127; Keith Guthrie, *Texas Forgotten Ports*, Vol. 2, *River Ports* (Austin: Eakin Press, 1993), 124.

53. Guthrie, *Texas Forgotten Ports*, Vol. 2, 124–37.

54. Ibid., 102–103; Michael Bailey, pers. comm., June 15, 2011.

55. Undated newspaper clippings, San Luis Pass, Brazoria County Historical Museum; *Brazosport Facts*, July 24, 1966; *Galveston Daily News*, June 13, 1909; Unpublished manuscript, Brazoria County Historical Museum.

56. "Old Station," *Handbook of Texas Online*, http://www.tshaonline.org/handbook/online/articles/hvo24; Craig H. Roell, "Linn, John Joseph," *Handbook of Texas Online*, http://www.tshaonline.org/handbook/online/articles/LL/fli12; *Galveston Daily News*, Feb. 10, 1895; Sept. 24, 1910; *San Antonio Ledger*, June 1, 1854; Guthrie, *Texas Forgotten Ports*, Vol. 1, 159–67.

57. *Galveston Daily News*, Sept. 24, 1910; Paul Freier, "Lookin' Back," *Port Lavaca Wave*, Mar. 15, 1979; Wayne H. McAlister, *Life on Matagorda Island* (College Station: Texas A&M University Press, 2004), 221; Guthrie, *Texas Forgotten Ports*, Vol. 1, 192; *Galveston Civilian and Gazette*, Dec. 15, 1857.

58. Murphy Givens, "Village on St. Joseph's Was a Victim of War," *Corpus Christi Caller-Times*, Dec. 6, 2006, http://www.caller.com/news/2006/dec/06/village-on-st-josephs-was-a-victim-of-the-war/; Halff, *St. Charles Bay Hunting Club*, 4; Maxwell, *Hobart Huson*, 8.

59. Neal, "Recollections of Dr. Neal," 95; J. W. Lockhart, "Fifty-Three Years Ago," *Dallas Morning News*, Feb. 27, 1893.

60. *Galveston Daily News*, Dec. 28, 1869; Nov. 23, 1879; Sept. 16, 1887; Dec. 23, 1901; March 29, 1904; *Flake's Bulletin* (Galveston), Nov. 1, 1867.

61. *Flake's Bulletin* (Galveston), Mar. 8, 1866.

62. Dilue Harris, "The Reminiscences of Mrs. Dilue Harris," Part I, *Southwestern Historical Quarterly* 4, no. 2 (1902): 85–127, digital images, The Portal to Texas History, University of North Texas Libraries, http://texashistory.unt.edu/ark:/67531/metapth101018/, crediting Texas State Historical Association, Denton, Texas; David G. McComb, "Houston, TX," *Handbook of Texas Online*, http://www.tshaonline.org/handbook/online/articles/hdh03; Andrew Forest Muir, "Destiny of Buffalo Bayou," *Southwestern Historical Quarterly* 47, no. 2 (1943), 91–106, digital images, The Portal to Texas History, University of North Texas Libraries, (http://texashistory.unt.edu/ark:/67531/metapth146054/, crediting Texas State Historical Association, Denton, Texas; *Dallas Morning News*, Feb. 27, 1893; Sept. 13, 1902.

63. Landmarks—Old Houston, http://www.houstonhistory.com/preservation/landmarks/history9a.htm (accessed June 28, 2011); W. A. Leonard, ed., *Houston City Directory for 1867–68* (Houston: Gray, Smallwood and Co., 1867), 67, Houston Pub-

lic Library, http://digital.houstonlibrary.org/cdm/compoundobject/collection/citydir/id/475/rec/4; *Flake's Bulletin* (Galveston), Nov. 15, 1867.

64. *Democratic Telegraph and Register,* Feb. 19, 1848; *Tri-Weekly Telegraph,* Oct. 18, 1860.

65. Guthrie, *Texas Forgotten Ports*, Vol. 1, 173–86.

66. *Houston Weekly Telegraph,* Sept. 1, 1858; Malsch, *Indianola,* 223; *Indianola [TX] Courier,* May 21, 1859, http://www.uttyler.edu/vbetts/indianola%20courier.htm; *Galveston Civilian and Gazette,* Dec. 15, 1857; *Galveston Weekly Journal,* June 4, 1852; *San Antonio Ledger,* May 4, 1854; Guthrie, *Texas Forgotten Ports*, Vol. 1, 178; *Galveston Weekly Journal,* Feb. 11, 1853, The Portal to Texas History, University of North Texas Libraries, http://texashistory.unt.edu/ark:/67531/metapth182234.

67. Guthrie, *Texas Forgotten Ports*, Vol. 1, 69–80.

68. Murphy Givens and Jim Moloney, *Corpus Christi—A History* (Corpus Christi: Nueces Press, 2011), 30; *Corpus Christi Star,* Mar. 10, 1849, The Portal to Texas History, University of North Texas Libraries, http://texashistory.unt.edu/ark:/67531/metapth80219; *San Antonio Daily Express,* Apr. 13, 1887; Guthrie, *Texas Forgotten Ports,* Vol. 1, 69–80.

69. Elizabeth Pettit Davenport, "Fort Brown," *Handbook of Texas Online,* http://www.tshaonline.org/handbook/online/articles/FF/qbf7.html; *Brownsville Herald,* Nov. 18, 1938; April 27, 1947; Murphy Givens, "King, Kenedy, Pierce: The Grandees of Grass," *Corpus Christi Caller-Times,* Sept. 2, 2008, http://www.caller.com/news/2008/sep/02/king-kenedy-pierce-the-grandees-of-grass/.

70. Guthrie, *Texas Forgotten Ports*, Vol. 2, 49; Jaques D. Bagur, *A History of Navigation on Cypress and the Lakes* (Denton: University of North Texas Press, 2001), 118; *Dallas Morning News,* Jan. 30, 1890.

71. University of Texas Institute of Texan Cultures at San Antonio, library photograph archive catalog, File No. A101-0066; *San Antonio Ledger,* Oct. 16, 1858; Eléanor Stuck, "Menger Hotel," *Handbook of Texas Online,* http://www.tshaonline.org/handbook/online/articles/MM/dgm2.html.

72. *San Antonio Ledger,* June 1, 1854; *Austin State Gazette,* Dec. 26, 1857, The Portal to Texas History, University of North Texas Libraries, http://texashistory.unt.edu/ark:/67531/metapth81325.

73. Hatcher, *Letters of an Early American Traveller,* 161; Guthrie, *Texas Forgotten Ports,* Vol. 2, 98; *Brownsville Herald,* Nov. 18, 1938; Abigail Curlee, "History of a Texas Slave Plantation, 1831–63," *Southwestern Historical Quarterly* 26, no. 2 (1922): 79–127, The Portal to Texas History, University of North Texas Libraries, http://texashistory.unt.edu/ark:/67531/metapth101084/m1/85/, crediting Texas State Historical Association, Denton; McNeir, *Forest McNeir of Texas,* 36.

74. Guthrie, *Texas Forgotten Ports*, Vol. 1, 182; Peel, "To Become a Texian," 107, Portal to Texas History, University of North Texas Libraries, http://texashistory.unt.edu/ark:/67531/metapth26718/; *Texas State Gazette,* Jan. 1, 1859; *Galveston Daily News,* Nov. 27, 1879; Flack, *A Hunter's Experiences,* 32; Oran Milo Roberts, *A Description of Texas, Its Advantages and Resources* (Saint Louis: Gilbert Book Co., 1881), 89.

75. *Chambers's Encyclopedia: A Dictionary of Universal Knowledge for the People, Illustrated,* Vol. 4 (Philadelphia: J. B. Lippincott and Co., 1862), 271.

76. *Galveston Daily News,* Sept. 24, 1910; Lyle Jordan narratives, 2001, private collection of Doug Pike.

77. Wiggins, *They Made Their Own Law*, 140; Addie Hudgins Follett, "Retrospect," Brazoria County Historical Museum Library Information Files (unpublished), 16; *Civilian and Galveston Gazette*, Jan. 24, 1851; Sept. 21, Nov. 23, 1852; *Galveston Daily News*, Dec. 12, 1869.

78. *Galveston Daily News*, Sept. 24, 1910; Flack, *A Hunter's Experiences*, 274.

79. James A. Tober, *Who Owns the Wildlife?* (Westport, Conn.: Greenwood Press, 1981), 6.

80. Walter B. Stevens, *St. Louis: History of the Fourth City, 1764–1909* (Saint Louis: S. J. Clarke Pub. Co., 1909), 640.

81. "The World of Sport," *Outing* 62, no. 4 (July 1913): 508.

82. Capooth, *Waterfowling America*, Vol. 2, 373–74; James S. Zachary, *New Orleans Guide* (New Orleans: Publisher's Agent, 1885), 102–4.

CHAPTER 3

1. Maria Parloa, "Keeping and Cooking Game," reprinted in *Texas Siftings* (Austin), Feb. 13, 1886; *Dallas Morning News*, Oct. 5, 1891; Nov. 22, 1903.

2. *Galveston Daily News*, Dec. 3, 1868; *Port Arthur News*, Nov. 18, 1928.

3. James A. Tober, *Who Owns the Wildlife?* (Westport, Conn.: Greenwood Press, 1981), 79; Frank M. Gilbert, "The Sale of Game," *Forest and Stream* 35 (1891): 312; *Galveston Daily News*, Feb. 26, 1893.

4. Charles Hallock, "Fishing in Southern Waters: A Generous Hospitality," *American Angler* 7, no. 1 (1885): 6.

5. *Oakland Tribune*, Nov. 9, 1903; Nov. 2, 1904; Nov. 19, 1910; Jeff Churan, pers. comm., Mar. 18, 2012; A. M. Cummings, *Sunset Magazine*, Dec. 1902; *Bakersfield Daily Californian*, Apr. 28, 1894.

6. *Dallas Morning News*, Jan. 22, 1897; *Galveston Daily News*, Nov. 21, 1897.

7. *Galveston Tri-Weekly News*, Nov. 15, 1872.

8. *Port Arthur News*, Jan. 21, 1927; *Galveston Daily News*, Dec. 29, 1898; *Brownsville Daily Herald*, Dec. 28, 1895, Chronicling America, Library of Congress and National Endowment for the Humanities, http://www.loc.gov/chroniclingamerica/lccn/sn86089174/1895-12-28/ed-1/seq-2.

9. *Galveston Daily News*, Dec. 1, 1871; Dec. 20, 1879; Oct. 13, Nov. 1, 1882; Dec. 12, 1883; Jan. 2, 1894; *Houston Daily Post*, Mar. 8, 1896, Chronicling America, Library of Congress and National Endowment for the Humanities, http://www.loc.gov/chroniclingamerica/lccn/sn86071197/1896-03-08/ed-1/seq-24; *Galveston Tri-Weekly News*, Dec. 25, 1872.

10. *Galveston Daily News*, Nov. 27, 1879; Jan. 22, 1893; Nov. 21, 1897; *Dallas Morning News*, Jan. 22, 1897; Murphy Givens, pers. comm., Feb. 25, 2009.

11. *Galveston Daily News*, Jan. 22, 1893; *Dallas Morning News*, Jan. 26, 1893; *Brownsville Daily Herald*, Feb. 21, 1893, Chronicling America, Library of Congress and National Endowment for the Humanities, http://www.loc.gov/chroniclingamerica/lccn/sn86089174/1893-02-21/ed-1/seq-4.

12. Harry M. Walsh, *The Outlaw Gunner* (Cambridge, MD: Tidewater Publishers, 1971), 59; *Houston Daily Post*, Dec. 8, 1895, Chronicling America, Library of Congress and National Endowment for the Humanities, http://www.loc.gov/chroniclingamerica/lccn/sn86071197/1895-12-08/ed-1/seq-15; *Lavaca Sea Breeze*, Nov. 3, 1887; *Galveston Daily News*, Jan. 10, 1879.

13. *Galveston Daily News,* Dec. 1, 1871; Nov. 5, 17, 1893; Dec. 13, 1896; Roy Swann, "Early Hunter Found Game," *Corpus Christi Caller Times,* Jan. 18, 1959.

14. *Flake's Bulletin* (Galveston), Nov. 1, 1867; *Galveston Tri-Weekly News,* Aug. 25, 1867.

15. W. T. Block, "A History of Jefferson County, Texas, from Wilderness to Reconstruction," http://www.wtblock.com/wtblockjr/History%20of%20Jefferson%20 County/chapter%207.htm; *Galveston Daily News,* Jan. 27, 1878; Dec. 18, 1910; P. Briscoe, "The First Railroad in Texas," *Southwestern Historical Quarterly* 7, no. 4 (1904): 279–85, digital images, The Portal to Texas History, University of North Texas Libraries, http://texashistory.unt.edu/ark:/67531/metapth101030/, crediting Texas State Historical Association, Denton; George C. Werner, "International-Great Northern Railroad," *Handbook of Texas Online,* http://www.tshaonline.org/handbook/online /articles/eqi04.

16. George W. Drury, "Railway Express Agency: Yesterday's Federal Express," *Trains: The Magazine of Railroading,* June 5, 2006, http://trains.com/trn/default. aspx?c=a&id=344; *San Antonio Light,* Aug. 23, 1884.

17. *San Antonio Express,* June 27, 1869; Oct. 29, 1929.

18. Matt Moffatt, "History of Ice Manufacturing at the Turn of the 20th Century," http://otal.umd.edu/~vg/amst205.F97/vj12/project5.html; *Galveston Daily News,* July 31, Aug. 31, 1878; Nov. 17, 1893;*United States Commission of Fish and Fisheries, Part XVII, Report of the Commissioner for 1889 to 1891* (Washington, DC: Govt. Printing Office, 1893), 4, and Stevenson, "Report on the Coast Fisheries of Texas," in ibid., 375.

19. Forest McNeir, *Forest McNeir of Texas* (San Antonio: Naylor, 1956), 80; J. C. Melcher interview, Mar. 19, 2009, Port Lavaca, TX.

20. Ralph Semmes Jackson, *Home on the Double Bayou: Memories of an East Texas Ranch* (Austin: University of Texas Press, 1961), 48; Melanie Wiggins, *They Made Their Own Law* (Houston: Rice University Press, 1990), 48; *Brownsville Daily Herald,* Aug. 8, 1893.

21. *Ice and Refrigeration* 3, no. 1 (1892): 449; *Forest and Stream* 73, no. 24 (1909): 934; Wiggins, *They Made Their Own Law,* 241.

22. *San Antonio Daily Express,* Oct. 15, 1886.

23. *San Antonio Daily Light,* July 20, 1889; *Dallas Morning News,* Jan. 15, 1897.

24. *Dallas Morning News,* Oct. 29, 1897; *Moberly* (Missouri) *Weekly Monitor,* March 2, 1899.

25. *Dallas Morning News,* Feb. 27, 1893.

26. Ibid., Dec. 7, 1891; McNeir, *Forest McNeir of Texas,* 31; *Galveston Daily News,* Nov. 21, 1903.

27. *Galveston Daily News,* Dec. 23, 1901.

28. William C. Hobaugh, Charles D. Stutzenbaker, and Edward L. Flickinger, "The Rice Prairies," in *Habitat Management for Migrating and Wintering Waterfowl in North America* (Lubbock: Texas Tech University Press, 1989), 368.

29. Lyle Jordan narratives, 2001, private collection of Doug Pike; Rollin H. Baker, *Tom Waddell, Texas Game Warden* (Halletsville, TX: Old Homestead Publishing Co., 2007), 139; Ronnie Luster interview, July 1, 2009, Houston, TX.

30. Charles Cardiff interview by Vernon Bevill, Bob Spain, and David Lobpries, Mar. 1994, tape 7326, Texas Parks and Wildlife Department Archives, Austin, TX; *Corpus Christi Times,* Nov. 23, 1937.

31. *The Louisiana Planter and Sugar Manufacturer* 40, no. 6 (1908): 84; Wayne Capooth, *Waterfowling America*, Vol. 2 (Memphis: privately printed, 2008), 442; Ike Handy, "Reflective Historical Narrative" (ca. 1960s), in Royce A. Strickland, *Ridgehaven and a Dunn Marsh Legacy: Photojournal of a Texas Coastal Outdoorsman, Lindsey H. Dunn Jr.* (Baytown TX: privately printed, 2004), 7; *Victoria Daily Advocate,* Oct. 1, 1903.

32. *Houston Daily Post*, Sept. 29, 1902, Chronicling America, Library of Congress and National Endowment for the Humanities, http://chroniclingamerica.loc.gov/lccn/sn86071197/1902-09-29/ed-1/seq-6/.

33. Walsh, *Outlaw Gunner,* 21; Shannon Tompkins, "Ghost Dance: Vision of the Waterfowling World in the Early 1900s Are Surreal, Haunting," *Houston Chronicle,* Nov. 2, 2000.

34. Tompkins, "Ghost Dance"; Shannon Tompkins, pers. comm., Mar. 25, 2011; John M. Taylor, "At the Touch of a Finger," *Wildfowl* 23, no. 5 (2008): 67; *Field and Stream* 112, no. 5 (2008): 95.

35. Yvonne Sutherlin, pers. comm., Apr. 15, 2009; *Sabine Pass News,* Feb. 16, 1899.

36. Emerson Hough, "Plover-Shooting," in *Shooting on Upland, Marsh, and Stream* (New York: Rand McNally, 1890), 205; Henry Hall, ed., *The Tribune Book of Open-Air Sports* (New York: Tribune Association, 1887), 423; Roy Swan, "The Sportsman," *Corpus Christi Caller-Times,* Nov. 24, 1957.

37. Lyle Jordan narratives, 2001, private collection of Doug Pike; *San Antonio Light,* Oct. 13, 1938.

38. Caspar Whitney, "The Sportsman's View-Point," *Outing* 41, no. 6 (Mar. 1903): 764; *Galveston Daily News,* Mar. 7, 1907; *San Antonio Light,* Feb. 26, 1922; Walsh, *Outlaw Gunner,* 95–108; "Uncle Sam Wars on Duck Bootleggers," *Popular Mechanics Magazine* 55, no. 5 (1931): 739–40; *Daily Bulletin,* Nov. 18, 1908.

39. William F. Mackey, *American Bird Decoys* (New York: Bonanza Books, 1965), 208–56.

40. Harris, M. Brown, "With the Ducks on the Texas Coast," *The Sportsman's Magazine* 1 (Oct. 1896–Apr. 1897): 493.

41. Capooth, *Waterfowling America*, Vol. 2, 9; *Galveston Daily News,* Nov. 30, 1902; Jack Holland, unpublished paper, Oct. 17, 2008, in collection of the author.

42. *Flake's Bulletin* (Galveston), Oct. 31, 1867.

43. *Dallas Morning News,* Nov. 16, 1886; *San Antonio Evening Light,* Sept. 18, 1882; *Galveston Daily News,* Sept. 5, Nov. 21, 1897; Keith L. Bryant Jr., "Stilwell, Arthur Edward," *Handbook of Texas Online,* http://www.tshaonline.org/handbook/online/articles/fst58.

44. *Hunter-Trader-Trapper* 42, no. 2 (1900): 128; *Galveston Daily News,* Sept. 21, 1898; Feb. 26, 1901; Bill Quick, pers. comm., Mar. 31, 2009; Ed Holder, "Market Hunters Took Their Toll," *Brazosport Facts,* Sept. 26, 1994.

45. J. P. Logan interview, Nov. 12, 2012, Houston, TX.

46. Charles Stutzenbaker interview, Oct. 24, 2008, Port Arthur, TX; Wiggins, *They Made Their Own Law,* 241; Herb Stafford, pers. comm., Jan. 19, 2010.

47. Yvonne Sutherlin, pers. comm., Apr. 15, 2009; Holder, "Market Hunters Took Their Toll"; Joe Rice, "A Pot Hunter in Texas," *Recreation* 41, no. 5 (May 1902): 371; *Sabine Pass News,* Feb. 16, 1899.

48. *Flake's Bulletin* (Galveston), Mar. 8, 1866; *Galveston Daily News,* Sept. 12, 1869; *Directory of the City of Galveston, 1899–1900* (Galveston: Morrison and Fourmy, 1899),

50; *Directory of the City of Galveston, 1881–1882* (Houston: Morrison and Fourmy, 1881), 30.

49. *Galveston Daily News,* Dec. 28, 1869; Nov. 18, 1873; Nov. 23, 1879; Oct. 9, 1885; Sept. 16, 1887; Dec. 19, 1893; *Flake's Bulletin* (Galveston), Nov. 1, 1867.

50. Charles H. Stevenson, "Report on the Coast Fisheries of Texas," in *United States Commission of Fish and Fisheries, Part XVII*, 403; Wiggins, *They Made Their Own Law*, 51.

51. *Galveston Daily News,* Nov. 23, 1879; Dec. 26, 1882; Nov. 3, 1885; Jan. 20, Dec. 22, 1893; April 25, 1897.

52. *San Antonio Daily Express,* Jan. 12, 1886; *Galveston Daily News,* Nov. 9, 1885; Mar. 3, 1887; Nov. 1, 1901; Feb. 12, 1909; Mary Jean Abshier, pers. comm.; McNeir, *Forest McNeir of Texas*, 57; *Galveston Tri-Weekly News,* Dec. 11, 1872; *Williamsburg Journal Tribune,* Feb. 1, 1887.

53. *Galveston Daily News,* Nov. 12, 1893; Sept. 19, 1896; Nov. 1, 1901.

54. Melanie Wiggins, pers. comm., Jan. 22, 2010; McNeir, *Forest McNeir of Texas*, 83; Claud Kahla interview, June 6, 2009, High Island, TX; *Galveston Daily News,* Jan. 2, 1909; Peter Stines interview, Sept. 5, 2008, Wallisville, TX.

55. *San Antonio Daily Express,* Jan. 12, 1886.

56. *Galveston Daily News,* Nov. 5, 1875; March 14, 1877; March 15, Oct. 11, 1878.

57. *Galveston Daily News,* Dec. 21, 1880; Nov. 5, 1888; Oct. 11, 1889; Sept. 27, 1894; Feb. 24, 1903; *Directory of the City of Galveston, 1899–1900*, 337; *Directory of the City of Galveston, 1881–1882*, 396; Robin W. Doughty, "Sea Turtles in Texas: A Forgotten Commerce," *Southwestern Historical Quarterly* 88, no. 1 (July 1984): 43–70, digital images, The Portal to Texas History, University of North Texas Libraries, http://texashistory.unt.edu/ark:/67531/metapth101210/, crediting Texas State Historical Association, Denton.

58. George C. Werner, "Galveston, Houston and Henderson Railroad," *Handbook of Texas Online,* http://www.tshaonline.org/handbook/online/articles/eqg07; *Galveston Daily News,* Jan. 27, 1878; Werner, "International-Great Northern Railroad".

59. *Galveston Daily News,* Aug. 27, 1865; Aug. 2, 1872; Oct. 27, 1875; Dec. 27, 1885; Aug. 5, Oct. 24, 1886; *Flake's Bulletin* (Galveston), Nov. 24, 1869; McNeir, *Forest McNeir of Texas*, 65–83.

60. *Heller's Galveston Directory: 1878 and Portion of 1879* (Galveston: John H. Heller, 1879), 41; *Galveston Daily News,* May 16, 1909.

61. *Galveston Daily News,* Sept. 14, 1883; Dec. 29, 1905; Ned Hardy, "When the Ducks Begin to Fly," *Dallas Morning News,* Sept. 27, 1908.

62. *Galveston Daily News,* Jan. 26, 1885; Roger Reed, "The Yellow-Legs or 'Telltale,'" *Sports Afield,* January 1898, 35.

63. *Galveston Tri-Weekly News,* Jan. 3, 1873; *Galveston Daily News,* Nov. 5, 1875; Mar. 14, 1877; Jan. 30, 1878; Feb. 10, 1894; Jan. 22, 1903; Roy Swann, "Early Hunter Found Game," *Corpus Christi Caller Times,* Jan. 18, 1959.

64. Joe Whitehead interview, Aug. 9, 2008, Smith Point, TX; McNeir, *Forest McNeir of Texas*, 97.

65. Peter Stines interview, Sept. 5, 2008, Wallisville, TX.

66. Frank W. Johnson, *A History of Texas and Texans*, Vol. 4 (New York: American Historical Society, 1916), 1,866.

67. Wiggins, *They Made Their Own Law*, 128–33; Melanie Wiggins, pers. comm.

68. *Galveston Daily News,* Nov. 24, 1920; Claud Kahla interview, June 6, 2009, High Island, TX; Wiggins, *They Made Their Own Law,* 241.

69. *Eagle Lake Headlight,* Feb. 17, 1917, roll 6 (Jan. 6, 1917–Dec. 28, 1918), microfilm image 30 of 478, Eula and David Wintermann Library, Eagle Lake, TX.

70. *Galveston Tri-Weekly News,* Nov. 17, 1865; Margaret S. Henson and Kevin Ladd, *Chambers County, a Pictorial History* (Norfolk, VA: Donning, 1988), 121; "Observations at Fort Anahuac," *Dallas Morning News,* Mar. 25, 1899.

71. Sylvia Lamb interview, Aug. 8, 2008, Wallisville, TX; Royce Strickland interview, May 31, 2009, Baytown, TX.

72. *Dallas Morning News,* March 25, 1899.

73. McNeir, *Forest McNeir of Texas,* 93–98.

74. Ann Quinn Wilson, *Native Houstonian, A Collective Portrait* (Norfolk, VA: Donning Co., 1982), 50; *Victoria Daily Advocate,* Mar. 29, 1904; *Galveston Daily News,* June 27, 1901; Capooth, *Waterfowling America,* Vol. 2, 421; Leo C. Harby, *Harper's Magazine,* 1890, reprinted in *Logansport* (Indiana) *Journal,* Aug. 15, 1890.

75. Priscilla Myers Benham, "Scanlan, Thomas Howe," *Handbook of Texas Online,* http://www.tshaonline.org/handbook/online/articles/fsc40; *Galveston Daily News,* Oct. 31, 1897.

76. *Morrison and Fourmy's General Directory of the City of Houston, 1889–90* (Galveston: Morrison and Fourmy, 1899), 53, Houston Area Digital Archives, Houston Public Library, http://digital.houstonlibrary.org/cdm/compoundobject/collection/citydir/id/3052/rec/2; *Morrison and Fourmy's General Directory of the City of Houston, 1899* (Galveston: Morrison and Fourmy, 1899), 397, Houston Area Digital Archives, Houston Public Library, http://digital.houstonlibrary.org/cdm/compoundobject/collection/citydir/id/4838/rec/5; *Morrison and Fourmy's General Directory of the City of Houston, 1900–1901* (Galveston: Morrison and Fourmy, 1900), 449–50, Houston Area Digital Archives, Houston Public Library, http://digital.houstonlibrary.org/cdm/compoundobject/collection/citydir/id/5114/rec/6; *Morrison and Fourmy's General Directory of the City of Houston, 1902–1903* (Galveston: Morrison and Fourmy, 1902) 549–50, Houston Area Digital Archives, Houston Public Library, http://digital.houstonlibrary.org/cdm/compoundobject/collection/citydir/id/5500/rec/13.

77. *Houston Daily Post,* Dec. 8, 1895, Chronicling America, Library of Congress and National Endowment for the Humanities, http://chroniclingamerica.loc.gov/lccn/sn86071197/1895-12-08/ed-1/seq-15; *Houston Post,* Nov. 12, 1899, ibid., http:/chroniclingamerica.loc.gov/lccn/sn86071197/1899-11-12/ed-1/seq-13; *Houston Post,* Dec. 30, 1899, ibid., http:/chroniclingamerica.loc.gov/lccn/sn86071197/1899-12-30/ed-1/seq-6; *Houston Daily Post,* Nov. 13, 1900, ibid., http://chroniclingamerica.loc.gov/lccn/sn86071197/1900-11-13/ed-1/seq-10; *Morrison and Fourmy's General Directory of the City of Houston, 1900–1901,* 41; *Morrison and Fourmy's General Directory of the City of Houston, 1899,* 52, 231.

78. Mooney and Morrison's Directory of the City of Houston for 1877–78 (Houston: Mooney and Morrison, 1877), 5, 47, Houston Area Digital Archives, Houston Public Library, http://digital.houstonlibrary.org/cdm/compoundobject/collection/citydir/id/1161/rec/7; *Houston Daily Post,* Jan. 5, 1902, The Portal to Texas History, University of North Texas Libraries, http://texashistory.unt.edu/ark:/67531/metapth85848; "Houston, a History and Guide," *American Guide Series* (Houston: Anson Jones Press, 1942), 102, The Portal to Texas History, University of North Texas Libraries, http://

texashistory.unt.edu/ark:/67531/metapth5865/?q=%E2%80%9CHouston%2C%2A%20 History%20and%20Guide%2C%E2%80%9D; *Galveston Daily News,* Dec. 26, 1894.

79. *Galveston Daily News,* Jan. 27, 1878; George C. Werner, "Houston and Texas Central Railway," *Handbook of Texas Online,* http://www.tshaonline.org/handbook /online/articles/HH/eqh9.html; *Morrison and Fourmy's General Directory of the City of Houston, 1899,* 41, 53, 175, 397; *Galveston Daily News,* Nov. 5, 1888; *Morrison and Fourmy's General Directory of the City of Houston, 1895-96* (Galveston: Morrison and Fourmy, 1895), 177, Houston Area Digital Archives, Houston Public Library, http:// digital.houstonlibrary.org/cdm/compoundobject/collection/citydir/id/4342/rec/12.

80. *Houston Daily Post,* Dec. 27, 1895, The Portal to Texas History, Chronicling America, Library of Congress and National Endowment for the Humanities, http:// www.loc.gov/chroniclingamerica/lccn/sn86071197/1895-12-27/ed-1/seq-11; Capooth, *Waterfowling America,* Vol. 2, 421; *Galveston Daily News,* Nov. 23, 1895; M. Whilldin, comp., *A Description of Western Texas,* (Galveston, TX: Galveston, Harrisburg, and San Antonio Railway Co., The Sunset Route, 1876), 32.

81. Edward T. Martin, "The Two Extremes," *Hunter-Trader-Trapper* 41, no. 1 (1920): 30; *Galveston Daily News,* June 25, 1885; Edward T. Martin, "Pintail Shooting in the Days Long Ago," *Hunter-Trader-Trapper* 32, no. 4 (1916): 22.

82. *The Texarkana Gateway to Texas and the Southwest: Issued Jointly by the Texas and Pacific Railway and the International and Great Northern Railroad* (Saint Louis: Woodward and Tiernan Printing, 1896), 179; *Galveston Daily News,* Oct. 31, 1889; Jan. 21, Nov. 11, 1892; Oct. 4, 1896.

83. *Velasco Times,* Nov. 21, 1891, The Portal to Texas History, University of North Texas Libraries, http://texashistory.unt.edu/ark:/67531/metapth185300; *Galveston Daily News,* Nov. 10, 16, 1893; *Dallas Morning News,* Feb. 4, 1892.

84. *Velasco Daily Times,* Dec. 27, 1891, The Portal to Texas History, University of North Texas Libraries, http://texashistory.unt.edu/ark:/67531/metapth185164; Dec. 29, 1891, ibid., http://texashistory.unt.edu/ark:/67531/metapth185165; Feb. 18, 1892, ibid., http://texashistory.unt.edu/ark:/67531/metapth185208; Jamie Murray, pers. comm., Feb. 26, 2012.

85. Neal McLain, Wayne LeCompte, Jim Williams, Jim Bohot, pers. comms., Feb. 25, 2012; Joe Jamison, "Reviewing the Past 75 Years," Brazoria County Historical Museum Library Information Files, courtesy Jamie Murray.

86. Doughty, "Sea Turtles in Texas," 60; *Galveston Daily News,* Nov. 9, 1885; Oct. 31, 1889; *Dallas Morning News,* Dec. 7, 1891.

87. Mary L. Griffin, "Palacios, TX," *Handbook of Texas Online,* http://www .tshaonline.org/handbook/online/articles/PP/hfp1.html; Matagorda County Museum Association, *Images of America: Matagorda County* (Charleston, Chicago, Portsmouth, and San Francisco: Arcadia, 2008), 100.

88. Brownston Malsch, *Indianola, the Mother of Western Texas* (Abilene: State House Press, 1988), 1-23, 43-48; Keith Guthrie, *Texas Forgotten Ports,* Vol. 1, *Mid-Gulf Coast Ports from Corpus Christi to Matagorda Bay* (Austin: Eakin Press, 1988), 173-86; *Indianola Weekly Bulletin,* Oct. 3, 1871, The Portal to Texas History, University of North Texas Libraries, http://texashistory.unt.edu/ark:/67531/metapth178913; *Dallas Morning News,* Oct. 15, 1885; Craig H. Roell, "San Antonio and Mexican Gulf Railroad," *Handbook of Texas Online,*"SAN ANTARANSAS PASS RAILWAY," lway," http:// www.tshaonline.org/handbook/online/articles/SS/eqs8.html.

89. *Galveston Daily News*, Sept. 12, Nov. 5, 1883; *Texas and Mexico, Showing Houston and Texas Central System of Railways* (Chicago: Rand, McNally and Co., 1885); *Dallas Morning News*, Oct. 15, 1885; *Galveston Daily News*, Sept. 22, 1905.

90. Roell, "San Antonio and Mexican Gulf Railroad"; *Galveston Daily News*, Feb. 28, 1887; *Lavaca Sea Breeze*, Nov. 3, 1887.

91. *Galveston Daily News*, Dec. 20, 1891; Oct. 30, 1895; Oct. 4, 1896; Paul Freier, "Lookin' Back," *Port Lavaca Wave*, Mar. 26, 1975.

92. *Lavaca Sea Breeze*, Nov. 3, 1887; Paul Freier, "Lookin' Back," *Port Lavaca Wave*, Mar. 19, 26, Apr. 2, 1975; *Brownsville Daily Herald*, Feb. 11, 1896, The Portal to Texas History, University of North Texas Libraries, http://texashistory.unt.edu/ark:/67531/metapth61902/; Calhoun County Museum photo reference no. A0081; *San Antonio Daily Express*, Dec. 15, 1893; *Galveston Daily News*, Sept. 11, 1896.

93. Carlos Smith interview, Apr. 26, 2009, LaPorte, TX; *Galveston Daily News*, Aug. 7, 1893; J. C. Melcher interview, Mar. 19, 2009, Port Lavaca, TX.

94. *Galveston Daily News*, Dec. 1, 1901; Guthrie, *Texas Forgotten Ports*, Vol. 1, 21–90; W. W. Wood, "History of Rockport, Fulton, Lamar and El Copano," unpublished (1953), collection of Aransas County Library, 57–60.

95. William Allen and Sue Allen Taylor, *Aransas: The Life of a Texas Coastal Community* (Austin: Eakin Press, 1997), 209; *Galveston Daily News*, Nov. 12, 1892; *San Antonio Daily Light*, Apr. 14, 1895; J. A. Allen, "On the Mammals of Aransas County, Texas, with Descriptions of New Forms of *Lepus* and *Oryzomys*," *Bulletin of the American Museum of Natural History* 6 (1894): 17; Janie White, pers. comm., Feb. 20, 2009.

96. *Galveston Daily News*, June 25, 1892; Sept. 6, 1893; *San Antonio Daily Express*, Jan. 28, 1893; Nov. 5, 1899.

97. *Galveston Daily News*, Sept. 6, 1893; June 4, 1894; *San Antonio Daily Express*, Jan. 28, 1893.

98. *San Antonio Daily Light*, Dec. 19, 1893; Allen and Taylor, *Aransas*, 214–15; *San Antonio Daily Express*, Dec. 15, 1893; Janie White, pers. comm., Feb. 20, 2009; *Galveston Daily News*, Mar. 22, 1900.

99. *Dallas Morning News*, Dec. 19, 1891; *Galveston Daily News*, Nov. 12, 1892; Roy Swann, "Early Hunter Found Game," *Corpus Christi Caller Times*, Jan. 18, 1959; Clark McAdams, "Following the Redheads to the Gulf Coast," *Ducking Days: Narratives of Duck Hunting, Studies of Wildfowl Life, and Reminiscences of Famous Marksmen on the Marshes and at the Traps*, ed. Charles B. Morss and William Chester Hazelton (Hazelton, PA: W. C. Hazelton, 1918), 27; Allen and Taylor, *Aransas*, 191; *Galveston Daily News*, Oct. 25, 1879; July 14, 1911.

100. *Galveston Daily News*, Jan. 5, 1889.

101. *Dallas Morning News*, Nov. 15, 1892; *San Antonio Daily Light*, Apr. 14, 1895; *Houston Daily Post*, Dec. 5, 1897, Chronicling America, Library of Congress, http://www.loc.gov/chroniclingamerica/lccn/sn86071197/1897-12-05/ed-1/seq-36.

102. Stevenson, "Report on the Coast Fisheries of Texas," in *United States Commission of Fish and Fisheries, Part XVII*, 412; Rick Pratt, pers. comm., Jan. 28, 2011; *San Antonio Daily Light*, June 6, 1890.

103. Judith Whipple, *Journal of Letters and History of George William Knight Mew*, (N.p.: Biography Press, 1975), 159, Corpus Christi Public Libraries Digital Archives, http://archives.cclibraries.com/cdm/compoundobject/collection/ifp/id/13256/rec/26.

104. Nancy Beck Young, "San Antonio and Aransas Pass Railway," *Handbook of Texas Online*, http://www.tshaonline.org/handbook/online/articles/SS/eqs6.html; *Brownsville Daily Herald*, June 26, 1895; *San Antonio Daily Light*, Dec. 19, 1893.

105. *Fort Worth Gazette*, Nov. 3, 1892; *Galveston Daily News*, Sept. 28, 1888; Murphy Givens, pers. comm., Oct. 16, 2011; *San Antonio Daily Express*, Dec. 24, 1889.

106. *American Angler* 28, no. 8 (1898): 147; *San Antonio Daily Express*, Sept. 23, 1900; *Galveston Daily News*, Nov. 21, 1891; Nov. 12, 1892.

107. A. C. Peirce, *A Man from Corpus Christi*, rev. ed. (1894; repr. Rockport: Copano Bay Press, 2008), 16–29.

108. Ibid., 29–66; *Galveston Daily News*, Mar. 8, 1883; Jan. 5, 1889; Nov. 12, 1892.

109. H. S. Canefield, "The Death of the Red-Winged Mallard," *Outing* 37, no. 4 (Jan. 1901): 427–31; *Galveston Daily News*, Nov. 21, 1891.

110. *San Antonio Daily Express*, Sept. 23, Oct. 14, 1900; *San Antonio Light*, Aug. 30, 1896; *San Antonio Daily Light*, Sept. 8, 1895.

111. *Brownsville Daily Herald*, Apr. 6, 1894; Edward L. N. Glass, reprinted in "Tidbits," Robert B. Vezzetti, ed., Cameron County Historical Association (ca. 1914), 50, courtesy Norm Rozeff; *Brownsville Herald*, Apr. 27, 1947; *Brownsville Herald*, June 26, 1915; *Brownsville Daily Herald*, Dec. 28, 1895, Chronicling America, Library of Congress, http://www.loc.gov/chroniclingamerica/lccn/sn86089174/1895-12-28/ed-1/seq-2; *Galveston Daily News*, Jan. 22, 1893; *Brownsville Daily Herald*, Dec. 13, 1892, Chronicling America, Library of Congress, http://www.loc.gov/chroniclingamerica/lccn/sn86089174/1892-12-13/ed-1/seq-3; ibid., Feb. 21, 1893, http://www.loc.gov/chroniclingamerica/lccn/sn86089174/1893-02-21/ed-1/seq-4.

112. *Brownsville Daily Herald*, Jan. 17, 1898.

113. Ibid., Aug. 13, 1894; Mar. 21, 1903; *Brownsville Herald*, Jan. 6, 1900.

114. *Brownsville Daily Herald*, Dec. 7, 1892, Chronicling America, Library of Congress, http://chroniclingamerica.loc.gov/lccn/sn86089174/1892-12-07/ed-1/; ibid., Feb. 28, 1893, http://chroniclingamerica.loc.gov//lccn/sn86089174/1893-02-28/ed-1/; *Brownsville Herald*, Oct. 24, 1940.

115. *Brownsville Daily Herald*, June 26, 1895; June 5, 1897; Feb. 16, 1900; *Galveston Daily News*, Nov. 24, 1901.

116. *Galveston Daily News*, June 12, 1888.

117. Ibid., Nov. 10, 1893; Stevenson, "Report on the Coast Fisheries," in *United States Commission of Fish and Fisheries, Part XLVII*, 415; Alex Sweet and Armory J. Knox, "Three Dozen Good Stories from Texas Siftings," *American Humor Series* 1, no. 1 (1887): 50–52.

118. *Brownsville Daily Herald*, Mar. 11, May 7, 1901; May 12, 1903.

119. *San Antonio Express*, Oct. 1, 1869; Dec. 12, 1876; *San Antonio Light*, Dec. 12, 1898; "Mitchell Lake," *Wikipedia*, http://en.wikipedia.org/wiki/Mitchell_Lake; *San Antonio Light and Gazette*, Nov. 30, 1909.

120. University of Texas Institute of Texan Cultures at San Antonio, library photograph archive catalog, File Nos. A101-0066 and A101-0049; *San Antonio Ledger*, Oct. 16, 1858; *San Antonio Light*, Apr. 23, 1930; *San Antonio Daily Express*, Dec. 1, 1870; *Galveston Tri-Weekly News*, Dec. 19, 1870; *San Antonio Daily Light*, Sept. 28, 1896.

121. *San Antonio Daily Express*, Oct. 5, 1886; May 11, 1887; *Dallas Morning News*, Feb. 26, 1888; *San Antonio Daily Light*, Sept. 21, 1886; Nov. 6, Dec. 7, 1889; Feb. 22, 1890; Dec. 19, 1893; Aug. 28, 1898; *San Antonio Light*, Dec. 2, 1885; Sept. 25, 1898; *San Antonio Daily Express*, May 11, 1887.

122. *San Antonio Daily Express,* Oct. 5, 15, 1886; Dec. 21, 1888; *San Antonio Daily Light,* Nov. 15, 1894; Dec. 2, 1895; Dec. 7, 1903.

123. *San Antonio Light,* April 26, Oct. 16, 1883; Dec. 2, 1885; *San Antonio Daily Express,* Jan. 23, 1886; *San Antonio Daily Light,* Jan. 12, 1886; Jan. 28, 1896; Apr. 4, 1898.

124. *San Antonio Daily Express,* Oct. 31, 1893.

125. *Dallas Morning News,* May 23, 1886; Nov. 24, 1899; Nov. 22, 1903.

126. Ibid., Dec. 17, 1900; Nov. 15, 1903.

127. Ibid., Nov. 9, 1902.

128. Kenneth Forree, "When Quail Sold for Bit in Dallas," ibid., Aug. 29, 1951.

129. *Fort Worth Register,* Oct. 23, 1897; Feb. 16, 1901; *Fort Worth Telegram,* Dec. 21, 1902.

130. *Dallas Morning News,* Mar. 4, April 23, May 3, 1887; *Fort Worth Daily Gazette,* Apr. 16, 1887, The Portal to Texas History, University of North Texas Libraries, http://texashistory.unt.edu/ark:/67531/metapth85408; *Fort Worth Register,* Feb. 16, 1901.

131. Wyatt Moore oral history by Thad Sitton, Feb. 12, 1983, Tape No. 150, File No. OH 150-5, James Gilliam Gee Library, Texas A&M University-Commerce; "Marshall and Texas Pacific Railway," Texas and Pacific Railway Museum History, http://www.marshalldepot.org/History.htm (accessed July 10, 2011); *Dallas Morning News,* Nov. 20, 1887; Feb. 25, 1900; *Dallas Weekly Herald,* Nov. 20, 1884.

132. *Dallas Morning News,* Nov. 15, 1893.

133. *Brenham Weekly Banner,* Nov. 6, 1890; Jan. 21, 1897; *Weimar* (Texas) *Mercury,* Nov. 29, 1902.

134. *Galveston Daily News,* Apr. 17, 1895; Aug. 11, Sept. 6, 1896.

135. *Morrison and Fourmy's General Directory of the City of Austin, 1889–90* (Galveston: Morrison and Fourmy,1889), 32, 61, Portal to Texas History, University of North Texas Libraries, http://texashistory.unt.edu/ark:/67531/metapth39150; *Morrison and Fourmy's General Directory of the City of Austin, 1900–1901* (Galveston: Morrison and Fourmy, 1900), 32, Portal to Texas History, University of North Texas Libraries, http://texashistory.unt.edu/ark:/67531/metapth61100.

136. *Waco Daily Examiner,* Dec. 24, 1881, The Portal to Texas History, University of North Texas Libraries, http://chroniclingamerica.loc.gov/lccn/sn84022109/1881-12-24/ed-1/seq-4/; *Waco Evening News,* Nov. 26, 1888; Jan. 2, 1892; Jan. 3, 24, 1893; *Waco Daily Examiner,* Oct. 18, f1885.

137. *Canadian Free Press,* Nov. 2, 1887, The Portal to Texas History, University of North Texas Libraries, http://texashistory.unt.edu/ark:/67531/metapth183623; *Laredo Times,* Feb. 29, 1888; Jan. 15, 1896; Dec. 30, 1899; University of Texas Institute of Texan Cultures at San Antonio, library photograph archive catalog, File No. 074-1114.

CHAPTER 4

1. *New York Times,* Nov. 10, 1891; Jan. 11, 1902; Jan. 12, 1904; *Galveston Daily News,* Mar. 24, 1890; July 18, 1894.

2. *Syracuse Standard,* Nov. 27, 1898; *Laredo Times,* Nov. 15, 1891; *Dallas Morning News,* Jan. 12, 1890; *San Saba News,* May 29, 1891; *Athens* (Texas) *Daily Review,* May 15, 1901.

3. Thomas F. De Voe, *The Market Assistant* (New York: Hurd and Houghton, 1867), 150; H. Frank Dabney, "Duck Shooting in Southern Waters," *The Sportsman's Magazine* 1 (1897): 100; Mayne Reid, *The Young Voyageurs* (Boston: Ticknor and Fields, 1853),

193; Arthur Cleveland Bent, *Life Histories of North American Wild Fowl* (New York: Dover Pub., 1987), 286; William Bruce Leffingwell, "The Canvas-back Duck," in *Shooting on Upland, Marsh, and Stream* (New York: Rand McNally, 1890), 408.

4. Elisha Jarrett Lewis, "Canvas-back," in *The American Sportsman* (Philadelphia: J. B. Lippincott and Co., 1857), 285; De Voe, *Market Assistant*, 150.

5. S. F. Baird, T. M. Brewer, and R. Ridgway, *The Water Birds of North America*, Vol. 2 (Boston: Little, Brown and Co., 1884), 34; Wells W. Cook, "Saving the Ducks and Geese," *National Geographic Magazine* 24, no. 1 (1913): 361–80.

6. *Galveston Daily News,* Feb. 26, 1893.

7. *Moberly* (Missouri) *Weekly Monitor,* Mar. 2, 1899.

8. *Galveston Tri-Weekly News,* Dec. 11, 1872; *Galveston Daily News,* Mar. 3, 1887.

9. Leffingwell, "The Canvas-back Duck," 412; Baird, Brewer, and Ridgway, *Water Birds*, Vol. 2, 32; Lewis, "Canvas-back," 272; *Logansport* (Indiana) *Pharos,* Jan. 21, 1890.

10. *Dallas Morning News,* Jan. 21, 1897; Fred Mather, "Canvasbacks and Terrapin," *Recreation* 7, no. 1 (1897): 479.

11. *Galveston Daily News,* Mar. 24, 1890; Nov. 12, 1892; July 18, 1894; July 18, 1897; *Dallas Morning News,* Jan. 22, Feb. 5, 1897; *New York Tribune,* Jan. 14, 1883, Chronicling America, Library of Congress and National Endowment for the Humanities, http://chroniclingamerica.loc.gov/lccn/sn83030214/1883-01-14/ed-1/seq-9/; Indiana *Democrat,* July 2, 1891; *New York Times,* Sept. 8, 1891.

12. Wayne Capooth, *Waterfowling America*, Vol. 2 (Memphis: privately printed, 2008), 426 ; "Observations at Fort Anahuac," *Dallas Morning News,* Mar. 25, 1899; *Galveston Daily News,* Feb. 10, 1894; Joe Whitehead interview, June 14, 2008, Smith Point, TX.

13. Capooth, *Waterfowling America*, Vol. 2, 427; Forest McNeir, *Forest McNeir of Texas* (San Antonio: Naylor, 1956), 74.

14. Capooth, *Waterfowling America*, Vol. 2, 424–29; *Galveston Daily News,* Feb. 26, 1893; Feb. 10, 1894.

15. Capooth, *Waterfowling America*, Vol. 2, 427.

16. *Galveston Daily News,* Feb. 26, 1893.

17. "Texas and the Southwest," *Forest and Stream,* 44 (1895): 85.

18. Patrick H. Butler III, "Moody, William Lewis," *Handbook of Texas Online,* http://www.tshaonline.org/handbook/online/articles/fmo21; "Observations at Fort Anahuac," *Dallas Morning News,* Mar. 25, 1899; *Galveston Daily News,* Jan. 30, 1909; Regina McElwain, "Murder at Lake Surprise," http://www.cchcnews.com/MurderAtLakeSurprise.pdf; Capooth, *Waterfowling America*, Vol. 2, 429; McNeir, *Forest McNeir of Texas,* 74.

19. McNeir, *Forest McNeir of Texas,* 73–83.

20. *San Antonio Daily Light,* Dec. 17, 1905; Capooth, *Waterfowling America*, Vol. 2, 429–30; McNeir, *Forest McNeir of Texas,* 84.

21. *San Antonio Daily Express,* Jan. 26, 1894; *San Antonio Daily Express,* Feb. 2, 1894; *Galveston Daily News,* Feb. 10, 1894; *San Antonio Express,* reprinted in *Galveston Daily News,* Jan. 31, 1894.

22. *Galveston Daily News,* Jan. 29, 30, 1909.

23. Ibid., Jan. 21, 1894.

24. Ibid., Feb. 10, 1894.

25. George Bird Grinnell, *American Duck Shooting* (New York: Forest and Stream Publishing, 1901), 598; Capooth, *Waterfowling America*, Vol. 2, 429.

26. McNeir, *Forest McNeir of Texas*, 91; Joe Whitehead interview, June 14, 2008, Smith Point, TX; Kevin Ladd, "Frost, John Lighter," *Handbook of Texas Online,* http://www.tshaonline.org/handbook/online/articles/FF/ffr21.html.

27. *Galveston Daily News,* Nov. 1, 1901; McNeir, *Forest McNeir of Texas*, 93; Joe Whitehead interview, June 14, 2008, Smith Point, TX.

28. Jim Sutherlin, pers. comm., Oct. 23, 2008; *Galveston Daily News,* Dec. 29, 1905; Ned Hardy, "When the Ducks Begin to Fly," *Dallas Morning News,* Sept. 27, 1908.

29. Roy Swann, "Early Hunter Found Game," *Corpus Christi Caller Times,* Jan. 18, 1959; *Lavaca Sea Breeze,* Nov. 3, 1887; *Dallas Morning News,* Dec. 19, 1891; *Galveston Daily News,* Nov. 12, 1892; Nov. 21, 1895; Henry P. Attwater, "Southwestern Game," *Ornithologist and Oologist* 16, no. 7 (1891): 109; *Houston Daily Post,* Nov. 23, 1901, Chronicling America, Library of Congress and National Endowment for the Humanities, http://www.loc.gov/chroniclingamerica/lccn/sn86071197/1901-11-23/ed-1/seq-12.

30. *Dallas Morning News,* Sept. 25, 1898; "Ducks on the Texas Coast," *Hunter-Trader-Trapper* 17, no. 3 (1908): 75–76.

31. Jamie Spears interview, Nov. 12, 2008, Port Aransas, TX.

32. McNeir, *Forest McNeir of Texas*, 84; *Dallas Morning News,* Nov. 15, 1892; Sept. 25, 1898; *Houston Daily Post,* Dec. 5, 1897, Chronicling America, Library of Congress and National Endowment for the Humanities, http://www.loc.gov/chroniclingamerica/lccn/sn86071197/1897-12-05/ed-1/seq-36; *Frank Leslie's Popular Monthly* 46, no. 1 (1898): 95.

33. T. S. Palmer, *Legislation for the Protection of Birds Bulletin*, US Dept. of Agriculture Division of Biological Survey, No. 12 (Washington, DC: Govt. Printing Office, 1900), 25; Robin W. Doughty, *Wildlife and Man in Texas: Environmental Change and Conservation* (College Station: Texas A&M University Press, 1983), 101–2; Murphy Givens, "Feather Merchants," radio column, *Corpus Christi Caller Times,* Nov. 21, 2003, http://www.caller.com/news/2003/nov/21/murphy-givens-radio-column-for-november-21-2003/; "Vintage Ladies Hats—How Ladies Hats Evolved Through History," http://www.vintageladieshats.net/.

34. *Fort Worth Gazette,* Oct. 15, 1887, Givens, "Feather Merchants."

35. *Fort Worth Gazette,* Aug. 4, 1889; *Fort Worth Weekly Gazette,* Oct. 7, 1887; *Galveston Daily News,* Sept. 20, 1896.

36. Palmer, *Legislation for the Protection of Birds Bulletin*, 25; N. O. Williams, "Destruction of Birds," *Transactions of the Iowa Horticultural Society, Proceedings of the Twenty-First Annual Meeting, 1886,* ed. G. B. Brackett (Des Moines, IA: Geo. E. Roberts, State Printer, 1887), 165.

37. *San Antonio Light,* Oct. 21, 1890; *Laredo Times,* May 21, 1901.

38. Joe Whitehead, pers. comm., July 26, 2010; Doughty, *Wildlife and Man in Texas,* 171–72; Capooth, *Waterfowling America,* Vol. 2, 18.

39. *A Visit to Texas: Being the Journal of a Traveller through Those Parts Most Interesting to American Settlers,* 2nd ed. (New York: Van Nostrand and Dwight, 1836): 145.

40. Frederic William Simonds, *The Geography of Texas* (Boston: Athenaeum Press, 1905), 71; Mark W. Harrington and A. Lawrence Rotch, *American Meteorological Journal* 5 (May 1888 to April 1889): 181–82; Capooth, *Waterfowling America*, Vol. 2 (Memphis: privately printed, 2008), 18; McNeir, *Forest McNeir of Texas*, 33; Williams, "Destruction of Birds," 165.

41. *Corpus Christi Caller-Times,* Jan. 18, 1959; *Brownsville Daily Herald,* Apr. 28, 1897; *Galveston Daily News,* May 14, 1891; Frank B. Armstrong company price sheet, from the collections of the Center for American History, The University of Texas at Austin, copy in the possession of the author; Doughty, *Wildlife and Man in Texas,* 100–101; Francis H. Kortright, *The Ducks, Geese, and Swans of North America* (Washington, DC: American Wildlife Institute, 1943), 225.

42. Walt Davis and Isabel Davis, *Exploring the Edges of Texas* (College Station: Texas A&M University Press, 2010), 91; Witmer Stone, "Report of the Committee on the Protection of North American Birds for the Year 1900," *The Auk* 28, no. 1 (1901): 74–76.

43. *Brownsville Daily Herald,* Dec. 27, 1899.

44. *Dallas Morning News,* July, 7, 1896; *Galveston Daily News,* Feb. 10, 1878; *Civilian and Galveston Gazette,* Sept. 23, 1855.

45. T. S. Palmer, "A Review of Economic Ornithology in the United States," *Yearbook of the United States Department of Agriculture, 1899* (Washington, DC: Govt. Printing Office, 1900), 271; George, B. Sennett, "The Eggers of Texas," *Audubon Magazine* 1 (1888): 34–35.

CHAPTER 5

1. Charles Hallock, "Fishing in Southern Waters—A Generous Hospitality," *American Angler* 7, no. 1 (1885): 6; Bland Simpson, "A Carolinian's Sound County Chronicle to the Inner Islands," (Chapel Hill: University of North Carolina Press, 2006), 45; "Game Preserving in Louisiana," *Outing* 11 (1888): 533.

2. *Galveston Daily News,* Oct. 4, 1896; *Houston Daily Post,* Nov. 30, 1902, Chronicling America, Library of Congress and National Endowment for the Humanities, http://www.loc.gov/chroniclingamerica/lccn/sn86071197/1902-11-30/ed-1/seq-2; *Victoria Advocate,* Dec. 25, 1899.

3. G. O. Shields, editor's letter to Mr. Chas. H. Smyth, Wichita, Kansas, *Recreation* 15 (1901): 446.

4. *Dallas Morning News,* Nov. 2, 1895; Jan. 15, 1897; Feb. 22, 1899.

5. *Frank Leslie's Popular Monthly* 46, no. 1 (1898): 99; Wayne Capooth, *Waterfowling America,* Vol. 2 (Memphis: privately printed, 2008), 20; *Brownsville Herald,* May 11, 1950; *Logansport* (Indiana) *Journal,* Mar. 26, 1904; James Cox, ed., *Notable St. Louisans in 1900* (Saint Louis: Benesch Art Publishing, 1901), 68.

6. Jay Vessells, "King of the Market Hunters," *Texas Game and Fish* 10 (1952): 12; *Western Field* 3, no. 1 (1903): 702; Capooth, *Waterfowling America,* Vol. 2, 19; *Hunter-Trader-Trapper* 42, no. 2 (1900): 128.

7. *Western Field* 3, no. 1 (1903): 702.

8. Elisha Jarrett Lewis, "Canvas-back," in *The American Sportsman* (Philadelphia: J. B. Lippincott and Co., 1857), 285; *Galveston Daily News,* Dec. 5, 1887.

9. Edward H. Forbush, *History of the Game Birds, Wild-Fowl, and Shore Birds of Massachusetts and Adjacent States* (Boston: Wright and Potter Printing, 1912), 515; William Temple Hornady, *Our Vanishing Wildlife* (New York: Clark and Fritts, 1913), 312.

10. Hornady, *Our Vanishing Wildlife,* 5–6; Capooth, *Waterfowling America,* Vol. 2, 380.

11. Capooth, *Waterfowling America,* Vol. 2, 28, 313; Forbush, *History of the Game Birds,* 513–14.

12. James A. Tober, *Who Owns the Wildlife?* (Westport, CN: Greenwood Press, 1981), 77–78; *Woodland* (California) *Daily Democrat*, Dec. 1, 1900; Capooth, *Waterfowling America*, Vol. 2, 22; Carolyn V. Platt and Gary Meszaros, *Creatures of Change: An Album of Ohio Animals* (Kent, OH: Kent State University Press, 1998), 91; Emma J. Welty, "Oregon Audubon Society State Report," *Bird-Lore* 7, no. 2 (1906): 269.

13. *Galveston Daily News*, Apr. 17, 1895; August 11, Sept. 6, 1896; *Houston Daily Post*, Dec. 5, 1897, Chronicling America, Library of Congress and National Endowment for the Humanities, http://www.loc.gov/chroniclingamerica/lccn/sn86071197/1897-12-05/ed-1/seq-36; S. W. Stanfield, "The League of American Sportsmen Report of the Texas Division," *Recreation* 21, no. 2 (1904): 182.

14. Caspar Whitney, "The Sportsman's Viewpoint," *Outing* 41, no. 6 (Mar. 1903): 764.

15. *Dallas Morning News*, Jan. 22, 1987; *Galveston Daily News*, Jan. 18, 1901.

16. Harold C. Bryant, "Survey of the Breeding Grounds of Ducks in California in 1914," *The Condor* 16, no. 1 (1914): 233; Ray Osborne, "Four-Legged Duck Blinds Are Banned," *Dallas Morning News*, Aug. 24, 1941.

17. Calvin Dill Wilson, "The Ducks of the Chesapeake," *Lippincott's Monthly Magazine* 55 (1895): 84.

18. H. L. Green, ed., "Editorial Department," *Free Thought Magazine* 14 (1896): 342; Harry M. Walsh, *The Outlaw Gunner* (Cambridge, MD: Tidewater Publishers, 1971), 34; Calvin Dill Wilson, "The Ducks of the Chesapeake," *Lippincott's Monthly Magazine* 55 (1895): 84.

19. Stephen M. Miller, *Early American Waterfowling, 1700s–1930* (Chicago: Winchester Press, 1986), 162; *San Antonio Daily Light*, May 22, 1886.

20. Hamilton W. Gibson, "Traps for Feathered Game," *Camp Life in the Woods and the Tricks of Trapping and Trap Making* (New York: Harper and Bros., 1881), 66–99.

21. *Baltimore American*, Oct. 29, 1887; *Woodland* (California) *Daily Democrat*, Dec. 4, 1903; *Galveston Daily News*, Oct. 1, 1893; H. P. N. Gammel, comp., *The Laws of Texas: Supplement Volume to the Original Ten Volumes, 1822–1897*, Vol. 12 (Austin: Von Boeckmann-Jones Co., 1904), 223, The Portal to Texas History, University of North Texas Libraries, http://texashistory.unt.edu/ark:/67531/metapth6695/.

22. *Oakland Tribune*, Jan. 27, 1903.

23. Robin W. Doughty, *Wildlife and Man in Texas: Environmental Change and Conservation* (College Station: Texas A&M University Press, 1983), 115.

24. *Galveston Daily News*, Nov. 20, 1876; Dec. 5, 1879; Oct. 26, 1881; Nov. 7, 1891; William Temple Hornady, *Our Vanishing Wildlife* (New York: Clark and Fritts, 1913), 9; "Carolina Parakeet," Conservation, All About Birds, Cornell Lab of Ornithology, http://www.birds.cornell.edu/AllAboutBirds/conservation/extinctions/carolina_parakeet.

25. Forbush, *History of the Game Birds*, 422; *Big Spring Herald*, Mar. 21, 1976; Frank Moore Colby, ed., *The New International Year Book* (New York: Dodd, Mead and Co., 1915), 473.

26. "The Snowy Egret," *Birds—A Monthly Serial* 2, no. 1 (1897): 39; T. S. Palmer, "A Review of Economic Ornithology in the United States," *Yearbook of the United States Department of Agriculture, 1899* (Washington, DC: Govt. Printing Office, 1900), 273; Frederic William Simonds, *The Geography of Texas* (Boston: Athenaeum Press, 1905), 71.

27. *Dallas Morning News*, Nov. 27, 1903; Francis H. Kortright, *The Ducks, Geese and Swans of North America* (Washington, DC: American Wildlife Institute, 1943), 224–25; John K. Strecker Jr., "The Birds of Texas," *Baylor University Bulletin* 15, no. 1 (1912): 13.

28. T. S. Palmer, *Chronology and Index of the More Important Events in American Game Protection, 1776–1911*, US Dept. of Agriculture Biological Survey Bulletin no. 41 (Washington, DC: Govt. Printing Office, 1912), 20–1; T. S. Palmer, *Legislation for the Protection of Birds Other Than Game Birds*, US Dept. of Agriculture Division of Biological Survey Bulletin no. 12 (Washington, DC: Govt. Printing Office, 1900), 11.

29. Palmer, "Review of Economic Ornithology," , 259–92; Palmer, *Chronology and Index*, 22–46.

30. Palmer, *Chronology and Index*, 22–46; Clinton Hart Merriam, *Directory of Officials and Organizations Concerned with the Protection of Birds and Game, 1909*, US Dept. of Agriculture, Bureau of Biological Survey, Circular no. 70 (Washington, DC: Bureau of Biological Survey, 1909), 4.

31. T. S. Palmer, "Lest We Forget," *Bulletin of the American Game Protective Association* 14, no. 1 (1925): 11; John B. Burnham, "The Old Era—and the New," ibid., 13.

32. Palmer, *Legislation for the Protection of Birds*, 17–22; Frank Miller, "Louisiana Audubon Society State Report," *Bird-Lore* 7, no. 2 (1906): 259; *Dallas Morning News*, Oct. 5, 1891.

33. Palmer, *Legislation for the Protection of Birds*, 14–20; Marvyn Davis, "Texas Audubon Society State Report," *Bird-Lore* 7, no. 2 (1906): 273; Forbush, *History of the Game Birds*, 515.

34. Palmer, "Review of Economic Ornithology," 283; Palmer, "Lest We Forget," 12.

35. Palmer, *Legislation for the Protection of Birds*, 167; Palmer, "Lest We Forget," 12.

36. Doughty, *Wildlife and Man in Texas*, 165; Palmer, *Legislation for the Protection of Birds*, 47, 167; Palmer, *Chronology and Index*, 30.

37. Palmer, *Chronology and Index*, 272; "Among the World's Workers," *World's Work* 12 (May–Oct., 1906): 8,137–38.

38. Rudolph Rosen, "The North American Model of Wildlife Conservation: A Century of Species and Habitat Management in America," presented at the Environmental Studies Colloquium, Whittier College, Whittier, CA, Mar. 17, 2010, 1–8; Palmer, "Lest We Forget," 12; Tober, *Who Owns the Wildlife?* 189; Harold Howland, *Theodore Roosevelt and His Times*, Chronicles of America Series, Vol. 47 (New Haven: Yale University Press, 1921), 130.

39. Palmer, *Chronology and Index*, 26–38.

40. Palmer, *Legislation for the Protection of Birds*, 44; *Hamilton* (Ohio) *Republican-News,* Nov. 1, 1898; *Washington Post,* May 7, 1907.

41. Rosen, "North American Model of Wildlife Conservation," 1–8; Jeff Churan, pers. comm., Mar. 16, 2012; Larry West, "What was the first national wildlife refuge in the United States?" Environmental Issues, About.com, http://environment.about.com/od/biodiversityconservation/f/What-Was-The-First-National-Wildlife-Refuge-In-The-United-States.htm.

42. *Special Laws of the Eighth Legislature, Convened Nov. 7th, 1859* (Austin: John Marshall and Co., 1860), 80; Palmer, *Chronology and Index*, 14.

43. *Galveston Daily News,* Nov. 16, 1876.

44. Stanley D. Castro, "Guessaz, Oscar Charles," *Handbook of Texas Online,* http://www.tshaonline.org/handbook/online/articles/fgu15; *Galveston Daily News,* May 5, 1891; Apr. 19, 1896; *Dallas Morning News,* Jan. 22, 1887.

45. Stanley D. Castro, "Davis, Mervyn Bathurst," *Handbook of Texas Online,* http://www.tshaonline.org/handbook/online/articles/DD/fda6o.html.

46. *Galveston Daily News,* Feb. 19, 1879; June 4, 1880; Apr. 14, 1881; Feb. 13, 1889; *San Saba News,* Apr. 8, 1882.

47. Palmer, *Legislation for the Protection of Birds,* 11–81; Doughty, *Wildlife and Man in Texas,* 165–70; Murphy Givens, "Feather Merchants," radio column, *Corpus Christi Caller Times,* Nov. 21, 2003, http://www.caller.com/news/2003/nov/21/murphy-givens-radio-column-for-november-21-2003/; *Galveston Daily News,* Mar. 15, 1891; Nov. 3, 1901; *Dallas Morning News,* Jan. 6, 1903; *San Antonio Daily Light,* Sept. 15, 1895.

48. *San Antonio Daily Light,* May 30, 1895; *Galveston Daily News,* Jan. 23, Feb. 13, 1893.

49. *San Antonio Daily Light,* June 30, 1895.

50. Ibid.; *Dallas Morning News,* Jan. 22, 1897; *San Antonio Light,* June 21, 1896.

51. H. P. N. Gammel, comp., *The Laws of Texas, 1822–1897* (hereafter cited as *Gammel's Laws of Texas*), Vol. 10 (Austin: Gammel Book Co., 1898), 1268, The Portal to Texas History, University of North Texas Libraries, http://texashistory.unt.edu/permalink/meta-pth-6733; *Dallas Morning News,* Jan. 22, 1897; *San Antonio Daily Light,* Sept. 13, 1896; *Galveston Daily News,* Dec. 30, 1896; *Houston Daily Post,* Jan. 25, 1897.

52. *Gammel's Laws of Texas,* Vol. 10, 1268; *Galveston Daily News,* May 21, 1897; *Dallas Morning News,* Oct. 4, 1897.

53. *Galveston Daily News,* Apr. 16, 1899.

54. Rosen, "The North American Model of Wildlife Conservation," 1–8; Gilbert T. Pearson, "Our Bird Treaty with Canada," Proceedings of the 27th Convention of the International Association of Game, Fish, and Conservation Commissioners (N.p.: The Association, 1935), 1–11.

55. Palmer, *Legislation for the Protection of Birds,* 49–53; *Dallas Morning News,* Dec. 1, 1920.

56. *Galveston Daily News,* Nov. 12, 1905; Palmer, *Legislation for the Protection of Birds,* 167; Doughty, *Wildlife and Man in Texas,* 166; "Report of Societies—Two New Audubon Societies," *Bird Lore* 1, no. 3 (1899): 103; "Report of Societies—Death of Miss Seixas," *Bird Lore* 2, no. 5 (1900): 166.

57. *Galveston Daily News,* Feb. 26, Nov. 11, 1901; *Dallas Morning News,* Apr. 20, 1901.

58. *Dallas Morning News,* Jan. 6, 1903; *Fort Worth Telegram,* Jan. 15, 1905; *Galveston Daily News,* Nov. 26, 1906.

59. Palmer, *Legislation for the Protection of Birds,* 30; Doughty, *Wildlife and Man in Texas,* 167; *Gammel's Laws of Texas: Supplement,* Vol. 12 (1904), 222–25.

60. *Gammel's Laws of Texas: Supplement,* Vol. 12 (1904), 223.

61. *Dallas Morning News,* Jan. 6, 1903; Castro, "Guessaz, Oscar Charles," *Handbook of Texas Online*; *Victoria Advocate,* June 20, 1903.

62. *Brownsville Daily Herald,* June 18, 1905; *Victoria Daily Advocate,* Nov. 22, 1905; *Galveston Daily News,* Dec. 10, 1903.

63. *San Antonio Gazette,* Jan. 5, 1905; *Dallas Morning News,* Mar. 12, 1906; *Galveston Daily News,* Sept. 16, 1928.

64. *Dallas Morning News,* June 28, 1905; Stanley D. Castro, "Attwater, Henry Philemon," *Handbook of Texas Online,* http://www.tshaonline.org/handbook/online/articles/AA/fat7.html.

65. *Dallas Morning News,* June 28, 1905.

66. *Galveston Daily News,* Mar. 27, Aug. 31, Sept 18, 1907; *Gammel's Laws of Texas: Supplement,* Vol. 13 (1907), 255–81; *Dallas Morning News,* Oct. 5, 1907.

67. Frank Moore Colby, ed., *The New International Year Book: A Compendium of the World's Progress for the Year 1909* (New York: Dodd, Mead and Co., 1910), 271.

68. *Victoria Advocate,* Nov. 14, 24, 1908; *Galveston Daily News,* Nov. 22, 1908; *Port Arthur Evening News,* Jan. 15, 1909.

69. *Galveston Daily News,* Nov. 19, 26, 1908; Jan. 21, 1909; July 31, 1910; *Weimar (Texas) Mercury,* Jan. 29, 1909.

70. Pearson, "Our Bird Treaty with Canada," 1–11.

71. "A Guide to the Laws and Treaties of the United States for Protecting Migratory Birds," Migratory Bird Program, US Fish and Wildlife Service, http://www.fws.gov/migratorybirds/RegulationsPolicies/treatlaw.html; *Galveston Daily News,* Sept. 14, 1913; Pearson, "Our Bird Treaty with Canada," 1–11.

72. Capooth, *Waterfowling America,* Vol. 2, 51; "A Guide to the Laws and Treaties of the United States for Protecting Migratory Birds"; *Galveston Daily News,* Sept. 14, 1913.

73. "A Guide to the Laws and Treaties of the United States for Protecting Migratory Birds"; Doughty, *Wildlife and Man in Texas,* 170; Pearson, "Our Bird Treaty with Canada," 1–11.

74. Castro, "Attwater, Henry Philemon," *Handbook of Texas Online*; H. P. Attwater, "Relation of Birds to the Farmer," *Houston Daily Post,* July 28, 1902, Chronicling America, Library of Congress and National Endowment for the Humanities, http://chroniclingamerica.loc.gov/lccn/sn86071197/1902-07-28/ed-1/seq-3/.

75. *Galveston Daily News,* Aug. 17, 1913.

CHAPTER 6

1. Early History of Fish Commission and Game, Fish and Oyster Commission, unpublished, courtesy Texas Parks and Wildlife Department; *Galveston Daily News,* Sept. 26, 1895; June 27, 1897.

2. Mike Bradshaw, *Texas Game Warden Chronicles* (Carrizo Springs, TX: Mesquite Bean Press, 2009), 6–8; *Dallas Morning News,* Sept. 5, 1897.

3. *Galveston Daily News,* Mar. 13, 1885; Sept. 23, 1892; Nov. 10, 11, 1905; Dec. 21, 1906; Oct. 4, 1908; *San Antonio Daily Light,* May 16, 1894; June 30, 1895; Oct. 15, 1905; *Dallas Morning News,* Sept. 5, 1897.

4. *Dallas Morning News,* Oct. 5, 1907; Sept. 22, 1909; H. P. N. Gammel, comp., *The Laws of Texas: Supplement Volume to the Original Ten Volumes, 1822–1897* (hereafter cited as *Gammel's Laws of Texas: Supplement*), Vol. 13 (Austin: Gammel's Book Store, 1907): 254–55, http://texashistory.unt.edu/ark:/67531/metapth6719/.

5. *Dallas Morning News,* Apr. 18, 1903; *Fort Worth Telegram,* Mar. 18, 1907; *Galveston Daily News,* Oct. 6, 1907.

6. *Dallas Morning News,* Oct. 5, 1907; Bradshaw, *Texas Game Warden Chronicles,* 8; *Fort Worth Telegram,* Aug. 18, 1907; *Galveston Daily News,* Sept. 10, 1907.

7. Bradshaw, *Texas Game Warden Chronicles,* 313; *Galveston Daily News,* July 25, 1897; *Dallas Morning News,* May 21, 1912.

8. *Galveston Daily News,* Dec. 2, 1908; Dec. 3, 1909; Frank M. Chapman, ed., *Bird Lore* 9, no. 1 (1907): 56.

9. *Galveston Daily News,* Feb. 9, 1911.

10. Ibid.; *Dallas Morning News,* Feb. 9, 1911.

11. William G. Sterrett, *Report of the Game, Fish, and Oyster Commission of Texas for the Period Ending August 31, 1912* (Austin: Austin Printing Co., 1912); *Galveston Daily News,* July 31, 1912; Nov. 20, 1913.

12. Bradshaw, *Texas Game Warden Chronicles,* 9; *Galveston Daily News,* Jan. 21, 1913.

13. *San Antonio Evening News,* Nov. 18, 1920; *San Antonio Light,* Oct. 31, 1916; *Mexia Evening News,* Dec. 18, 1922.

14. *Dallas Morning News,* Nov. 12, 1903; *Dallas Morning News,* Nov. 15, 1903; *Galveston Daily News,* Nov. 6, 1904.

15. Judith Linsley, pers. comm., May 1, 2009; Bill Blair, pers. comm., May 9, 2009; Rollin H. Baker, *Tom Waddell, Texas Game Warden* (Hallettsville, TX: Old Homestead Publishing Co., 2007), 68; *Galveston Daily News,* Dec. 6, 1912.

16. Harry M. Walsh, *The Outlaw Gunner* (Cambridge, MD: Tidewater Publishers, 1971), 1, 45.

17. J. C. Melcher interview, Mar. 19, 2009, Port Lavaca, TX; Jim Warren interview, Mar., 19, 2010, Hockley, TX.

18. *Galveston Daily News,* Dec. 5, 1906.

19. Ibid., Mar. 27, 1907; Bradshaw, *Texas Game Warden Chronicles,* 8; *Galveston Daily News,* Sept. 18, Oct. 26, 1907.

20. *San Antonio Daily Express,* Dec. 16, 1908; *Victoria Advocate,* Dec. 5, 1908.

21. Byrd Minter Jr., pers. comm., Feb. 8, 2011.

22. *Forest and Stream* 66, no. 14 (1906): 548.

23. *Galveston Daily News,* Jan. 6, 1910; Edward H. Forbush, *History of the Game Birds, Wild-Fowl, and Shore Birds of Massachusetts and Adjacent States* (Boston: Wright and Potter Printing, 1912), 513; Frank M. Chapman, ed., *Bird Lore* 9, no. 1 (1907): 56–57.

24. *Wichita Daily Times,* Dec. 8, 1911; *San Antonio Light,* Dec. 12, 1911; *Galveston Daily News,* Nov. 14, Dec. 22, 1912; Feb. 20, 1913.

25. *San Antonio Express,* Apr. 30, 1950; *Mexia Evening News,* Dec. 18, 1922; *Dallas Morning News,* May 30, Dec. 17, 1919; *San Antonio Evening News,* June 19, 1920; *Lubbock Avalanche,* Mar. 20, 1919.

26. *Fort Worth Telegram,* Jan. 10, 1904; *Galveston Daily News,* Dec. 21, 1906; Nov. 23, 1907; Sept 16, 1928.

27. *Victoria Advocate,* Nov. 18, 1911; *Galveston Daily News,* Dec. 3, 1909; Nov. 20, 1912.

28. *Brownsville Herald,* Oct. 13, 1914; *Victoria Daily Advocate,* Oct. 14, 1914; *Galveston Daily News,* Jan. 15, 1920; Feb. 16, 1921.

29. *Dallas Morning News,* Nov. 3, 1901; *Galveston Daily News,* Dec. 3, 1905.

30. *Colorado Citizen,* Nov. 15, 1928; Baker, *Tom Waddell,* 65; Robin W. Doughty, *Wildlife and Man in Texas: Environmental Change and Conservation* (College Station: Texas A&M University Press, 1983), 177.

31. *Galveston Daily News,* Jan. 7, 1913; Apr. 17, June 16, 1925; Oct. 23, 1930.

32. J. R. Jefferson, "Annual Report of the Game, Fish, and Oyster Commission of Texas for the Fiscal Year Ending August 31, 1920" (Austin: Von Boeckmann-Jones Co., 1921), 6.

33. Alex Wolff interview, June 28, 2008, Houston, TX; James Smock, pers. comm., Jan. 22, 2009.

34. Randy Chatagnier, pers. comm., Mar. 14, 2009.

35. Lillian Chatagnier Richards interview, Mar. 27, 2009, Port Neches, TX.

36. Evelyn Standley, untitled and unpublished manuscript, 1992, private collection of John Kemp.

37. Evelyn Standley interview, July 5, 2012, Anahuac, TX, courtesy John Kemp.

38. Louis Schorlemmer interview, Apr. 1, 2010, Eagle Lake, TX.

39. Rick Pratt interview, Sept. 24, 2009, Port Aransas, TX.

40. Billy Shika interview, Jan. 31, 2010, Corpus Christi, TX; "Ducks Unlimited Institute for Wetland and Waterfowl Research Scholarship," http://www.ducks.ca/assets/2012/06/fellowship11.pdf.

41. Fred Dahmer oral history by David Todd, June 7, 1997, Uncertain, TX, Conservation History Association of Texas, Texas Legacy Project, Reel No. 1010; *Galveston Daily News,* June 2, 1912; William Sterrett, *Report of the Game, Fish, and Oyster Commission of Texas for the Period Ending August 31, 1914* (Austin: E. L. Steck Press, 1914), 27; Wyatt Moore oral history by Thad Sitton, Feb. 2, 1983, Tape No. 150, File No. 150-1, James Gilliam Gee Library, Texas A&M University–Commerce.

42. Wyatt Moore oral history by Thad Sitton; Thad Sitton and James H. Conrad, eds., *Every Sun That Rises: Wyatt Moore of Caddo Lake* (Austin: University of Texas Press, 1985), 104.

43. Wyatt Moore oral history by Thad Sitton.

44. Joel Kirkpatrick, "Morning Cup," *Galveston Daily News,* Mar. 26, 1984.

45. Ray Osborne, "Four-Legged Duck Blinds Are Banned," *Dallas Morning News,* Aug. 24, 1941; Lyle Jordan narratives, 2001, private collection of Doug Pike.

46. Bill Womack interview, Nov. 4, 2009, West Columbia, TX.

47. J. C. Melcher interview, Mar. 19, 2009, Port Lavaca, TX; Steve Fisher interview, Nov. 18, 2009, Port Lavaca, TX.

48. Johnny Atwood interview, Apr. 3, 2009, Rockport, TX; Rick Pratt, pers. comms., Oct. 2, 2009; Jan. 23, 2012.

49. Forrest West, pers. comm., Sept. 2, 2012.

50. *San Antonio Light,* Feb. 23, 1938; *Dallas Morning News,* Feb. 23, Mar. 15, 1938.

51. Bob Brister and Ben East, "Texas Man Trap," *Outdoor Life,* December 1956, 79; *Corpus Christi Times,* Apr. 18, 1956.

52. *Galveston Daily News,* Sept. 19, 1956; Ed Zern and Tom Lineaweaver, "The Biggest U.S. Raid against Market Hunting Bags 53 Texans," *Sports Illustrated,* April 30, 1956, 46, SI Vault, The Outdoor Week, http://vault.sportsillustrated.cnn.com/vault/article/magazine/MAG1130787/index.htm; Bob Brister and Ben East, "Texas Man Trap," *Outdoor Life,* December 1956, 48.

53. Brister and East, "Texas Man Trap," 48; *Corpus Christi Caller-Times,* Apr. 18, 22, 1956.

54. Freddie Abshier interview, Anahuac, TX, June 13, 2008.

55. Brister, and East, "Texas Man Trap," 48, 77–80; *Galveston Daily News,* Apr. 19, 1956.

56. *Corpus Christi Caller-Times,* Apr. 18, 1956; Brister and East, "Texas Man Trap," 79.

57. Brister and East, "Texas Man Trap," 51.

58. Zern, and Lineaweaver, "The Biggest U.S. Raid."

59. *Corpus Christi Caller-Times,* Apr. 22, 1956; Zern, and Lineaweaver, "An SI Special"; *Corpus Christi Caller-Times,* Apr. 22, 1956.

60. Brister, and East, "Texas Man Trap," 80; *Galveston Daily News,* Sept. 12, 1956.

61. *Galveston Daily News,* Apr. 19, 1956; *Corpus Christi Caller-Times,* Sept. 13, 1956; Pete Flores, pers. comm., Sept. 28, 2011; Brister, and East, "Texas Man Trap," 51; *Galveston Daily News,* May 3, 1928; Oct. 19, 1956; Jan. 2, 1957; Oct 26, 1958.

62. *Mexia Daily News,* May 22, 1956; *Abilene Reporter-News,* May 22, 1956; Lyle Jordan, pers. comm., May 1, 2010.

63. Brister, and East, "Texas Man Trap," 51, 80; *Corpus Christi Caller-Times,* Apr. 18, 1956; *Galveston Daily News,* Apr. 28, 1956; Sylvia Lamb interview, Aug. 8, 2008, Wallisville, TX.

64. Don Holloway to Royce A. Strickland, pers. comm.; Kendon L. Clark, "Memoirs, or, Fulfilling My Obligation," unpublished, 77, courtesy Kendon L. Clark.

65. Clark, "Memoirs," 77–78; Chester Rogers, [Title illegible], *Houston Chronicle Magazine,* Oct. 27, 1946, Wallisville Heritage Center collection; *Deer Park Progress,* Nov. 18, 1981.

66. *Corpus Christi Caller-Times,* Apr. 18, Sept. 13, 1956.

67. Kendon L. Clark, pers. comm., Jan. 30, 2010.

68. Joe Whitehead interview, June 14, 2008, Smith Point, TX; Anonymous.

69. Brister and East, "Texas Man Trap," 51; Charles Stutzenbaker interview, Oct. 24, 2008, Port Arthur, TX.

CHAPTER 7

1. Greg Keddy interview, Aug. 9, 2008, High Island, TX; Eugene Linden, "Wildlife Cops on a Bust," *Time,* Feb. 20, 1989, 18; Texas Waterfowl Investigation Briefing Material—Branch of Special Operations, Dec. 15, 1988, courtesy Shannon Tompkins; Joe Doggett, "Rogue Guides an Exception, Not Rule," *Houston Chronicle,* Dec. 15, 1988.

2. Gene Campbell interview, May 2, 2009, Anahuac, TX; Jamie Spears interview, June 22, 2008, Aransas Pass, TX.

3. Clyde "Boots" Faggard, pers. comm., Apr. 18, 2009; Grand jury indictment, *United States of America vs. Charles Lane Plauche,* Criminal Case No. B-88-104-CR, US District Court, Eastern District of Texas, Beaumont Division; Miscellaneous US Fish and Wildlife Service records, courtesy Shannon Tompkins.

4. Charles R. "Doc" McCallum, unpublished notes to author, Aug. 1 to 21, 2009; O. D. LaBove to President Richard Nixon, Mar. 2, 1971, collection of Charles R. "Doc" McCallum; J. P. Linduska, Associate Director, US Fish and Wildlife Service, to O. D. LaBove, Mar. 23, 1971.

5. *Port Arthur News,* Jan. 19, 1975; Eugene Linden, "Wildlife Cops on a Bust," *Time,* Feb. 20, 1989, 18; Miscellaneous USFWS records, courtesy Shannon Tompkins.

6. Bob Brister, "Story of Sting Isn't Over Yet," *Houston Chronicle,* Dec. 18, 1988; Texas Waterfowl Investigation Briefing Material—Branch of Special Operations, Dec. 15, 1988, courtesy Shannon Tompkins.

7. Greg Keddy interview, Aug. 9, 2008, High Island, TX; Jamie Spears interview, June 22, 2008, Aransas Pass, TX; Doug Bird interview, Feb. 19, 2010, Corpus Christi, TX; Gene Campbell interview, May 2, 2009, Anahuac, TX; Billy Sheka interview, Feb. 19, 2010, Corpus Christi, TX; Ralph Leggett interview, May 2, 2009, Anahuac, TX; Forrest West, pers. comm., Sept. 7, 2008; James Fox interview, Oct. 17, 2008, Rockport, TX.

8. *Beaumont Enterprise,* May 21, 1989.

INDEX

Abadie, John M., 79
Abozo, Joe, 83
Abshier, Freddie, 137
acorns (mast), 18, 107
Adams Express Company, 45, 61
African American hunters and workers, 4, 25, 26
agriculture and game, 4, 50–51, 116, 132
alcohol, baiting with, 106
Alhambra House, 34
alligators, 16, 18, 66
Alvord, Menry E., 47
Ambolt, Herman E., 112
American Angler, 78
American Game Protective and Propagation Association, 110, 119
American Hotel, 30
American Ornithologists' Union (AOU), 110, 115
ammunition, historical overview, 22, 23
See also firearms
Anahuac National Wildlife Refuge, 144
Anderson, William, 99
Antarctic Refrigerator Market, 85
Aransas, 80
Aransas Bay, 10, 31, 74–76

Aransas Bay Fish, Oyster and Game Depot, 82
Aransas Harbor Terminal Railroad, 76
Aransas Pass, 14–15, 74, 76, 127
A. R. Hillier Packing Company, 71
Armstrong, Clarence, 75
Armstrong, Ed, 46
Armstrong, Frank B., 99
Armstrong, William, 75, 123
Army, US, 34
arrests under game protection laws, 120, 127, 128, 129, 130, 136, 138–41, 143–45
artists, wildlife, 38
Arto, John and son, 67
Artusy, Eugene, 67
Ashland Hotel, 79
Atlantic coast market hunting
    canvasbacks, 88–89
    and decline of species, 101
    game laws, 108
    historical overview, 4, 36–37
    punt guns, 52–53
    and railroad development, 40
    restaurants, game market for, 40
    sink boxes, 53–55
See also individual states/cities

Attwater, Henry Philemon, 115, 116, 117–18, 120
Atwood, Johnny, 135
Audubon, John James, 37, 38
Audubon Society, Texas, 115, 116
    See also National Association of Audubon Societies (NAAS)
Austin, Texas, 35, 85
Austin's (Stephen F.) colony, 4, 9, 15, 16–17, 27, 29–30

Back Bay (Virginia), 88, 104
Baffin Bay, 11
bag limits, 111, 118, *124*
Bailey, Florence Merriam, 99
baiting of fowl, 6, 106, 144
Balcones Escarpment, 9
Baltimore Sun, 90
barrels, packing, 5, 27, 46, 74
bartering system, 35
Bauer, Frank, 123
Beaumont, Texas, *42*, 50, 56–57, 129
Belbaze, J. L., 60
Bell, Ben U., 84
Bellis's Market, 82
Berry brothers, 78
Berwick, Luther and Walter, 139, 141

Big Flats, 95
big guns, 108
  See also punt guns; swivel guns
Big Prairie, 10
Biological Survey, US. See Bureau of Biological Survey, US
Black, Richard, 139
black brant, 20
"black legged" ducks, 36
black powder guns, 22
Bladeone, Bard, 119
blizzards, 60
Bludworth, Jim and Jed, 76
bluebills (scaup), 20, 104
blue geese, 20
bluewing teal. See teal
boats
  buy boats, 47, 49
  and hunting strategies, 24–25
  mosquito fleet, 59–60, 128
  schooners, 24–25, 75, 79–80
  steamships, 29, 41, 61, 70, 80
  transporting game to markets, 28–29
bobolinks, 109
bobwhite quail. See quail
Bolivar Peninsula, 59, 65, 133
Bolivar Plantation, 17
Bond and Company, 82
Bond and Whitcomb Commission Company, 91
"bonnet martyr," 6, 99
Boone, M. H., *139*
Boone and Crockett Club, 110
Boortz, Johnny, 138, 140, 141
"bootleg hunting," 132
Boyle, James S. and David, 45
Brazoria, Texas, 29
Brazoria County, 4, 21, 27, 69–70
Brazos River and floodplain, 9, 14, 30, 69–70
Breitz, E. A., 62
Brenham, TX, 85
Brewster, C. E., 123, 128
Briers, Joe, 140
Briggs, Robert Lee, 78

Brister, Bob, 137, 138, 141, 144
Broussard, J. J., 129
Brower House, 30
Browning firearms, 51–52
Brownsville, Texas, 34, 43–44, 79–81, 129
Brownsville Daily Herald, 43
Brundrett, Ancel, 135
Brundrett, Jeb, 135
Bryant, Charles, 119
Buffalo Bayou, 14, 32
Buffalo Bayou, Brazos and Colorado Railroad, 68
buffleheads, 19, 20, 41
bull-hunting, 105
  See also steers/oxen, hunting over
Bureau of Biological Survey, US, 125, 136
burning (clearing), 20
Burridge, Charles, 70
butterballs, 41
buy boats, 47, 49
Byrd, Mark, 111

Caddo Lake, 34–35, 84–85, 133
Cade, Charles T., 123
Cajuns, 40, 56
Calhoun County, 73
  See also Indianola, Texas; Matagorda Bay/Island; Port Lavaca, Texas
Calhoun County News, 116
California, 40–41, 104, 106, 108
Campbell, Gene, 143, 144
Campbell, J. W., 128
Campeche outpost, 16
Canada, treaty with, 120
Canada geese, 20, 24, 43
Canadian (River) Sportsmen's Club, 122
Canfield, A. L., 46
canning industry, 80–81
canvasbacks
  Atlantic market and hunting grounds, 88–89
  culinary demand for, 5, 87–88
  diet and habitat overview, 19–20, 88

Galveston Bay area highlights, 61–63
  hunting highlights, 13, 14, 95
  Texas hunting grounds, 90–96
  Texas market, 89–90
  wildfowl trade/distribution highlights, 96
Capitol Hotel, 67
Caplan, John, 67
Capooth, Wayne, 66, 91, 103, 104
Cartwright, Gary, 16
Casimir House, 34
Cates, W. T., 33
cattle industry, 44, 62, 75
celery, wild, 20, 88, 89, 95
Central Flyway, 9
Central Market (Houston), 66–67
chain of lakes, Chambers county, 62, 91–95
Chambers County, 17, 62, 91–95, 136–41
Chambers Encyclopedia, 36
Chapman, Frank, 111
Charles Demack and Company, 127
Charles Fowler, 89
Charlie's Chop House, 70
Chatagnier family, 130, 131
Chesapeake Bay, 53–54, 88, 89–90, 102, 104, 106
Chicago markets, 37, 40, 91, 104, 108–9
China Grove Plantation, 14
Christopher, Garth, 138
City Market (Dallas), 83
Civil War, 4, 5, 39
Clapper, Russell, 21
Clark, Kendon, 140–41
Clark, Manson, 140–41
Clarkson, Frank, 138, *139*
Clear Lake, 13, 21, 62
Clopper, J. C., 13
closed season laws, 108, 111, 114
"clubbing" birds, 25–26
Coastal Bend, 10–11, **12**, 95, 96
Coastal Plains, 9–13, 13–15
Cobolini, Louis, 60, 75, 80, 96

Colby's Café, 67
cold storage, 5, 60, 61
collector's markets, 5, 97, 99, 100
Colonial Dining Room, 35
Colorado, 106
Colorado County. *See* Eagle Lake area
Colorado River, 4, 9, 29, 85
    See also Matagorda Bay/Island
Colosia and Radanovich, 60
Comanche Indians, 30
commission hunters, 55, 70, 91–93, 102–3
commission merchants. *See* forwarding agencies
commodity reports, 42–43, *90*
competition
    crop destruction by waterfowl, 50–51
    Fisherman's Union, 75
    hawkers *vs.* markets, 32–33, 79
    sportsmen *vs.* market hunters, 6, 92, 102, 111–19
    wild fowl *vs.* domestic foragers, 18
    wild game market *vs.* farm-raised domestic market, 44
    See also crop destruction by waterfowl
Conally, Ben C., 139–40
conservation movement, 6, 101, 109–11, 112
Constantine, Nic, 85
contract hunters. *See* commission hunters
Copano Bay, 10, 31, 74–76
Cora Dean, 59–60, 66
Cordier, Albert E., 67
corn, baiting with, 106
corn crops, *50*
"cornfield ducks," 20
Corpus Christi Bay area
    ecology and geomorphology of, 10
    hunting highlights, 15, 132–33
    marketplace/restaurant profile, 34
    volume of exports from, 104–5
    wildfowl trade/distribution highlights, 77–79

Corpus Christi Caller, 77
Corpus Christi Hotel, 34
Corpus Christi Oyster, Fish, and Game Company, 77, 80
Corpus Reef Fish and Oyster Company, 77
cotton culture, 4
county game laws, 101
Cox, J. D., 129
Crain, W. H., 72
cranes, 14, 21, 23–24, 99, 120, 128
Crenshaw, James A., 59
crop destruction by waterfowl, 50–51
Cross, Bob, *139*
crude oil killing method, 106–7
curlews, 4, 5, 21, 23, 52, 107, 120
Currituck Sound, 88–89, 102–3, 104

Dahmer, Fred, 133
Dallas, Texas markets, 35, 68, 83–84, 126, 136
Dallas Morning News, 39, 83, 84, 103, 113, 114, 118
David, J. M., 130
Davis, Mervyn Bathhurst, 111–12, 115, 116, 117–18, 120
dead decoys, 26
deadfall traps, 4
declines in waterfowl, 6, 99–100, 101, 102–3, 103–5, 105–7
decoys, hunting over, 26–27, 52, 53–55
Decrow's Point, 14, 30, 36
Delaware, 108
Demack, Charles, 128
de Vaca, Cabeza, 30
De Voe, Thomas F., 37
DeWitt's colony, 15, 30
Dickinson Bayou, 13
diet and habitat overview, 18–22
distribution. *See* shipping of game; wildfowl trade/distribution highlights
diving ducks, 5, 19–20
    See also canvasbacks
Dixon, Joe, 133
Dodd, J. C., 84

Dodge, Henry, 60
dollar ducks, 41
Dorsa, Frank, 83
Dorsa Fish, Oyster, and Produce Company, 83, *84*
Dorsett, William J., 75, 95
Doughty, James M., 75
Doughty, Robin, 99, 107, 129
Douglas, Mary, 79
doves, 4
dowitchers, 22
Dreyers, Lloyd, 132
drop shot, 22
duck policemen, 108, 110–11
ducks, diet and habitat overview, 18–20
Ducks Unlimited, 133
Duke, Holmes, 128
Dutcher, William, 110
dynamite in hunting, 133

Eagle Lake area, 10, 21, 64, 68, 85, 129
Eagle Lake Headlight, 129
East, Ben, 137, 138, 141
East Bay (Galveston Bay area), 62, 64, 90–91
East Coast market hunting. *See* Atlantic coast market hunting
East Texas, 15, 34
    See also Caddo Lake
ecology and geomorphology of Texas coast, 9–13
eelgrass, 88
Eggerst, Theo, 60
eggs (wildfowl), 5, 31, 97, 100, 112, 116
egrets, 5–6, 98–99, 107, 112
electricity, proliferation of, 66–67, 84
    See also ice for preservation; refrigeration
electronic recorders, 143
Elite Restaurant, 57, 82
Ellis, Bill, 132
Enabling Act of MBTA, 120
enforcement of game laws
    1956 sting, 136–41
    1988 sting, 143–45

enforcement of game laws (cont.)
    difficulties in, 108–9, 112–13, 119, 120, 129–30
    Great Depression profile, 130–33
    historical overview, 7
    increasing emphasis on, 110–11
    private associations, 122
    by railroads, 116, *117*, 124–25
    against restaurants, 128–29
    Terrell's Game Warden Act, 108–9, 118, 122
    See also laws, game protection; outlaw hunters; wardens, game
"English callers," 53
Epicurean Restaurant, 57
Eskimo curlews, 21, 107
European markets, 5, 89, 90
Exchange Restaurant, 85
exportation of game. *See* shipping of game
express shippers, 45
    See also forwarding agencies
extended magazines, 105

factory-loaded shotgun shells, 39, 51
Faggard, Boots, 143
Fannin, James, 4
fashion industry. *See* plumage market
fat/grease (cooking), 36, 100
feathers, 37
    as bride price, 35, 36
    for fly fishing, 107
    game laws, 116, 120
    quills, market for, 5, 100
    uses and prices, 36
    See also plumage market
federal game laws
    1956 sting, 136–41
    1988 sting, 143–45
    game wardens, 125
    historical overview, 6–7, 111, 115, 119–20
Federal Migratory Bird Act (FMBA) (1913), 6, 119–20
Fergusen, Jim, 140
"figure of four" traps, 4

fines paid for game violations, 122, 123, 140
firearms
    gun powder, 22, *23*, 51–52
    historical overview, 22
    in outlaw hunting, 132–33, 133–36
    pump guns, 51–52, 133, *134*
    punt guns, 6, 52–53, 105, 114, 134–36
    semiautomatic shotguns, 52, 105, 133
    swivel guns, 6, 52, 53, *54*, 103, 105, 114, 134–35
    technological advances in, 5, 39, 51–53
fire hunting, 108
fire pots, 26
Fish and Oyster Commission (FOC), Texas, 7, 121, 122
Fisher, Steve, 135
Fisherman's Union, 75, 79
fishing flies, feathers for, 107
Fishkill Landing, 88
Flack, Frank W., 18, 20, 24, 25
flavor of game birds (table appeal)
    canvasbacks, 87–88
    cranes, 21
    ducks, 19, 20, 36
    geese, 19, 20, 24
    pelicans, 100
    shorebirds, 21–22
    songbirds, 109
flickers, 109, 144
flies, nuisance of, 17
flintlocks, 22
floating market (Galveston), *48*, 57, *58*
floodwaters, importance to ecosystem, 12
Florida, 107, 111, 112
Flower of France, 99
FOC (Fish and Oyster Commission, Texas), 7, 121, 122
Follets Island, 30
Foree, Kenneth, 83
Forest and Stream, 91, 92, 94, 106, 110, 111

Forest McNeir of Texas (McNeir, F.), 92
Fort Brown, 34
Fort Worth, Texas, 35, 83–84, 136
forwarding agencies, 45, 60–61, 68, 82
    See also game merchants; shipping of game
Fox, James, 145
Frank Ford and Company, 70
Franks, Burrell, 16
Franks, Ike, 138, 141
Freeman, William "Bill," 139–40
fresh water, importance of in ecosystem, 12–13
Frontier Fish and Oyster Company, 81
Frontier Ice Works, 46
Frost, John Lighter (Sheriff), 94
Fuller, Tom C., 128, 129
Fulton, TX, 74, 75
Futch, Ed, 133
Futch, Jimmy, 132–33

gadwalls, 19, 41
Gaido, S. J./Gaido's Café, 130
Galbraith brothers, 133
gallinules, 22, 50
Galveston, Harrisburg, and San Antonio Railway, 60–61, 68
Galveston, Houston, and Henderson (GHH) Railroad Company, 60
Galveston, Texas
    buy boats, *49*
    decline of waterfowl, 105
    dependence on hunting, 4
    floating market, *48*
    game prices in, 42–43
    illegal markets in, 127–29
    marketplace/restaurant profile, 31–32
    origins of, 16
Galveston Bay/Island
    ecology and geomorphology of, 10
    hunting highlights, 13–14
    hunting laws, 111
    swans, abundance of, 21
    wildfowl trade/distribution highlights, 57–64

See also East Bay (Galveston Bay area)
Galveston Daily News, 36, 72, 76, 88, 94, 95, 112–13
Galveston Fish and Oyster Company, 60
Galveston Game Protection Association, 122
Galveston Game Protective League, 128
Galveston Ice House, 28
Galveston News, 119
Game, Fish, and Oyster Commission, Texas (GFOC), 105, 122–25, 133
game birds (other than waterfowl), 6, 29, 37–38, 39, 81, 101
   See also songbirds
game hawkers, 16, 32–33, 41, 79
   See also roadside marketing
game laws. *See* laws, game protection
game markets. *See* marketplaces
game merchants
   and commission hunters, 55
   Galveston Bay area, 60–61
   and game law enforcement, 127
   post–Civil War overview, 47–49
   See also forwarding agencies
game protective associations, 122
Game Warden Act (Terrell), 108–9, 118, 122
Garriga, Frank, 80
gasoline engines, 49
G. B. Marsan and Company, 60
Geeo, George L., 83
geese, diet and habitat overview, 20, 24
Gengler, Peter, 58
Gentry, Flavius, 74
Gentry Fish and Oyster House, *48*
geomorphology of Texas coastal plains, 9–13
GFOC (Texas Game, Fish, and Oyster Commission), 105, 122–25, 133
Gieselman, John M., 128
Gingham Inn, 136
Giozza, Frank, 57

Givens, Murphy, 43, 77
Givens, S. S., 30
Glen, John, 145
Globe House, 35, 82
Golden Crescent Oyster Company, 73
goldeneyes, 19, 20, 41
gold rush, 34
Goodfellow, Robert, 124, 129, 133
Good Housekeeping, 39
grackle skins, demand for, 100
Grand Central Hotel, 67
Grand City Hall and Market House (Houston), 66
grass plover, 22
gray brant, 20
gray ducks, 19, 41
gray geese, 20, 41, 43
Grayson, Tom, 35
Great Depression, 130–33
"great resorts" of canvasbacks, 88–89
greenheads/greenhead mallards, 18, 43, 82
Green Lake, 10
greenwing teal. *See* teal
Griggs, Billy, 91, 92, 94, 99
Grinnell, George Bird, 110
grouse. *See* prairie chickens
Guadalupe River and Bay, 35, *54*
Guessaz, Oscar Charles
   chain of lakes access issue, 92, 93
   game law activism, 111, 113, 114, 115, 116, 117–18
   and lead poisoning of birds, 94
Guggenheimer, Randolph, 40
Gulf, Western Texas, and Pacific Railway (GWTP), 71
Gulf City Co-Operative Manufacturing Association, 60
gunning lamps, 26, 108, 115
gun powder, 22, *23*, 51–52
guns. *See* firearms
Gus Zuercher, J. R. Scott and Company, 82

Haag and Auderer, 68
habitat destruction, 6, 101, 107

habitat profiles, 18–22
Hallock, Charles, 110
hammerless firearms, 51
Harbor Island (Chambers County), 55, 95–96
Hargraves, Sam Sr. and Jr., 138–39, 141
Harris and Morgan Steamship Line, 71
Harrisburg, Texas, 32
Harris County Fish and Game Protective Association, 129
Harris County Game Protective Association, 113
Harris County Sportsmen's Association, 122
Hart, Bill, 132
hats, feathers for. *See* plumage market
Haun, Goebl, and Company, 85
Havre de Grace, 103–4, 106
hawkers, game, 16, 32–33, 41, 79
   See also roadside marketing
Hawley's Refrigerator, 60
Haywood, John, 34–35
Heiman, Robert, 94
Henry and Joe's Restaurant, 57
heron plumes, 128
Hettie May, 80
Hewetson, James, 15, 30–31
High Island (Galveston County), 59, 64, 123, 127, 128, 136–41
H. N. Tanner and Company, 84
Hogg, James, 92, 93–94
Holder, Ed, 56
Holland, Jack, 55
Holley, Mary Austin, 17
hooks, baited, 106
Horatio, 70
Hornaday, William Temple, 104
Horner, Jack, 136
horses, hunting over/from, 23, 52
hotels, colonial Texas, 30
   See also restaurants, game market for
Hough, Emerson, 91, 94
House Bills in Texas game legislation, 111, 114, 118
Houston, Texas, 14, 32–33, 56, 66–69
   See also San Jacinto River

Houston and Texas Central Railroad (HTC), 68, 72
Houston Chronicle, 144
Houston Daily Post, 62, 76
Houston Gun Club, 122
Houston Ice House, 28
Houston Prairie, 10
Houston Telegraph and Texas Register, 13-14
Houstoun, Matilda, 4
H. Runge and Company, 33
Hubby, Turner, 114
Hudson River, 88
Hudspeth, Roy, 138
Huff's Hotel, 30
Hughes, Edwin, 64
Hughes, Lee, 84
Hughs, W. A., 64
hummingbird feathers, 98
A Hunter's Experiences in the Southern States of America (Flack), 18
hunting culture, overview, 126
hunting grounds of note
    canvasbacks, 88-89, 90-96
    Galveston Bay area, 61-64
    Laguna Madre area, 79
    San Antonio area, 81
    San Jacinto River/Houston, 68-69
    Trinity River delta, 65-66, 83
hunting methods/strategies
    and agriculture, 50-51
    historical overview, 6, 23-27
    outlaw hunters, 130-33
    questionable practices of market hunters, 105-7
    See also firearms
hunting syndicates, 88
huntsmen, definition, 3, 17
hurricanes, 16, 18, 60, 70, 72, 74, 95, 99, 115
Hynes Bay, 95, 102
Hynson, Henry, 60

ice for preservation
    historical overview, 5, 27-28, 30, 39
    ice-making, 45-46, 61, 69, 74, 81

Ida Mae, 59
illegal hunting. *See* outlaw hunters
Illinois, 104, 108-9
Indianola, Texas, 33-34, 70, 71-72
Indianola Courier, 33
Indianola Ice House, 28
Indianola Market House, 33
Indians, American, 16, 17, 27, 30
indoor markets, 42
insects, nuisance of, 16, 17
Institute for Wetland and Waterfowl Research, 133
International Association for the Protection of Game, 109-10
International-Great Northern Railroad Company, 61
Intracoastal Canal, 133

jackdaw skins, demand for, 100
Jackson Ranch, 63
Jamison, Joe, 70
Japan, 120
J. C. Crippe market, 85
J. D. White and Company, 60
Jefferson, J. R., 130
Jefferson, Texas, 34-35, 45
Jefferson County, 18, 52, 56, 143-45
J. I. Griffith, 49
Johnson, Charlie, 76
Johnson, Herman, 46, 64
Johnson, John J. "Jack," 52, 56-57
Johnson, Lewis Lowell, 56
Johnson, Peter, 27, 31
Johnson, Theodore "Charlie," 31
Johnson, Tiff, 80-81
Johnston, Albert Sidney, 14
Jordan, Henry, 36
J. R. Berry and Son, 84

Kahla, Barney Edward, 64
Kahla, Claud, 60
Kahla, Fred, 24, 64, 65
Kahla, Vernon, 138, 139
Kansas City markets and railroads, 56
Karankawa Indians, 16, 27
Keddy, Greg, 143

Keith Lake, 95
Kellogg, Mr., 70
Kenedy, Mifflin, 27, 34
Kennedy, William and Lee, 94
Kibbe, Isaac P., 121, 123
Kilber, A. L., 128
killdeer, 22
King, Richard, 34
"King of the Market Hunters," 103
Kinney, Henry L., 34
Kozick, J. A., 128
Krieble, Don, 139

Labadie's Wharf, 60
LaBove, O. D., 143-45
LaBove's Shooting Resort, 143-45
Lacey, John F., 115
Lacey Act (1900), 6, 115, 119, 144
Laens, John M., 57
Lafitte, Jean, 4, 16
LaFour, Emmet, 65
LaFour, Gerald "Buddy," 140
LaFour, Morgan, 140
Laguna Madre, 11, 27, 79-81
Lake Austin, 25
Lake Stephenson, 62, 88, 89, 91-95
Lake Surprise, 55, 62, 88, 91, 92-95
Lamb, Sylvia, 140
lamps, hunting with, 26, 108, 115
Lane, J. D., 52, 56
Lang, John H., 60, 68
Lang, P. A., 89
lanterns (lamps), hunting, 26, 108, 115
Laredo, TX, 85-86
La Salle (René-Robert Cavelier, Sieur de La Salle), 9
Lavaca, Texas, 14, 30
    See also Port Lavaca, Texas
Lavaca River and estuary, 9-10, 30
Lavaca Sea Breeze, 44
laws, game protection, 6-7, 108-11, 111-19
    See also federal game laws; state game laws
lead poisoning of birds, 94
League and Company, 57

League of American Sportsmen (LAS), 105, 110, 111
Lee, C. B., 61
legends. *See* lore and storytelling
Lettes, Ben, 75, 95
Lewis, John, 35
Lewis Monroe and Sons, 83
Liberty Fish and Oyster Company, 71
licensing, hunting, 111
Lincecum, Gideon, 21
Lineaweaver, Tom, 137, 141
Linn, John J., 30
Linnville, Texas, 30
live decoys, 52, 53
Lockett, R. R., 114
Logan, J. P. "Pink," 56
Logan James Pinckney, 56
London markets, 5, 89, 90
Long, James, 29
Lorance, R. W. "Bob," 123
lore and storytelling, 14, 18, 76
Lost Lake, 95
Louisiana, 16–17, 40, 104, 108
Louisiana Ice Manufacturing Company, 45
Louisiana Planter and Sugar Manufacturer, 50
Louisiana State Game Commission, 104
Loustenban, John, 82
lower coast, ecology and geomorphology, 10–11
Lozano taxidermy, 98, *99*
Luster, Ronnie, 50

MacMullan, Boyd Buford "B. B.," 135–36
Maley, Harley, 140–41
Maley, Joe F., 64
mallards, 18, 43, 61, 63–64, 82, 104
Mallory Line steamers, 61
Malsch, A., 14
A Man from Corpus Christi (Peirce), 78
Marion, John Priour, 78
Market Hall (Corpus Christi), 77
Market House (Galveston), 31, 57

Market House (San Antonio), 35, 81
market hunters
    commission hunters, 55, 70, 91–93, 102–3
    culture of and law enforcement, 126–27
    historical overview, 3–7
    hunting culture, overview, 126
    numbers of, 102
    profiles, 16–18, 55, 70, 75–76, 78–79, 83, 84
    See also hunting methods/strategies; outlaw hunters
marketplaces
    Austin, TX, 85
    Brazos River corridor, 70
    colonial Texas, 29–31, 36–37
    Dallas/Fort Worth area, 83–84
    East Coast profiles, 37
    East Texas, 84
    Galveston Bay area, 57–58
    historical overview, 4, 29
    Houston, TX, 66–68
    Laguna Madre area, 79, *80*
    post-Civil War Texas, 42
    pre-Civil War Texas, 31–35
    San Antonio area, 81–83
    Waco, TX, 85
    See also restaurants, game market for; wildfowl trade/distribution highlights
market reports, 42–43, *90*
Market Square (Houston), 32–33, 66, *67*
Marsan, G. B., 60
Marshall, TX, 84–85, 133
martelles, 41
Martin, Edward T., 69
Marty, Joe, 56–57
Mary Ann, 80
Maryland, 103–4, 106, 108
Mason and Dodge decoys, 53
Massachusetts, 108
mast (acorns), 18, 107
Matagorda, Texas, 29–30
Matagorda Bay/Island, 10, 14, 30, 70–74

Matagorda (Bay) Fish and Oyster Company, 69, 73–74
Mathies Brothers, 82
Matlock, Joe, *139*
McCallum, Charles R., 144
McClintock, William, 15
McCulloch, Champe Carter, 112
McCulloch House, 33
McFaddin, W. P. H., 18
McIlvain and Dunn's English Kitchen, 70
McNamara, J., 128
McNeir, Forest, 46, 49, 59–60, 63, 66, 92–93, 99
McNeir, Pascal, 92–93
McNelly's Rangers, 79
meadowlarks, 29, 83, 109
Melcher, Ed, 74, 135
Melcher, J. C., 126–27
Menger Hotel, 35, 82
menus, confidential, 128–29
methods, hunting. *See* hunting methods/strategies
Mexican currency, 35, 44
Mexican hunters, 17
"Mexican tree ducks," 41
Mexican War, 4, 15, 34
Mexico, 120
Michigan, 37, 104
middle Texas coast, ecology and geomorphology, 9–10, 11
Migratory Bird Treaty Act (MBTA) (1918), 6, 120, 125, 130, 143–45
Military Plaza market, 81
Miller, J., 55
Miller, William, 75
Miller Brothers Fish and Oyster Company, 73, 75, *76,* 77, 82
Miller Hotel, 79, 129
millinery trade. *See* plumage market
milo (sorghum), 132
Minnesota, 37, 89, 104
Minter, Granville Elias "Bill," 127
Mississippi River, 37, 40
Missouri game laws, 127
Missouri River, 37

Mitchell Lake, 81
Model Game Law, Texas (1903), 6, 116, 117–18, 121–22
"model law" of AOU (1886), 110, 116
Model Market, 57
Mohr, J. P., 68
Moke's Millinery Parlor, 98
monopolies, market, 44
Monroe, Lewis and sons, 83
Moody, William Lewis, 92–95, 96
Moore, Wyatt, 133
Morgan, Antonio, 33
Morgan, Emily West, 14
Morgan, James, 13–14
Morgan City Fish, Oyster, and Game, 82
Morgan's Point, 13, 32, 69
Morgan Steamship Line, 70, 80
Morton, Barney, 129
Moses, Asa, 30
mosquitoes, nuisance of, 16, 17
  See also yellow fever
mosquito fleet, 59–60, 128
"mosquito" slip, 57
Mother of Texas, 29
mottled ducks, 18, 43
Mustang Island, 10
muzzle-loading guns, 22, 23

names of bird species, *19*
National Association of Audubon Societies (NAAS), 110, 112–13, 115, 123, 128
national park system, 110
national wildlife refuges, 111
natural history collector markets, 5, 99–100
N. B. Jaas, 57
Neal, Benjamin Harris, 14
Nebraska, 104
Needville, Texas, 42
Nelson, William G., 57, *58*, 60, 62, 73, 91, 95
nesting sites and plumage hunting, 98
netting of fowl, 6, 106

New Orleans
  high-volume kill examples, 104
  ice-making plants, 45
  marketplace/restaurant profile, 37–38
  numbers of market hunters, 102
  and railroad development, 40
  steamship routes, 29
  wildfowl trade/distribution highlights, 56
New York Association for the Protection of Game, 109
New York markets, 47, 87–88, 97
New York Telegraph, 87–88
New York Times, 87
nicknames of bird species, *19*
night hunting
  game laws, 108, 113, 114, 115
  historical overview, 6
  nongame birds, 109
  outlaw strategies, 134–35
  sportsmen against, 105
  strategies for, 25–26
Noessel, George, 34
nongame species, protection of, 109
North American Central Flyway. *See* Central Flyway
North Carolina, 88–89, 102–3, 104, 108
northern shovelers, 19
Nueces River, 15

Oak Hall Restaurant, 85
O'Brien, John, 68
O'Farrell, William, 57
Offatts Bayou, 61–62
O. J. Miller market, 85
Old Reliable Game Stand, 57, *58*, 62
opium, baiting with, 106
Orange, Texas, 56
Orange County, 56–57
Orchard Lake, 10
Oregon, 41
osprey feathers, 98
Our House Restaurant, 33
Outdoor Life, 137, 141

Outlaw Gunner, 106
outlaw hunters, *131*
  1956 sting, 136–41
  1988 sting, 143–45
  Great Depression profile, 130–33
  historical overview, 6–7, 126–28
overgrazing, 20
oxen/steers, hunting over, 6, 52, 105, 134
Oyster Bayou, 136, 138
oyster luggers, 19
oysters, popularity of, 87–88

Pacific Coast markets, 40–41, 104
packing companies. *See* game merchants
Padre Island, 11
Palace Coffee Saloon and Restaurant, 67
Palacios, TX, 70–71
Palmer, Henry, 99
Palmer, Theodore Sherman, 108
Pamlico Sound, 104
Panhandle area, 85
papabots, 22, 44
partridges. *See* prairie chickens; quail
passenger pigeons, 4, 81, *90*, 107, 109
Pauri, Frank, 72
Peach Point Plantation, 4
Peirce, A. C., 78
Pelican Island, 111
pelicans, 31, 100, 112
Penny, James, 34–35
percussion locks, 22
Permanent Game Law (1907), 6, 119, 122
Perry, James F., 4
Pherobe, 92
Phillips, Mertie, 37
Pier 19, Galveston, *48*, 57
pigeons. *See* passenger pigeons
pintails, 18–19
pipe guns, 136
piping plovers, 22
pit blinds, 144
Pitchford, J. J., 83

planter culture, 4
plovers, 4, 5, 21, 22, 23, 52, 79, 83–85
plumage market
    and game laws, 109, 111, 112, 116, 120, 128
    market overview, 5–6, 96–99, 107
    See also feathers
Poindexter Ice Company, 28, 30
Point (Port) Isabel, 34, 79–81
Pollepel's Island, 88
ponies. *See* horses, hunting over/from
Pope, Judge, 119
Popular Saloon and Chop House, 85
Port Aransas, 74, 132
Port Arthur, Texas, 56, 130
Port Bay Hunting Club, 123, 133
Port Lavaca, Texas, 30, 47, 70, 72–74, 125
Port Lavaca Fish and Oyster Company, 74
Port Lavaca Ice Factory, 74
possession limits, 118
Post Office Exchange Restaurant, 82
poultry industry, 44
powder. *See* gun powder
Power, James, 15, 30–31
prairie chickens, 4, 12, 33, 114, 117
Pratt, Rick, 132, 135
preservation methods
    barrel packing (no salt), 5, 27
    brining/salting, 5, 27, 46
    canning, 80–81
    cold storage, 5, 60, 61
    during hunting trips, 46
    lard, 56
    limitations of, historical overview, 4–5
    refrigeration, 5, 45, 46–47, 60, 89
    See also ice for preservation
prices
    bird skins, 99–100
    canvasbacks, 88, 89–90
    feathers, 36
    game, early Texas, 35–36
    game, post-Civil War Texas, 41–44, 81–82, 83, 84, 85

ice, 45, 46
plumage, 99
quills, 100
restaurant, 57
salt, 27
upper Texas coast, 56, 57
Prior, F. W., 79
"providence rice," 50
puddle ducks, overview, 18–19
Pueschel, Charles, 82
pump guns, 51–52, 133, *134*
punt guns, 6, 52–53, 105, 114, 134–36
Pye, Ebenezer, 60

quail, 12, 29, 111
quills, market for, 5, 100

raids. *See* seizures of illegal game; sting operations
Railroad House, 35
railroads
    Brazos River corridor, 69, 70–71
    East Texas, 85
    Galveston Bay area, 60–61
    and game laws, 111, 113, 114, 116, 117, 124–25
    historical overview, 5, 39
    Houston markets, 68
    Laguna Madre area, 79–80
    Matagorda Bay area, 70–71, 72
    post-Civil War expansion, 40–41, 45
    Rockport area, 75
    San Antonio area, 82
    upper Texas coast, 56
rails, 22
rattlesnakes, 4, 16, 18
Ray, Tom, 103
Recreation, 102
redheads, 3, 5, 19, 20, 88, 104
refrigeration, 5, 45, 46–47, 60, 89
"Refrigerator Meat Market," 82
Refugio County, 102
Remington firearms, 52
repeating firearms, development of, 39, 51

restaurants, game market for
    Brazos River corridor, 70
    Brownsville, TX, 79
    and game protection laws, 117
    during Great Depression, 132
    Houston, TX, 67
    inland areas, 85
    and outlaw hunting, 128–29, 135, 136, 138
    post-Civil War, 39–40
    San Antonio area, 82–83
    See also marketplaces
Rhode Island, 108, 110
rice crops, 50–51
Rice Hotel, 67, 129
Richards, Lillian, 132
ring-necked ducks, 19, 20, 41
ringneck plovers, 22
Rio Grande corridor, 79, 85–86
Rio Grande Railway, 79–80
Ritter, W. E., *139*
Riverside Café Restaurant, 82
roadside marketing, 4, 16, 32–33, 41–42, 130, *131*
Robertson, James, 33
robins, 29, 41, 109
Rock, Jim, 13
Rockport, Texas, 75–76, 104–5, 116–17, *118*
rookeries and plumage hunting, 98, 111
Roosevelt, Theodore, 110, 111
roseate spoonbill, 120
Rosen, Rudy, 115
Rowena, 89
Royer, Clovis and Nelson, 138, 140
ruddy ducks, 20
Runge, Henry, 33
Rupert, Charles and Company, 73
Russia, 120

Sabine River and estuary, 9–10, 17, 49, 56, 143–45
Sadler, A. D., 60
Sadler and Meunier, 60
sailing skiffs, 24–25

Saint Claire Lake, 91
　See also Wallis Lake
Saint Louis markets, 37, 40, 91
Saint Mary, TX, 74
St. Charles Restaurant, 67
St. Charles Saloon and Restaurant, 85
St. John, Percy, 14–15
St. Joseph Island, 10, 14–15
St. Mary's Wharf and Warehouse Company, 74
Salcedo, Jesus, 76, 78
sale of game birds, game laws for, 114, 115, 124–25, 126–28
salt for preservation, 5, 27, *28*, 46
salt water, ice from, 61
salt water influx and habitat destruction, 95
San Antonio, Texas area, 35, 60–61, 81–83
San Antonio and Aransas Pass Railway (SA&AP), 68, 75, 76, 77, 82
San Antonio and Mexican Gulf Railroad, 72
San Antonio Bay, 10
San Antonio Daily Express, 93
San Antonio Daily Light, 76, 114
San Antonio Daily Times, 111
San Antonio Express, 94
San Antonio Gun Club, 114, 122
San Antonio Ice Factory and Fish, Oyster, and Game Depot, 82
San Bernard River, 4
sandhill cranes, 14, 21, 23–24, 128
sandpipers, 21, 22
San Jacinto River, 13, 14, 32, 66–69
San Luis, Texas, 30
Santa Anna, 14
Santa Anna (schooner), 15
Saturday Evening Post, 94
Scanlan, Thomas, 66
scatterguns, 6
scaup, lesser, 20, 104
Schallert, Robert, 78
Schember, Louis, 128
schooners, 24–25, 75, 79–80
Schorlemmer, L. C., 132

Schorlemmer, Louis, 132
Schultz's Palm Garden, 83
Schwartz, August, 33
Scott, J. R., 82
Sea Breeze Hotel, 30
sea salt "mining," 27
seasons, hunting, 108, 110, 111, 112, 118, 119–20
Sea View Hotel, 123
Seixas, Cecile, 115
seizures of illegal game, 127–28, 128–29
　See also enforcement of game laws
"self-poisoning of ducks," 94
semiautomatic shotguns, 52, 105, 133
Sennett, George B., 100, 110
Sens, Otto, 129
Shamrock Hotel, 135
shells, shotgun, 39
Sherwood, M. E. W., 39, 109
Shields, George O., 102, 111
Shika, Billy, 132–33
shipping of game
　in-state markets, 41–44
　national markets, 45–49, 59–60, 87–93
　post–Civil War overview, 39–41, 55
　sale of birds, game laws for, 114, 115, 124–25, 126–28
　volume of exports, 104–5
　See also transport of game to markets; wildfowl trade/distribution highlights
Shiras, George III, 119
shocks, rice, 50–51
shorebirds, 4, 21–22, 23–24, 52, 107
　See also eggs (wildfowl); plumage market
Short Order Restaurant and Lunch Counter, 82–83
shot (ammunition), 22, *23*
shotguns, 22
Shupee, George C., 128
Silver King Market, 82
Simmary and Hampel's Restaurant, 82
Simon's Restaurant and Oyster Parlor, 85

Singleton, Bob, 137
sink boxes, 53–55, 96, 104
Sitton, Thad, 133
skiff hunting, 24–25, 108
skins (bird), market for, 5, 97, 99–100, 116
sloops, 24–25, 59–60, 128
　See also sink boxes
small birds, protection of, 109
"small ducks," 41
Smith, Captain, 14
Smith, George, 85
Smith, W. H. "Will," *73*
Smith Point, 62–63
Smock, James, 130
smokeless powder, 51–52
snakes, 4, 16, 18
snaring of fowl, 106
sneak hunting, 23, 52, 135
snipe, 4, 21, 22, 23, *43*, 66
snow geese, 20, 41
snowy egrets, 5–6, 98–99, 107
songbirds, 4, 29, 109, 112, 144
Sorenson, Andrew "Pop," 123
sorghum, 132
South Bay Hunting Club, 96
South Carolina, 104
Southern Pacific Railway, 70–71, 115
Southern Steamship Company, 71
Spears, Gordon "Pop" and family, 96
Spears, Jamie, 143
species profiles, 18–22
specklebelly geese, 20
Spencer firearms, 51
spiking of bait, 106
spoonbills, 19
sport hunters
　access and intimidation issues, 92, 93–94
　disdain of market hunting methods, 105
　and enforcement of game protection laws, 122, 123
　as market hunters, 55
Sports Illustrated, 137, 141
sprigs/sprig tails, 18–19, 43

Srivner, David, 75
Stafford, Herb, 56
stalking, 23
Standley, Linnie Evelyn Stephenson, 132
Standley, Morris, 132
Stanfield, S. W., 105
Starr, Frank, 82
state game laws
  vs. federal laws, 115, 119
  historical overview, 6–7, 101, 108–9, 110–11
  Texas profile, 111–19
steamships, 29, 41, 61, 70, 80
steers/oxen, hunting over, 6, 52, 105, 134
Stefano, Anthony Marc, 136–41
Stephenson, Eliza, 91
Stephenson, George "Bud," 91–92
Stephenson, W. C., 124, 126, 129, 133
Sterrett, William G., 123–25, 128, 133
Stert, Arthur, 84
Stevens, George W., 123, 127
Stillman, Charles, 34
Stilwell, Arthur, 56
Stilwell, Hart, 137
Stines, Peter, 63
Stines, Will, Jr., 63
Stines, Will, Sr., 59, 60, 63
sting operations, 136–41, 143–45
Stone, Jerome, 130
storms. See weather dangers
Strachan, Robert, 75
Strand, The (Galveston), 57
stranding, dangers of, 17
street vendors. See roadside marketing
Studeman, Henry, 132
Stutzenbaker, Charles, 141
subsistence hunting, 15, 126, 130–33
sugarcane culture, 4
"sugared" duck ponds, 144
  See also baiting of fowl
Sullivan, Henry, 60, 128
Superach, John and Company, 77, 82
Susquehanna Flats, 88, 90, 103–4, 106, 108

swans
  decline of, 104
  diet and habitat overview, 20–21
  game protection legislation, 120
  hunting highlights, 13, 14–15
  quill market, 100
Sweetwater Lake, 61–62, 95
swivel guns, 6, 52, 53, 54, 103, 105, 114, 134–35
Sydnor, J. S., 32
Sydnor House, 32
syndicates, hunting, 88

tagging violations, 145
Talley, T., 82
tangle birds, 50
Tarpon Inn, 132
tattler, 22
taxidermy, 98, 99
Taylor, Anson, 16
Taylor, J. H., 84
Taylor, Zachary, 4, 15, 34
teal, 18, 19, 43
Teller, Henry M., 115
tell-tale, 22
tenders (skiffs), 25
Tennessee, 104
terrapins. See turtles, market for
Terrell (Senator), 116, 122
Texas and New Orleans Railway, 56
Texas and Pacific Railway, 85
Texas Express Company, 45, 61, 68
Texas Field, 111
Texas Field and Sportsman, 111
Texas Fish Commission, 121
Texas Game, Fish, and Oyster Commission (GFOC), 105, 122–25, 133
Texas Game Protective Association (TGPA), 111, 113, 114, 115
Texas House, 30
Texas Ice and Cold Storage Company, 61
Texas Model Game Law (1903), 6, 116, 117–18, 121–22
Texas Parks and Wildlife Department (TPWD), 7, 121

Texas Revolution, 4
Texas Shooting Club, *113*
Texas State Fish and Oyster Commission (FOC), 7, 121, 122
Texas State Sportsmen's Association (TSSA), 92, 111, 115
Texas Wells Fargo Express Company, 45
Tex's Oyster saloon, 85
Tiller, Barney, 128
T. M. Bagby, 41
Tod, John G., 13
Top Hat restaurant, 138, 140
torch hunting, 25–26
trans-Atlantic shipping, 5, 41, 60, 89, 90
transport of game to markets
  colonial era, 31
  early methods and challenges, 28–29
  and game laws, 113, 114, 115–16, 119, 124–25, 127–28
  limitations of, historical overview, 4–5
  See also shipping of game; wild-fowl trade/distribution highlights
trapping of fowl, 4, 6, 106
tree ducks, 20
Tremont Hotel (Chicago), 40
Tremont House (Galveston), 31, 128–29
Trinity River delta, 64–66, 83
trotlines, hunting strategies with, 133
trumpeter cranes, 21
trumpeter swans, 20–21
tundra swans, 20–21
Turf, Field and Farm, 111
turkeys, wild, 4, 29
Turner, Neal, 79
Turner and Dingee, 84
turtles, market for, 35, 60, 87–88

undercover operations, 136–41, 143–45
Union Fish Company, 75, 96
upper Texas coast, ecology and geomorphology, 9–10

INDEX → 183

US Fish and Wildlife Service (USFWS), 136–41, 143–45

Vaca, Cabeza de, 30
Valisneria spiralis, 88
"vegetable" slip, 57
Velasco, TX, 69–70
Velasco Fish and Oyster Company, 69
Velasco Terminal Railway, 69
Victoria, Texas, 35, 85
Victoria Daily Advocate, 119
Villenueve, Casimir, 34
Virginia, 88, 104, 108
Vogelsang, August, 64
Volk, W., 33

Waco, TX, 85
wading birds and plumage market, 87, 97, 100, 107, 112
Walcott, Ben, 69
Waldorf Astoria, 40
Wallis Lake, 62, 91, 92–95
Wallisville, TX, 64–65
Walsh, Harry, 106, 126
wardens, game, 7, 110–11, 121–25
   See also enforcement of game laws
Warrach, H., Jr., 73
Warren, Jim, 127
Waterfowling America, 91
water moccasins, 18
weapons. *See* firearms
weather and spoilage, 25
weather dangers
   blizzard of 1886, 60
   early profiles, 17–18
   Galveston Bay, 13
   hurricanes, 16, 18, 60, 70, 72, 74, 95, 99, 115
   ice storms, 63
Weekly Times, 111
Weeks-McLean Law (1913), 6, 119–20
Wells Fargo Company, 33, 45, *48*, 61, 64, 74
West, Forrest, 135–36, 145
Western Commission Company, 103
Western Field, 103
Western Poultry and Game, 103
Wetzel, Nat, 50–51, 103
Wheat, J. P., 117
whistling ducks, 20
whistling swans, 20–21
white brant, 20
white-fronted geese, 20, 41
Whitehead, Addison, 62–63
Whitehead, Joe, 63, 94, 141
White's Lake, 91
   See also Lake Stephenson
whooping cranes, 21, 23–24, 99
wigeons, 19
Wiggins, Melanie, 57
wild celery, 20, 88, 89, 95
wildfowl trade/distribution highlights
   Aransas/Copano Bays, 74–76
   Brazos River corridor, 69–70
   Corpus Christi Bay area, 76–79
   Galveston Bay area, 58–64
   inland areas, 81–86
   Jefferson County, 56–57
   Laguna Madre area, 79–81
   Matagorda Bay area, 70–74
   Orange County, 56–57
   San Jacinto River/Houston area, 66–69
   species overviews, 18–22
   Trinity River delta, 64–66
Wildlife and Man in Texas (Doughty), 107
wildlife preservation. *See* conservation movement
"Willie Nelsons," 143
Wilson, Alexander, 38
Wilson's snipes, 21, 22, *43*
Winchester firearms, 51
wing feathers, market for. *See* quills, market for
Wisconsin, 37, 88
Wolff, Alex, 130
Womack family, 134
Wood, Richard, 123, 129
Wood, Richard H., 75
Wood, William W., 125
woodcocks, 4, 25, 26
wood ducks, 19, 41, 99, 107
Woodland Daily Democrat, 104

yellow fever, 34, 44
yellowlegs, 21–22
Yellow Rose of Texas, 14

Zern, Ed, 137, 141
zones, hunting, 110

About the Author

R.K. Sawyer has been a waterfowl hunter since 1964, the seeds of his lifelong passion sown on Maryland's Chesapeake Bay. He currently resides in Sugar Land, Texas, with his wife Wendy and Matagorda Mattie, a black Labrador Retriever. A retired petroleum geologist, Rob has since been working with waterfowl habitat projects and freelance writing. He is the author of four historical hunting books: *A Hundred Years of Texas Waterfowl Hunting* (2012), *Texas Market Hunting* (2013), *Images of the Hunt* (2020), and *The Tarpon Club of Texas* (2022) and numerous magazine articles.

www.ingramcontent.com/pod-product-compliance
Lightning Source LLC
Chambersburg PA
CBHW062138160426
43191CB00014B/2321